BRIAN ROBINSON:
PIONEER

BRIAN ROBINSON:
PIONEER

Graeme Fife

Brian Robinson:
Pioneer

Copyright © Graeme Fife, 2010

First published in 2010
by

Mousehold Press
Victoria Cottage
Constitution Opening
Norwich NR3 4BD

and

Sport and Publicity
75 Fitzjohns Avenue
Hampstead
London, NW3 6PD

www.mousehold-press.co.uk

www.sportandpublicity.co.uk

This edition published in 2014

Cover design by Terry Batsford

ISBN 978-1-874739-73-9

Cover images:
front – Brian Robinson after winning the Critérium du Dauphiné Libéré, 1961

back – Tour de France 1958. Stage thirteen 230 kms from Dax to Pau.
Brian Robinson leads legendary Tour winners Louison Bobet and Jacques Anquetil
on the Col de l'Aubisque.

Printed by Page Bros. Norwich

CONTENTS

WELCOME TO YORKSHIRE
TOUR DE FRANCE, 2014

We breed a special kind of man in Yorkshire. The qualities that we hold dear are those of honesty, integrity, humility, generosity and sheer hard graft. If there is one man who embodies these qualities it is Brian Robinson.

A number of years ago, as we were working towards bringing the Tour de France to Yorkshire, I had the pleasure of meeting Brian and hearing his amazing story. I do not use the word superstar lightly, but in addition to being the first Briton to win a stage in the Tour, Brian has tirelessly given of his time as a *Grand Départ* ambassador, sharing his vast knowledge of the sport with everybody he meets, and always with his gentle good humour. He has been an inspiration to me and my team and I know how special it will be to see the race that meant so much to him, racing on the roads he and his brother rode in their youth.

Over the next 210 pages you will discover, as I have, what an amazing man, competitor and athlete Brian was and continues to be. I hope you enjoy this new edition of the book as much as I have and that you enjoy the Tour de France in Yorkshire as much as I know Brian will.

Gary Verity
CEO Welcome to Yorkshire

PUBLISHER'S NOTE

This book, long overdue when it was first published in 2010, was the result of many people, over the course of many years, trying to convince Brian that he should publish an autobiography. However, when it became obvious he was never going to write such a book, the only alternative had to be a biography written by a professional writer. When Brian and I talked on the subject he finally agreed, but with one essential proviso – that it could only be written by Graeme Fife.

That was fine: Graeme was a good friend whom I very much liked and respected. Furthermore he was an outstanding writer, with a deep understanding of European cycling history, who had been published by major publishers. He, himself, was very enthusiastic about the project and I was delighted when he agreed to bring his book to us. That enthusiasm is evident on every page of "Brian Robinson: Pioneer".

The book contains much information that you might find surprisingly candid. Brian was a great racing cyclist and a man well ahead of his time: he was the first to make European road cycling more international, although its stubborn traditions still took another two or three decades to be fully overcome. Brian's unpretentious manner and personality might be looked down upon by many of Britain's present day cycling stars, but his humility and his pioneering spirit (which he was probably unaware of himself at the time) should serve as a reminder to them of the opportunities which they currently enjoy, and which he never did.

As co-publisher, I would like to extend my thanks to Graeme and Brian, of course, and to my co-publisher, Adrian Bell, and to Mick Clark for their efforts in bringing this wonderful book to publication.

This book is now being reprinted in a special paperback edition that celebrates the Tour of France starting in Britain. Yorkshire will host the first two stages on British soil and then it moves South. The third stage begins in the university town of Cambridge and finishes on the Mall in central London, very close to Buckingham Palace.

Yorkshire is Brian's home county. He is a Yorkshireman through and through, so it could not be more fitting that Brian, our first pioneer in the world of professional road racing and our first Tour de France stage winner should have been so instrumental in bringing the great race to Britain.

Richard Allchin
Sport and Publicity

PUBLISHERS' ACKNOWLEDGEMENTS: We would like to thank the following: Robert Garbutt, Editor of *Cycling Weekly* for giving us permission to use a number of photographs from their excellent archive, as they have done so often before, and Keith Bingham for helping us select and identify those photographs; Mick Clark, who compiled the *Palmarès*, and Terry ('El Tel') Batsford for the new cover design; Phil Liggett MBE, who kindly agreed to write the *Foreword*, and Alan Mercer and Tony Mackertich who, learning of the book, offered us a number of their photographs. Many people continue to encourage us to keep extending our list of cycling titles and to all those we send our thanks, and in this regard we owe a special debt of gratitude to David Harmon. We would also like to thank André Darrigade, Raymond Poulidor, Barry Hoban, Vin Denson and Paul Sherwen for taking the trouble to send us a recollection of Brian Robinson. Many people continue to encourage us to keep extending our list of cycling titles and to all those we send our thanks, and in this regard we owe a special debt of gratitude to David Harmon who also worked hard with the Welcome to Yorkshire CEO, Gary Verity. We would also like to thank André Darrigade, Raymond Poulidor, Barry Hoban, Vin Denson and Paul Sherwen for taking the trouble to giving us their recollections of Brian Robinson. Thanks also must go to David Reed for his continued support and advice not only with this book, but though the years.

AUTHOR'S ACKNOWLEDGEMENTS:

My thanks to Adrian Bell for the loan of Jock Wadley's indispensable chronicle of Robinson's continental riding in his magazine *Coureur*. Thanks, too, to Richard Allchin for his gift of copies of the *UCI Encyclopédie* of professional riders which supplied timely, recherché information and for his support throughout this work, as well as for the full list of Robinson's *palmarès,* which he and Mick Clark compiled.

Nigel Dick, a filmmaker based in Los Angeles, sent me transcripts of interviews he conducted with Tony Hoar, which provided insight into the 1955 Tour and Hoar, himself, gave me further help via e-mail. I talked to Tony Hewson, Bob Maitland, Bernard Pusey and Ian Steel and they were generous with time, reflection and souvenir. Mike Thorogood gave me valuable insights into certain mechanical aspects of the bike which added to the story. Geoff Evans gave me useful data. Mme Danielle Couzot, the archivist of *L'Equipe* in south-west Paris, afforded me free access to the microfiche of back copies of the journal and uncomplainingly reset the ancient viewing apparatus when it seized up, as it did frequently. I'm grateful for the information on wool and polyester mix provided by the textile department of the Victoria and Albert Museum and to Peter Donovan for a touching vignette (p179).

Many thanks, too, to Phil Liggett, both for the Foreword and for that superb route over the High Peaks, Robinson's turf, which we and other friends have ridden together.

To Brian and Audrey, for hospitality and hearty welcome in Yorkshire and fielding endless phone calls, my hearty gratitude, of course. And to Brian himself, for his tip about lawn sand and for putting up with the whole thing, what can I say? 'Now you can relax', perhaps.

For Duncan

Thanks to one friendship, my godson,
Thanks to our own acquaintance, my dear friend and companion.

Yours G

FOREWORD

As I was being born on what would become known as Merseyside, in 1943, Brian Robinson and his family were moving on from Ravensthorpe to Mirfield, where both his father and mother would spend 24 hours a day between them working in the Halifax bombers factory, readying operations for World War II. Cycling was on neither of our minds, least of all mine.

Forty-eight years later, in a tent on the Knavesmire in beautiful York and on a sunny June day, I was the principle guest of the Yorkshire Road Club as it celebrated 100 years. I was sitting alongside 'Mr Cycling' himself, the irreplaceable Ron Kitching.

I said to Ron: 'Is Brian Robinson here?' 'Of course,' replied Ron, 'he's sat over there,' pointing to the depths of an overcrowded tent, there to celebrate a centenary with one of the most famous cycling clubs in White Rose country.

I stood and said: 'I'd like to take wine with a man whom I have never seen in my life, but who has been one of the most influential men in my career and one of the most remarkable in our sport – Brian Robinson.'

Brian, his round face and balding head his trade mark, stood and replied: 'And it is very nice to meet you too.' His personality was revealed in these few words.

A family man, a cyclist, a builder and a gardener, probably in this order, Brian to this day would make any high achieving British cyclist envious of his career. Yet, if perhaps he had not been such a nice man, with moral standards and an inherent code of honour second to none, then he would have won many more races.

He was, as you will read, one of the first ever British riders to finish the Tour de France in 1955. Fifty years on, when he was 74, Brian paid for a party to mark the occasion. He invited as many British riders who had taken part as he could locate and they came from far and wide for an evening never to be forgotten.

How glad I am that this book, so ably written by author Graeme Fife, will detail Brian's life. As you read you will gather the same feelings that greeted me in York. Brian was often too nice and generous. When he won Britain's first ever stage of the Tour de France in Brest in 1958 it was after the Italian Arigo Padovan had switched him in the sprint and forced his way over the line in first place. He was relegated and Brian was crowned the champion of the day.

A year later Brian was going into the history books, winning another stage, but this time with the added codicil of one of the Tour's greatest margins. On the road to Chalon-sur-Saone he won by over 20 minutes! Today this feat still counts as the fourth largest victory margin on any stage of the Tour de France. Ironically, Padovan again finished second.

Racing in the same era as Brian was an outstanding Belgian Classics specialist called Fred De Bruyne. Unlike Brian, I never knew Fred when he was a racer, but I met him on the Tour de France when we came together as television commentators in the early '80s. He spoke excellent English and was proud that his son was attending Cambridge University, but it was about Brian we talked. Sadly, Fred died in 1992, but Brian will remember Fred as the rider who, in 1957, beat him for second place (behind the Spanish star Miguel Poblet) in the longest unpaced Classic race of them all, from Milan to San Remo. Before then, no British rider had ever stepped onto the podium of such an important race and Robinson had made it happen by a late breakaway with De Bruyne, the winner the previous year, and Poblet.

A lifetime passed before I got to ride with Brian. I found myself climbing the Peak District mountain of Holm Moss behind him during my 'Phil and Friends' CTC Charity ride in the August of 2004. Brian has always joined in as one of the Friends. Having earlier asked what I thought of his new bike with straight handlebars, but very light, I'd said it looked nice. He replied: 'First one I've had to pay for since I was 18!'

Two hours later, I was gazing across the barren moors of The Moss, happy to be unashamedly holding on to the back wheel of one of Britain's greatest riders, notwithstanding he was in his mid-seventies (74, in fact), when he said: 'You know, Phil, I think I may still hold the record for the fastest time up this mountain.' Words said with pride but most definitely not with conceit. It was no time to remind me of this, and although he wasn't sure of the time he set that distant day in the Huddersfield RC Hill Climb, he was still riding up at the same speed as far as I was concerned.

In modern times, British cycling has made enormous progress. In 2010 there was a commercial British team once again in the Tour de France. The following year Mark Cavendish won the Tour's points competition and in 2012 Sir Bradley Wiggins became the first British overall Tour winner. The following year, it was the turn of another Briton, Chris Froome, to wear the yellow jersey on the the the Champs Elysées. But how many will remember that the first British team in this great race was in 1955, and that Brian Robinson was the pioneer who would continue to lead the way in British road racing for the next eight years?

To any aspiring racing cyclist I say: equal the feats of Brian Robinson and you can look back in pride at having been among the very best racing cyclists that Brtitain has ever produced.

It must warm Brian's heart to know the Tour de France is visiting his home county of Yorkshire this summer. He has worked closely with the organizers in the UK as a figurehead despite his debut in the great race being nearly sixty years ago! It proves that Great Britain's first ever Tour stage winner is still held in such high regard with the French organisers, a remarkable achievement after all this time.

Chapeau, Brian

Phil Liggett, MBE
Hertford

Pioneer: French pionnier, originally foot-soldier. 1. One of a body of foot-soldiers who march with or in advance of an army or regiment, having spades, pickaxes etc to dig trenches, repair roads and perform other labours in clearing and preparing the way for the main body. (*Oxford English Dictionary*)

'Camerado, this is no book,
Who touches this, touches a man.'

Walt Whitman, *So Long*

INTRODUCTION

I first met Robinson in January 2001, at Combloux, during the annual Arc-en-Ciel Trophée Robic ski-fest attended by a bunch of former pro riders. A week's fun and reunion, combining conviviality at table and two competitions: downhill slalom and eight-kilometre cross-country. Combloux, 'the pearl of Mont Blanc', nestles beneath the towering ranges of the highest mountain in Europe, along the valley from Sallanches, home of the Worlds in 1964 and 1980. The list of overall winners of the Trophée, founded as a tribute to Jean Robic, killed in a car crash in 1980, includes some of the greatest names in cycling: Adorni, Jacques Anquetil, Alain Bondue, Gianni Motta, Charley Mottet, Raymond Poulidor, Bernard Thévenet. Motta, who won the Giro d'Italia in 1966, had won it for the past four years.

I'd already spoken to Robinson on the phone a number of times. First, when I interviewed him for an article in *Cycle Sport* and on other subsequent occasions when he helped me with information about the era in which he rode. He encouraged me to come to the Alps, I contacted the Combloux Tourist Office and they booked me into the hotel where Robinson was staying, along with André Darrigade, Henri Anglade, Joseph Groussard, Nicolas Barone, Michel Jouahnnet...These last two, Barone a particular friend from the peloton, had taught Robinson the rudiments of skiing five years earlier, when he was sixty-five, told him how to get going and left him to it. They came back in the afternoon to find him hurtling flat out down the slope like a runaway cart and then introduced him to that second most useful of skills: how to stop. Formal training over, now get on with it. He was utterly assured by the time I went out on the slopes with him and I realised, of course, that the aptitude for plunging off down a gurt great mountain at breakneck speed once you'd got up it, had been inbuilt for a long time.

The first evening, I sat to eat on my own in the dining room where the others with Darrigade's wife Françoise and Anquetil's widow, Janine, were installed. Robinson had cautioned me, gently, to wait until I was invited to join them...or not. In fact, I hadn't even been served when I was beckoned across to sit at the table.

I skied with them – Motta, who, for some reason, insisted on calling me Andrew, gave me a memorable private lesson on one finishing slope – and spent one evening after supper talking with Robinson, about nothing much, friendly conversation over a beer, when the others had gone to town.

It was the start of a firm and enduring friendship.

Robinson is unaffected, modest and unassuming. Indeed, his remarks about Coppi later in this book – how could such a mild-mannered man be so aggressive on a bike? – might equally apply to him. There have been people who, whilst admiring the man himself, felt that he lacked aggression. This is to misread him. If he was disinclined to puff himself and talk a good ride off the bike, that is no more than the grounded, sane attitude of a man who knows that words alone mean nothing. What you do on the bike is what counts and the testimony of riders who rode against and were beaten by him is more eloquent than any reservations about his apparent lack of spike. Considering what he achieved, in the circumstances in which he had to operate, he took on the job of professional cyclist in the continental peloton and the Tour de France itself with all the fight and tenacity of a Yorkshire terrier. He was, too, the great pioneer, in what Jean Bobet calls 'la belle époque' of a hard sport in a very tough era, the trail-blazer for a succession of British riders who followed him to the continent.

1: MY KIND OF COUNTRY

I walk from the car across the gravel driveway to the Robinsons' house on the fringe of Mirfield, east of Huddersfield. Robinson has spent most of his life in this corner of West Yorkshire. He began his working life as a joiner and carpenter, continued as one in the winter lulls of his career as a professional bike rider and, after he retired from racing, set up and ran a building firm. He built this house, where he and his wife Audrey live, a few years past, the walls of handsomely dressed local sandstone, some of the blocks scored lengthwise with a parallel punch, round the shell of what had been a stone cart-shed attached to a pub called The Horseshoes, now gone. In the open porch, in which the caravan used to be parked, there's a small work-bench, cupboards for tools, and a bike on a turbo trainer. That's a bald statement of the obvious: life without a bicycle is unthinkable. In 2005, a crowd of family and friends gathered in this porch for drinks before a banquet at the local golf club, where he and Audrey met, to celebrate the men who'd ridden the 1955 Tour de France and the other Britons who'd followed them. Phil Ligget gave the address and, next day, Robinson, Liggett and I joined the annual 'Phil and Friends' CTC ride, a big loop from just outside Sheffield, across the High Peaks, a terrain of austere beauty, on roads and climbs that helped shape Robinson as a bike rider. 'My kind of country,' he says, without a hint of nostalgia or sentimentality. Just fact. 'My kind of country.'

And it was one day in 1938 that he first sallied out into a small pocket of it by bike, a nondescript 14-inch machine, 'an anybody's bike' as he puts it, 'no crossbar, just a down tube'.

There was a park in Batley, three or so miles from the family house in Ravensthorpe along the way from Mirfield, the cobbled main road through latticed with tramlines, a bit of an assault course for a junior boneshaker. Some of his pals came by the house. 'Let's got to Batley Park, come on, Brian, ask yer mother.'

He asked his mother: 'Can I go? Can I go?' His father was out on a shop-fitting job. He was a keen cyclist, he'd have said yes, for certain sure he'd have said yes. He'd have spotted the passion in the nipper, the desire, the need to explore, to cut loose and test the freedom of two wheels, safe enough to go on his own in those days, and he'd have to venture out there sometime, but his mother was adamant. 'Oh no, you're not to go there, it's too far.' Dewsbury Moor which lay athwart the way was no barren lonely waste of a Dartmoor, beset with Grimpen Mires and phantom monster hounds, but three miles was three miles and eight years old was eight years old. No. His mother was quite strict, her kindly nature a bit crimped by the burden of physical disability, a drooping foot, the result of infantile paralysis, which hampered her with a limp.

Robinson went anyway. It was a spacious public park where a lot of people went, by bus or tram, for a leisurely sprawl in a green acre. The kids had a great time. And, when the truant slunk back, his mother glared at him. 'Where've *you* been?' (Blush.) 'You've been to Batley Park, haven't you? I'll give you what for' and he got a hiding. That, he says, was an early and important lesson of how to get on. Afterwards, he didn't bother to ask, he just went. If they don't see you go you can likely slip back without anyone knowing. There is, isn't there, in any devoted cyclist a streak of pig-headedness? Of incurious adventure, for sure. And, of course, in Yorkshire, obduracy, grit, is not so much prized as reckoned to be an essential part of any self respecting individual's make-up. 'Hear all, see all and say nowt. Eat all, sup all and pay nowt. And if ever thee does owt for nowt, do it for thee-sen (ie yourself)' may count as the extreme credo of the no-nonsense spirit. There is, it must be said, no trace of that implied tight-fisted parsimony in Robinson. Phlegmatic he may be but his warmth, generosity and good humour is of the sort bred by intelligent practicality, accepting that things are what they are and must be worked with, not against, deeply imbued with a downright common sense whose immediate response to a problem is 'What's to do?' rather than a defeatist 'Oh no.......'

In the course of one of our intermittent telephone conversations long before this book was mooted, staying in touch, sharing news, asking after this and that, we touched on the vicissitudes of life as a freelance – whether as a professional rider, builder (part of my own background) or writer – the setbacks, the constant need to steel yourself against disappointment, shrug it off and press on regardless – Robinson said, memorably: 'That's right – you care but you don't worry.'

One example: during his time on National Service in the army with the King's Own Light Infantry, stationed in York, he had leave to ride the Army Championship time-trial in Aldershot. Taking a train was not an option – the fare was too expensive – so he rode as far as Grantham and then tried to thumb a lift. He stood at the side of the A1 – the main trunk road to the south, at that time a two-lane highway – him and his bike, watching the traffic go past, indifferent, regardless. After a lot of futile waving of his thumb, he decided to bike not hike. Approximately 180 miles. He got to the Aldershot barracks, a vast complex of military installations and had a day's rest. The start was at 11am and he recorded the best time he'd ever done, 59m 52s. 'It was a good preparation ride,' he says, with characteristic disregard for obstacles. Put up and shut up is one way of expressing it. In his words: 'Life is what it is, better get on with it.' It is the professional's central maxim. No complaint about circumstances, conditions or obstacles, just get on with the job. He rode back, too. 'A good training ride' he called it. On another occasion, stranded somewhere after a race, he cadged a lift home in an RAF transport plane heading back to the base in Acaster Malbis, just outside York. The charge master, Ted Gerard, also a cyclist, was a pal of his. That said, everyone in the cycling world knew everyone else. Ted hailed from south London, an archetypal spiv, into all sorts, bit of this, bit of that, ducking and diving, bobbing and weaving. He eventually bought an island off Scotland where he lived for ten years, presumably scanning the straits with binoculars for the approach of the bailiffs in a revenue cutter.

After the great Batley Park misdemeanour, young Robinson got an upgrade: a positive luxury, an 18-inch bicycle built up by his father with bits from three old bikes that had lain in a garage, unused and neglected. He bought them – five bob* (ie shillings) the lot – from their owner, a wealthy client for whom he was doing a job, and fettled them into a couple of serviceable machines, one for young Robinson, one for his big brother Des, Desmond, three years older.

It was about this time that he was diagnosed with possible diabetes. Every playtime at the Junior School, which lay some six or seven hundred yards from the family house in Day Street, his mother brought him a cup of Bovril or Oxo or plain beef broth as a tonic. The scare didn't seem to discommode him and it was a false alarm. The beef broth? Mother making sure to build him up against infection. He and his friends roared off on their bikes, heading for the pit stacks of the collieries, riding up and down their steeps, a bit of cyclo-cross to the top and daredevil skidding back on the slopes' loose surface. One of Robinson's uncles was a miner and he remembers him always scrubbed and pink. Fond of a pint, too. The Miners' and Working Mens' Institutes had special opening hours so that the pitmen could stop off on their way home from a shift to slake their thirst. 'By, those lads could drink,' Robinson told me. 'I had friends who worked in the mines and they could shift nine pints on a Saturday night – it never seemed even to touch the sides.'

Robinson's father Henry, born in 1904, came from a long line of joiners. Early records show one of his ancestors living at Old Laund in Lancashire, just north of Burnley in 1459. Laund, linked to the original root 'land', means 'an open space among woods, a glade, untilled ground, pasture. The name of the locale fits the people who lived there, for the early Robinsons were small-holders, pastoral and arable, who, by canny dealing, gradually extended their property, became entrepreneurs and branched out into the textile trade. They

---

* The origin of bob as slang for a shilling is obscure. Shilling itself is probably from a Teutonic word rendering the Latin solidus the silver coin whose abbreviation 's' features in our old money, l s d. For a summary of counting in old money – pounds, shillings and pence – see *Appendix II.*

got wealth and, in settlement of an unpaid debt, took ownership of a fine manor house, Swinsty Hall, in the village of Clifton, south-west of Harrogate, some 25 miles from Old Laund. Thus the Robinsons arrived in Yorkshire in 1590 and, for seven generations, the Robinson men were designated 'joiners and journeymen' – that is, they worked at day's wages (French *journée*). The title of joiner is generic but in this case the trade was, foremost, that of wheelwright – a valuable asset to someone whose main enterprise is in producing crops and has a need for a cart to ferry them to market, along with the cattle they'd reared. Brian Robinson's grandfather, Henry – and the name Henry predominates for the eldest son in the family genealogy – interrupted the succession of wheelwrights. His death certificate names him 'farmer'. Interestingly, echoing the apparent oddity of Shakespeare's will in which he bequeathed his wife, Anne Hathaway, his 'second best bed', grandpa Henry details a 'feather bed and bedstead and bedding' as part of his bequest to his widow, Charlotte, along with (presumably a favourite) 'corner cupboard'. (This is all noted in the spidery copperplate of the solicitor's clerk's relief nib pen on a slightly foxed and age-jaded white page.) These items were to be set aside for her to inherit 'after my disease' [ie decease] should she prove to be 'the longer liver'. Their eldest son, Henry, Robinson's father, resumed the family tradition as a joiner and journeyman, a tradition which his younger son continued.

Henry married Milly Backhouse in 1927 when he was 23 and she, a cotton winder at a local mill, was 21. She was employed to attend a massive machine which spun out cotton thread onto cones, for the warp in the fabric, or else onto smaller tubes, or cops, for the weft. As soon as a cone was full she had to reach over the working gear to lift it clear, snip the thread, replace it with an empty cone and stack the full cone on a rack on top of the machine. She needed a quick eye, nimble fingers and steady concentration. It was disconcerting, potentially dangerous, work. There was not much in the way of safety guards or rails. The demon mill ground on, champing its remorseless jaws at speed.

Robinson was born in 1930 and grew up in Henry and Milly's first house, in Ravensthorpe, three rooms upstairs (one bedroom scarce big enough for a bed), one main room downstairs plus a scullery, with an outside loo, no garden but a back yard shared with other houses in the row, front door opened straight onto the pavement. It stood adjacent to the workshop in which Robinson senior worked as a joiner/shopfitter and belonged to the boss of the firm. Power for the various machines – lathes, saws, drills, planers, dust extractors and so on – came from a single-cylinder gas engine and when the drone of the motor wound up early every morning, it was the signal for father to leave for work. Robinson remembers sneaking into the big timber store – a large building on three floors, open to the winds – after all the men had gone home, to play, him and his brother Des and their pals.

All manner of games. Hide and seek among the stacks, king of the castle on the tops, the exhilaration of climbing the piles of wood drying out ready for working, games of tag all round the place, the excitement of running free in the grown-ups' outsize world when the grown-ups had gone.

In the narrow alleyway along one side of the house, his father had a hen run for laying birds, clutches of eggs to eat or sell as a supplement to the family income. In the garage next to the house, he kept a motorbike and side-car, just big enough to squeeze in the two boys for a weekend trip out into the country or a jaunt to the coast. After the motorbike came a Raleigh three-wheeler, and, finally, a four-wheel Ford 8. When petrol rationing was imposed early in the war, the car had to be laid up and partially dismantled.

Beneath the house was a cellar. In one corner, below a lidded chute down from ground level, a heap of coal. In another corner, a pile of wood. To one side, by a chimney breast, the copper for boiling the linen. The cellar was a dank, grimy, murky place, filled with the smell of coal-dust and that indefinable damp must of decay that lingers in dark underground places and lit by a single grimy window, its glass opaque with filth and barred across with a wire mesh grille. It was the horror dungeon of any child's febrile imagination and it gave Robinson the creeps when he was a kid. He has a recurring dream, even today, which must be rooted in his dread of the sooty gloom in that subterranean hole. 'I'm back down there, it must be that place, and there's a bogey man coming for me. It's horrible. Apparently I wake up gasping *Err...errr....*'

Mirfield is encircled by a number of big cities in the industrial heartland of Yorkshire: Wakefield, Leeds, Bradford, Halifax, Huddersfield, long famous for textiles, engineering (plant for the mills), tool-making, manufacturing. (Mirfield itself was known for its tanneries, maltsters and large railway marshalling yard.) Immediately beyond the perimeter of the dense mass of the urban labyrinths packed with warehouses, mills, factories, houses, lies the open country of the great shire with its three Ridings (Old English *thriding*, third) that might be called England's broad chest. This was Robinson's playground as he grew up, later his training ground. In summer and spring, when school finished, he and Des and their friends spent the holidays roaming at will, across the fields, in the local woods, in Batley Park, or foraging out on their bikes. They'd set off with a picnic, sandwiches and a bottle of drink and, in the way of kids who don't know how time works nor how long a day is going to be, nor yet how to count or gauge its interminably long hours as they pass, but, in the way of cyclists, eat before they're hungry and drink before they're thirsty, the grub was usually eaten and the fizzy pop drunk by 10.30 in the morning.

At 11am on Sunday 3 September 1939, the Prime Minister Neville Chamberlain declared war in a broadcast to the nation from Downing Street. 'I remember that,' says Robinson. 'We were round at my grandma's to listen to the announcement on the radio. She was a bit of a tartar, a bit "kids should be seen and not heard", if you like. I was sat on her horsehair sofa, wearing shorts, and there were stiff horsehairs poking up through the cover and scratching the backs of my legs. It was that itchy. Like a coconut mat. I kept wriggling about against the prickliness and grandma glared at me and said: "Sit still, we're trying to listen." That was what she'd always say "sit there and be still". She couldn't bear fidgeting. Of course I didn't know what it was all about, being at war, I mean.'

Sister Jean had been born in April 1937. The house was, plainly, too cramped to accommodate them all, and, just after the war broke out, they moved to a larger place on nearby Dewsbury Moor, which overlooked Ravensthorpe, about two miles distant. A council house with three sizeable bedrooms. A bathroom. A bathroom –'would you believe it?' At the time most houses had only a single, cold water tap supplying a copper in which to boil water for clothes washing or kettles to boil water on a gas stove or coal-fired range to fill a tin tub for a bath in front of the fire. An outside midden, or earth closet, served as a loo.

Robinson stayed at the same school. 'We mostly walked or, if I could, I cadged a ride on a pal's bike, me in front working the pedals and him sitting on the saddle.'

The new house also had a large back garden. Something in the atavistic Robinson memory triggered, or maybe it was genetic, for Henry and Milly began to supplement their income through an enterprise which went back five centuries to the Old Laund: small-holding. The land behind the house, about 100 square yards in size, bounded by a railway line with open fields beyond, became an allotment. They grew vegetables – cabbages, sprouts, potatoes (which often came up riddled with worm-holes, says Robinson remembering the eyes in the spuds) – they kept two pigs and set up a large shed full of hutches which were home, eventually, to forty rabbits…for sale and for their own pot, of course. They started out with two Dutch does and a Flemish buck which, true to their reputation, bred like rabbits.

Robinson senior made a greenhouse in sections at the workshop and he and the two boys carted it back to the new house on his bike: the bottom half of the frame resting on one pedal, Des and Brian guiding the bike either side, father pushing on the saddle. The bed for the greenhouse they laid from used bricks, of which there were plenty in a dump halfway between workshop and house. They loaded Jean's old pram, converted as a trolley, and humped them back, trip after trip. 'That kind of thing is what makes your legs strong, I suppose.'

GF   Did you help in the garden, too?

BR   Well, I did, because I had to, it wasn't a question of being asked, it was expected, but I was a bit of a reluctant gardener, shall we say? Anyway, being coerced, it rubs off on you.

The greenhouse supplied prolific quantities of tomatoes and lettuce plants – Robinson used to cycle round delivering pounds of tomatoes at a time to family friends round about the district.

Robinson senior, as a skilled tradesman, and now aged 42, was exempt from call-up to the services. Instead he did a number of jobs related to the war effort – driving wagons transporting supplies and provisions from railway stations to one military depot or another and helping clear bomb damage in Sheffield – before being directed to work in a local cotton mill, now converted into a factory making doors for Halifax bombers. The Halifax of Yorkshire shared night-raid duties over Germany with that other famous bomber, the Lancaster. Thus, the two inveterate warring houses of England, whose rivalry had once torn the realm apart, were now united in its defence.

Robinson remembers, one summer holiday, going with his father on a trip to Sheffield to clear bomb damage. 'Sheffield's in a deep bowl of land, as you know, and when we got to the top of the rim of it and looked down, we could see all these steel girders sticking up from the wrecked buildings, twisted and bent in all kinds of magical shapes. Magical to me, as a youngster, not to anyone caught up in the devastation, of course.'

All back gardens had been partly excavated to take an Anderson shelter, named for John Anderson, the minister in charge of air-raid precautions. These were made from six curved sheets bolted together at the top, with steel plates at either end. Half buried in the ground with earth heaped on top, the entrance protected by a steel shield and an earthen blast wall, they measured 6ft 6in by 4ft 6in (1.95m by 1.35m) and could accommodate six people. The shelters were free to families earning less than £5 per week, otherwise, they cost £7. They were always dark, damp and disagreeable and especially chilly in winter. In fact, as he said wryly, the Robinson rabbits almost certainly had a more comfortable berth.

They stayed there overnight a few times until the uncertain charm of being up all night huddled in a cellar wore off and they ceased to bother when the sirens began to wail. Luckily, few bombs were dropped on Dewsbury or the surrounding districts. The Luftwaffe was routinely making for the major port at Liverpool and the larger industrial centres of Manchester and the vital steel plants in Sheffield. Following the railway lines across country as a marker back to the North Sea and home, they might jettison some of their unused lethal cargo on the way and did so once or twice – 'they must have had a couple of spares for us' – but they seem not to have known about the converted cotton mills-aircraft plants and the Dewsbury factories were a missable target. They produced shoddy – yarn obtained by tearing to shreds refuse wollen rags, the waste of the factory floor – which, with the addition of new wool is made into a kind of (inferior) cloth used in padding, carpets and so on. As to Wakefield, not far along the Calder valley, the biggest local enterprise was, and still is, rhubarb, forced in the dark of big sheds, rhubarb to eat, rhubarb pills against constipation and rhubarb to plump out jam when the juicier fruit is in short supply. The great cyclist Beryl Burton worked in a Wakefield rhubarb shed and since the rhubarb shed knew not day from night – it was always night-work, as it were – she and the boss of the rhubarb farm, Norman 'Nim' Carline, another outstanding time-triallist, could pick their moment to go out training on the bike. There's no evidence that the Germans knew about this or, if they did, cared.*

As soon as Jean was old enough to go to school – Robinson, now in the senior school, taking and collecting her – Milly, too, was drafted in to work in the factory. Women played a crucial wartime role in replacing male factory workers called to arms. As in so many spheres, the work such women did won no medals, was barely even recognised, and, after the war, largely and shamefully glossed over and forgotten. Indeed, it has only recently had mention and belated honourable thanks. Henry worked a twelve-hour night shift and, cycling home, used to wave to Milly as she went past in the bus on her way to the factory to start her twelve-hour day shift. (When I asked him 'Who looked after Jean?' Robinson paused. 'She must have been in with the rabbits,' he said.)

Tending the allotment and the livestock, meantime, fell to the two boys. The job was there to do so they did it. 'We mucked in and my life ever since has been like that – mucking in whatever has to be done, whatever's going on'. That included culling dandelions from the nearby fields on the way home from school to feed to the rabbits. There was a sewage farm across the field at the back of the house in whose well-manured soil the dandelions grew prolifically and abnormally large, up to two feet tall, their bright yellow heads not infrequently capped with a discarded French letter. The Robinson boys mixed tea grounds with the few oats that they could scrounge from pet shops and animal feed traders. In Jean's old pram they barrowed sacks of 'sewage muck' dug out of the settling beds a couple of fields away back to the garden.

Home from school, the boys peeled potatoes and got the basics ready for their father's tea before he left for the night shift and, every Saturday, went off to the market in Dewsbury to buy what they could in the food line.

---

* Once, when actors had to gather backstage to make the 'noise without' of a mob, they intoned the word 'rhubarb, rhubarb, rhubarb…' They were known as rhubarbers rhubarbing. A suggestive 19th century music hall comic song has a line 'Is your rhubarb up?' (a man to a woman or vice versa) meaning 'how about it?'

Traders flocked in from the Blackpool area, small-holders, salad-growers, nurserymen, wholesalers, and the kids joined the queues for anything they could get – a packet of biscuits, whatever. To begin with, the stall-holders wouldn't serve them. It was already an old trick: to beat rationing, mothers would send their children out one by one to plead hunger and come home with three or four times their share when the young scavengers reassembled. It took a visit by father Robinson to establish their credentials as bona fide representatives of just the one domicile.*

Robinson was still providing urine samples because of the suspected diabetes and, in lieu of his sugar ration, got extra bacon and cheese. He says this may have done him good in the long run and he still doesn't eat much sugar.

Between work at the factory, the calls of family and allotment, there was little time to do anything extraneous. In any case, father and mother were free at weekends only. Social life centred on the family home. The Robinsons didn't go out, they didn't buy clothes, they saved money. Frugality and busy busy hard work…it was no bad conditioning for a lad who eventually had to scrap for a living as a professional cyclist.

School, says Robinson, was so-so but books were never much of a lure. He and a couple of pals used to cycle along a path across the fields the two miles from the new house to the senior school they attended in Ravensthorpe. On a bike you could take short cuts and save time. There was no bike shed, they just propped the machines against a wall. Indeed, the bike lock is a relatively recent necessity. Not that former ages were less villainous but, somehow, the respect for a bicycle as an essential adjunct of anyone's existence protected it from common thievery. Bikes must have been stolen, but in certain communities the idea was unthinkable.

He liked and excelled at gym and sports and, aged thirteen, having failed entry to the grammar school – he'd had no expectation of passing – he went to the technical college in nearby Dewsbury to study for a trade qualification. Practical and theory in metalwork and woodwork, plus chemistry, English, mathematics, algebra, sports. Next door to the college, was what used to be called the Assistance office, for payments of the dole and other subventions. Robinson had to call in every week with half a crown, from his father, to help support his grandmother. Her husband, Robinson senior's father, had left her and there was, as yet, no state pension. Since Robinson's father was in full employment, he was obliged to contribute to his mother's subsistence. He was glad to do so, but this only exacerbated his vindictive feelings towards his father. Whenever they drove past a building site with the name Robinson on the board, he'd stop to find out if it was the absconder. 'If I ever catch that

---

* For wartime rationing, see *Appendix III.*

bastard...' he growled. The intention ducked the opportunity. Once the old man did turn up at the house and, suddenly disinclined to take a swing, his son merely refused to let him in.

In 1945, at the end of the war, Robinson's father took over an old joinery firm a quarter of a mile down the road from the aircraft factory. He'd been looking for such a place and, after the owner of this small firm died, Henry discussed buying the workshop with the man's widow, who lived in a house next door and was managing the business as best she could. There were only two old codgers working there at the time – the young men were away at the war. Henry negotiated the purchase and the sale was clinched in 1944. He was still working at the factory but called in at the workshop whenever he could to oversee the work – general house repairs and coffins. It was quite common for joinery firms to double as coffin-makers – they had the requisite skills and ready access to wood – which meant that they also commonly performed the duty of undertakers, especially in rural districts and for the urban poor. Funeral directors, where they operated, were too expensive for most people. Taking on duties for the disposal of the dead carried the bonus of a petrol allowance, when fuel was still under ration. The Ford 8 was reassembled and emerged from the garage.

In the way of making money wherever it was to be made, Robinson senior turned his adeptness with machines to profit after the war, buying up ailing motors at auction and repairing them to sell on. Purchase price: £30, sale price: £35...in the words of Mr Micawber, 'Result, happiness.' (An average weekly wage at the time was around £5.)

There is no better way to learn mechanicing than by watching and being guided by an expert and it was from his father that Robinson learned the skill, vital to him as a professional cyclist, of fixing bikes. The French have a saying: 'Quand j'entends, j'oublie; quand je vois, je me souviens; quand je fais, je sais.' When I hear, I forget; when I see, I remember; when I do, I know. These are the basics of apprenticeship (from the French word *apprendre* 'to learn'), being told how it's done, watching someone do it, then doing it yourself. I once stood by, after a ride with him out from Mirfield, as Robinson set my bike on a stand in the outside porch and casually repaired its broken mudguard with a riveter.

Robinson left technical college – top in his year in carpentry and joinery, second in metalwork – and began work in the workshop which Henry had now taken over completely. One of the old guys there, Harry, long past retirement age, kept on when the young men went off to war, got him started. The old lady took to the new people and when she moved from the house and offered to rent to the Robinsons they didn't hesitate. After they moved in, Robinson embarked on a formal seven-year apprenticeship under his father. Learning the trade at the bench, getting accustomed by daily practice to the use of tools – chisels, planes, saws, drills, squares and rules, straight edges and gauges, sharpening and setting, working from drawings and jigs, preparing and finishing wood, sanding and polishing, mixing glue and seeing to the routine chores which always fell to the youngest member of the workshop: keeping it swept, stoking the stove, pushing the handcart loaded with tools from site to site and, when he was still green, searching the shelves vainly for rubber mallets and brass tacks, left-handed screwdrivers, sky hooks, skirting board ladders, tartan paint and diamond hammers ('hardest substance known to man, lad, is a diamond, common knowledge, that') and 'fetch us a long wait, lad', till he twigged and saw the nascent sly smile on the older men's faces, pulling his leg as theirs had been pulled when they were tykes. Early on, he spent a lot of time reclaiming timber, particularly from big houses where beams had been used to shore up and reinforce cellars as air-raid shelters. (Timber was still rationed and when it did come off ration, the material on offer was generally second-rate, unseasoned stuff.) This entailed a lot of heavy work, heaving out the baulks, extracting the nails and dragging the wood up onto the machine bed to go through the mechanical saw. The more interesting work involved general repair of mills and property, re-cording sash windows and, answering a vogue for modernisation, making flush doors and boarding out banister rails with hardboard panels.

His father was a hard taskmaster but a good teacher – all the men he taught turned into good tradesmen – although inclined to flares of impatience. Perhaps he got it from his mother. He was short-tempered with fiddling about, bodging or slackness. But, an occasional 'Get done and bugger off' had no anger in it, rather it was a reminder that time was money and a regular tradesman not only needed to do good work he needed to do it fast. The apprenticeship in the workshop was supplemented by three sessions per week of night school, studying for the City and Guilds trade qualification, a three-year course in technical drawing, carpentry and joinery theory and practical work. They made models of window frames, door frames, different sorts of door, a roof – gables, hips, various pitches to acquaint themselves with the complex jointing required for the structure of beams, rafters, purlins, cross members, wall-plates. For the nights on technical drawing, Robinson strapped the large drawing board to his back for the bike ride into Dewsbury.

In the years immediately after the war, the Robinson joinery shop was called on by more and more people asking for space in their house to be converted into a bathroom. Out with the old tin tub and a farewell to the Council night-soil cart making the rounds of the earth closets. It was part of a wider social trend to better living conditions as the country faced the enormous task of building new housing to replace what had been bombed to rubble in vast tracts of towns and cities bombed flat. The Robinson enterprise did a lot of work repairing and fitting out houses to accommodate Latvians and Poles, displaced by the ravages of war and come to work in the textile and carpet factories.

2: BASH-UPS UP THE DALES

Yorkshire and the Midlands had long been a breeding ground for top-flight cyclists. The list of champions bred and tempered on the central spine and outspill of the Pennine Range and High Peak is long. Using England's central upland chain as a springboard west into the Lake District, east into the Wolds, the men and women of the region, have trained and continue to train on these hills for a multiplicity of events run by the numberless local Clubs and Wheelers.

From the age of 13, when he started college, Robinson began to pitch up for junior rides with the Huddersfield Road Club and, when he was 14, the earliest age permissible, he joined his brother as a member. (Father had been a member before the war.)

GF   I guess you were itching to go.

BR   Oh, yes. I didn't appreciate, at the time, why the Club didn't let youngsters join till 14 but looking at the run sheets – out into Derbyshire, Bakewell, Matlock and all over – well, they're some fair distance to ride. It's beyond me today.

The family trio, father and two sons, was already well established on the road. During Robinson's time at the technical college, they frequently cycled some 23 miles northwards through the gap between Bradford and Leeds past Otley and Bramhope to North Rigton, south of Harrogate, to visit an elderly aunt, sole survivor of his father's branch of the family. (The area – scenic moorland, villages of stone houses, gaunt crags dominating a patchwork of fields, sheep grazing – has been much used as a setting for Yorkshire television dramas and featured as the backdrop to the opening credits for Emmerdale.) It was these rides, he says, which really stirred and ingrained his passion for the bike. His father was a good rider, his brother Des became one of the best amateurs in the country and, if there was none of that humourless kick-arse, keep up or drop off mentality that has so often marred if not blighted the relationship between established cyclists and the tiro, there was unquestionably a huge boost of stimulus – the best sort of encouragement – for a stripling to be riding with older, faster men in friendly companionship. In a born cyclist, the impulse to compete is never far away and the Robinsons did their bit and bit and jostled for notional primes as part of the cheerful camaraderie and the natural drive in all cyclists to half-wheel and rack up speed.

Race you to the sign...first to the junction...beat you to the oak tree... Robinson wins, holds up his arms as his father sails past and sings out, 'Wrong tree'.

Robinson says he owed much to those early outings, the family three-up making the long spin there and back, geeing each other on, laying the foundation of racing spirit, fitness and muscle power. Exuberance, too. Cycle-racing may call on an endless capacity to absorb suffering, but it is rooted in and sparked by enjoyment, the need to ride the bike, the irrepressible desire to make the two wheels hum.*

The local Ravensthorpe Cycling Club had become (temporarily) defunct – all the young riders were away at the war. Since Robinson senior had been a Huddersfield man before the war and brother Des was now working there, as an engineering draughtsman at Hopkinson's Mechanical Valves, the HRC was the obvious choice. One of the old members, Stanley Smith, performed the invaluable role of looking after the younger riders. Men like Smith were invaluable to clubs, a friendly bridge between the skinny new kids and the established seniors, as well as carrying a roll of tools in their saddlebag to get riders out of trouble. Club runs set off at 9 o'clock and, come the warmer months, were out pretty well all day, if not at a particularly rapid pace. Stanley, slower and more leisurely in his ways by now, shepherded the juniors from 10 o'clock onwards. There was much to be said for this gentler initiation. Stanley had never been a racer but he was a solid club man, an anchor, and, if any youngster got dropped, Stanley was there to sweep them up and lend them the comfort and support of his presence alongside. In the absence of the young men in the forces, there was a preponderance, at the time Robinson first turned up, of 'youngsters, rejects and oldies' as he puts it. In those early days before he was earning, he had sixpence a week pocket money, enough for two cups of tea on a club run. Equivalent values of purchasing power, past and present, are always impossible to pin accurately, nor does it help to say that sixpence in old money equals two and a half pence in new. However, two cups of tea and your pocket money is gone...it gives some idea.

The first really substantial expedition he remembers came in the glorious summer of 1945, not long after he'd become a member. They rode off for a week to the Lake Districts, over all the passes, round all the lakes and one night stayed in a farmhouse – the Youth Hostels were full. They came down to breakfast and were goggle-eyed: bacon and eggs, apple pie, lashings of bread and butter, jam and marmalade aplenty...that morning's ride to lunchtime was, in consequence, a rather sedate affair.

Even as a junior, he became more and more involved with the club programme: longer rides, steadily boosting the pace, pitching up for club

---

* Most pros continue to ride a bike after they retire, if not immediately, with some notable exceptions. Jacques Anquetil didn't and, when he was racing, he said, alluding to his bike: 'What miner loves his pick?'

time-trials, passing up bottles and food to the senior men. There were club nights, too, a cup of tea, hanging around talking about cycling, getting enthused by the stories of races won, races that ought to have been won, the rivalries with other clubs, the year ahead, the events to go for, the best bikes to be had, the opposing claims of componentry, the traditions and folklore of cycling, the banter and chaffing which informs and feeds the conversation off the bike as well as on it.

The club runs, a hundred miles or so, headed to most points of the compass from start points outside pubs which, more or less routinely, were taken as direction finders. They'd originated as hostelries and travellers' rests, after all, and served a more ecumenical purpose than simply as ale-houses, offering tea and sandwiches as well as beer. The meet at The Fleece in Berry Brow, on the A616 some distance south of Huddersfield, sent them into the High Peak district of Derbyshire, via Holmfirth, Holme Moss, Saddleworth Moor, on to Bakewell and Matlock Bath – known as 'a seaside town without the sea', being replete with fish'n'chippies and amusement arcades – and back, perhaps over The Shivering Mountain – Mam Tor – (favoured venue for a big end-of-season hill climb). The George Hotel in Brighouse led westward across the Pennine Way into Lancashire and Heptonstall Moor, Wadsworth Moor, the Forest of Trawden or else north to Keighley Moor and the dales: Airedale and Wharfedale, Garsdale, Swaledale, Arkengarthdale, Coverdale, Nidderdale and a loop round Ripon.

The terrain – whether closer dales or the open moorland spread along the flanks and across the tops of the big rounded hills, outcrops of the Pennine chain, dipping into and out of the strines (an Old English word meaning 'the meeting of waters'), namely the deeper cuts hewn by rivers teeming out of the limestone – makes superb country for riding. Long climbs on the exposed roads, withering lifts up the steep twisting lanes out of the spouts, where the water has cut further and further into the rock. Into the basin and up out again, it's like riding the inner surface of a cauldron. Robinson hit the haul out of Strines Dike, below Foulstone Moor, for the first time when he was thirteen. He walked. Sixty years later, I followed him as he rode steadily up it, in the saddle, inured to the nastiness of it, giving away nothing of what he was thinking, which may have been coarse. The gradients are either extreme or plain wearisome. The landscape often unsheltered to winds. The continual switch from climbing to descending is a rare conditioner for lungs and legs. Once Robinson joined the serious club runs, he found himself part of a line of succession that had produced some of the finest amateur riders in Britain. The code among the top club riders was that anyone was welcome to join the ride but if you got dropped, you got dropped, that was that. When Des started racing at the age of 18, Robinson, then 15, went training with him, did all the rides that the older boy did, mixed it with the older clubmen and other guys from across the region, men like Gordon Thomas and Peter Procter, the Poole brothers, Jack Fancourt. Many of them had been racing before the war so had bags of experience. Robinson held his own, too, and he says that those training rides were a lot harder than many of the races he rode later. As a result, when he did start racing, he weathered the shock of the high pace much more easily than he might have done.

His father had told him that he couldn't start racing until he was 18 and, as in so many aspects of his life at that time, he didn't bitch. Father's word was law and the prohibition had a salutary effect. When he did start racing against opposition in open events he had (he recalls) so much pent-up energy, it was like letting a greyhound out of the trap. That said, his first time-trial, a club race over the hills round Mirfield, he did nothing. Nerves? Inexperience? Not parcelling out his effort well? Whatever the reason, the time was rubbish and without a decent qualifying time he had no credentials for inclusion in any race. The first junior event he rode, with two of his close pals, a 25 mile time-trial, was undersubscribed so they were allowed in, to make up the numbers. By this time, Robinson was fizzing: the innate dissatisfaction with the only time he had on record, the hard training he had put in with Des, the desire to make a showing, the sheer class already in his young legs. He and his two friends came first, second and fourth, grabbed all bar one handicap prize, and they were off.

He began to record his times and placings:

Dinnington Institute Road and Path Cycle Club 25, June 1948: winner, 1h 3m 52s.

Sheffield Sports CC July 1948: won by brother Des, Robinson 2m 32s down.

In May 1949, his first massed start race on the Team Valley circuit, a Trading estate outside Newcastle-upon-Tyne, built on a government initiative and completed in 1938. Robinson came 9th helping his team to the overall win…and so on, results he noted on a sheet of plain foolscap paper, neatly lined across and down with a pencil.

Brother Des was prominent in the wins, so, too, R. J. 'Bob' Maitland, with whom Robinson later rode the Tour de France in 1955, named (for instance) as winner of the Richmond Road Race in June 1949. In this mass-start event, on a circuit round Swalesdale out of Hipswell, Robinson came 12th out of 74 finishers and the Hudderfield RC took away a prize of £3. Two weeks later, Maitland won the Isle of Man time-trial – Robinson was 5m 30s down on the winning time but first on handicap – for age. Maitland was six years older.

The Isle of Man week was a high point of the British cycle-racing year. The hilly main road round the island could be closed to traffic, so, too, the roads across its waist and up and over the main height of Snaefell, which squats in the centre like the ornamental boss of a shield. Most important, since the Isle of Man has its own parliament, the Tynwald, which dates from around 979 AD, it lay outside the jurisdiction of Great Britain and therefore, beyond the reach of the NCU and its ban on massed racing on the roads.

Motor racing had begun on Man in 1904 for a similar reason. A speed limit of 20mph had been imposed on the mainland in that year and, seeking a more indulgent climate of regulation, the fast crowd approached the Tynwald, which agreed to the staging of the inaugural Gordon Bennett Car trial. The first of the famous Tourist Trophy (TT) for motorbikes followed in 1911, using the Snaefell mountain course later used by the cyclists.

The cycle racing on the island grew into The Manx Cycling Week. The biggest races were the Manx International Trophy, over three laps of the Snaefell TT course, and the Manx Premier for professional riders, using a shorter circuit through Clypse. The Snaefell course, 37.75 miles long, runs north from Douglas to Ramsey, up over the road below the mountain and back to Douglas. The first winner of the Manx Trophy, in 1936, over one lap, was Charley Holland who, the following year, became the first Briton to enter the Tour de France. (See my Inside the Peloton for that story.) The Frenchman Pierre Chazaud won in 1937 and, following the win by the Englishman Bill Messer in 1939, it wasn't until 1963 that another Briton won – Tom Simpson. His predecessors on the podium included some of the greats of the continental peloton: Ercole Baldini, Italy, '56, Seamus 'Shay' Elliott, Ireland, '59, André Darrigade, France, 1960, Jo de Roo, Holland, '61, Rudi Altig, Germany, '62. Simpson's second win, not much more than a month before his death on Mont Ventoux, 1967, bracketed Elliott's reprise ('64) and Jacques Anquetil's victory, in 1965. Four of those Manx winners also won the World champion's rainbow jersey on the road: Baldini, 1958, Darrigade, 1959, Simpson, 1965, Altig, 1966. That Anquetil, le Maître, the first five-times winner of the Tour de France, could be lured to the Isle of Man – for a whacking purse, no doubt – gives some indication of just how prestigious the meeting and its main prize were.

In 1949, Robinson competed in the Mannin Veg (literally the 'little one' in Manx), for juniors – a single lap of the mountain course – and came 10th. After the Isle of Man week, the pain of appendicitis that had first bitten earlier in the season recurred and was so severe that he went to see the doctor. He walked into the surgery, the physician examined him, poked him in the inflamed area, confirmed the diagnosis and rang the hospital. Robinson set off walking, straight away, and by the time he'd got to the infirmary the appendix had burst and infection had set in. He was in bed for a week. The weather was hot, the ward so stifling, that he crawled out of bed to sit on the balcony for some relief of whatever breeze there was. When his father came in to visit, he was aghast at the scar: the surgeon had cut the lad straight up the middle. He rounded on the doctor. 'Bloody hell, why did they have to cut through that thick wall of muscle?'

The appendectomy put paid to the rest of the season.

In 1950, brother Des won the 'big one', the main Manx International Trophy, and Robinson himself then competed in the Mannin Veg.

'I was on song and won the three primes on the way into the final sprint, well-placed, and I moved over to the right of the road ready for the downhill run-in. Suddenly, the gear jammed, the chain dropped between the little sprocket and the chainstay and locked solid. I still had enough momentum to keep me going and I freewheeled over the line for fourth. It was a real disappointment, although just as well, probably, because Dad had come over on a day trip and I think he'd have gone completely crazy if we'd done the double.'

He was riding his first new bike, that day, a hand-built, bespoke frame – 'a gen [genuine] iron' he calls it – made by Johnny Berry in Manchester, the favoured frame-builder of the moment – tone, style, line. He rode across to get measured and order colour – yellow…folie de grandeur? – and, when it was ready, collected it and rode home with it over his shoulders. It cost 15 guineas and Robinson had to save a long time to get the money. There was not a lot of good equipment to be had or spare cash to buy it, so he'd begged and borrowed components. The gear that jammed was an old, single pulley Simplex. When he banged it into the big gear for the final sprint, the change was too much for it to cope with and the chain slipped the little sprocket. Years later, he cautioned young riders against faddish obsession with and spending too much on this bit of fancy kit over that bit of fancy kit. What counts is technical efficiency, dependability.

For five years running, the Isle of Man week was Robinson's annual holiday, putting up at Mrs Clark's Guest House, lash-up breakfasts and high teas and, in the years he went there as an amateur, cloudless blue skies and warm sunshine. Twenty of them went from the club. It was a young cyclist's heaven. All the racing men and women of note turned up, internationals and top club riders, so there were plenty of high quality races to watch when they themselves weren't out on the road, either training or racing. Afternoons in pleasure boats, rowing them around like dodgem cars, having sea battles and running fights with water pistols. In the evening, it was off to the Villa Marina in Douglas, girls on one side of the ballroom, blokes on the other and that long walk across the open floor between, ostensibly to ask a girl for a dance but really to chat her up. Joe Loss and other bands giving it the works on the platform. A few beers to get the courage up, pretending to be able to waltz and quick step to impress the girls. It was a rare interlude of complete let-go and leisure. He can't remember any bad weather. Was it the perfect summer idyll when no rain fell nor grey skies blotted the high spirits? With neither complaint nor dismay, Robinson says that he didn't have much in the way of idle time when he was an apprentice. And, having become a qualified tradesman after that seven-year stint at the bench and the drawing board, he faced the obligatory two-year National Service (which ordinarily began at 18 and had been deferred till he had finished his apprenticeship). He would not, therefore, be free of service of one sort or another until he was 23 years old. Until then, his life revolved round work and cycling.

After the racing had finished for the year, there followed what he calls 'the social season' until the end of January when, shaking off the indulgence of the winter, they had to start thinking about getting some miles in. From one of the local rendezvous on Sunday morning, they'd set off at 8am and build to a regular 100 mile ride, back by two and meet up again in the cinema at 3pm for the matinee. Three nights of the week were taken by night school. Monday night was given over to fettling the bike and on the two remaining nights they'd do a 25 miles chain-gang with the clubmen, or else he and Des would do a flat-out 25 on their own. That was the pattern until Easter and the first belter, a group of eight riders on a four day round trip to the south coast organised by Des – first overnight in Warwick, second in the New Forest – a four-day, no holds barred mile-eater. The group included Peter Bates, an international who'd ridden the Paris-London in 1947, one of the first races on open roads in Britain. It was won by George Fleming, a time-trialler at heart, who later managed Robinson and his brother in the Route de France stage race.

In the summer of 1948, London hosted the Olympic Games and Robinson and a gang of others, rode down to Windsor Park to watch the road race, a three hundred and sixty miles round trip. Their pal Bob Maitland was riding. This, he said, gave him the bug for road racing.

After Easter, as night-school sessions tailed off, training began to get serious and the longest ride they did was the Wednesday Bash-up up the Dales. Twenty-six miles round trip from Mirfield to the Ellis Briggs shop in Shipley and from there a ride of forty miles, sixty-six all told. Home from work for two poached eggs on brown toast and off to join the others, forty guys heading off at sink-or-swim speed. There was always a real hell-for-leather dash off the front up the narrow road, round the turn on the sharp hill overlooking Bolton Abbey – those who got shelled out on the ascent racing to join on the downhill. Another sprint up the last climb on Hollins Hill down into Shipley Glen across Charlestown Bridge on a wide road, forty racing cyclists going for it, flat out on a wide road, taking all manner of risks, the blood running high, adrenaline pumping, it was wild. The local police finally got wind and, one night, they were out waiting for the stampede. Not that any member of the stampede paid a blind bit of notice and they vastly outnumbered the constabulary, anyway.

GF   I think you've mentioned that ride to me before.

BR It's still one of my favourite rides. Not on the roads we used then, you can get smaller roads, much prettier. It's just 100km and makes a good evening ride because we do that regular, now, or did, before I got crocked.*

There might be a weekend outing stopping overnight in a Youth Hostel, or a one-day club ride from Mirfield to Blackpool, sandwiches and a drink as they rode down the promenade and straight back home. They did the same ride for fun, too, eight or a dozen of them setting off on the round trip of some 180 miles at 8 am. Blackpool, 'a famous seaside place…that's noted for fresh air and fun.' The Golden Mile promenade between the two piers, North and South, either gale-swept or sun-kissed and always patrolled up and down by green and cream municipal trams. Holidaymakers and day trippers lounged in striped deck chairs or, in inclement weather, still getting their full dose of fresh air, huddled up against the burly gust of the wind off the Irish Sea. The famous Tower, 158 metres high, inspired by the Tour Eiffel in Paris and opened to the public in 1894. Resident organist in the Tower ballroom, Reginald Dixon, 'Mr Blackpool', vamped away at the celebrated Wurlitzer organ, but that had been a cosier entertainment for their family outings along with tea and cakes in a seafront café. On day visits with the club set, the Galleon Bar in the Winter Gardens served a pint of 'old ale and sandwiches, too'. Champagne on tap at Yates' Wine Lodge. Candy floss and lipstick pink and white rock with the name all the way through from booths along the Front. Donkey rides on the sands, kiss-me-quick hats and souvenirs, What the Butler Saw machines, amusement galleries and penny arcades. Into the Pleasure Beach across the foyer where jets of compressed air blew the girls' skirts up round their knickers, and inside, the fairground noise of the mighty steam organ accompanying stomach-curdling rides on the Big Dipper, the Grand National, the Ghost Train. Distorting mirrors, wobbly cakewalks and the Haunted House followed by beer for the lads and Babycham in a lady's glass for the lasses at Fanlight Fanny's across the road. Blackpool, the Mecca for working class outings and escapees from the retired miners' home just up the road in Bispham. Guest Houses and lodgings where the bath plugs were jealously guarded by sharp-nosed landladies putting a curb on excessive use of hot water and prone to turfing their guests out after breakfast at 9 o'clock on the dot to get off for their daily ration of holidaymaking 'And don't come back while teatime'. The treeless cliff top verge afforested with painted wooden, Council-owned stand-up substitutes during summer and still in

---

* In November 2009, Robinson came off his bike during the weekly ride with friends, spent two months in hospital and, at the time of writing (April 2010), is riding again, stints upwards of 40 miles, after getting back in shape on the turbo, but, inevitably, fretting about the length of time it is taking him to recover fully.

full artificial pasteboard leaf come autumn for the annual influx to see the famous illuminations – another draw for family trips. For the wheelers from Mirfield, a film at the cinema in the afternoon, fish and chips on the promenade and the long ride home into dusk and twilight. In the harsher months, they wore tailored shorts, based on a French pattern and made by an ex-cyclist in Huddersfield, buttoned at the knee over long socks; shirt and a long continental sweater which fell below the waist and had pockets on the chest and back. These sweaters were expensive, imported from France and not so easy to get hold of. Otherwise, it would be government surplus bomber jackets or the common or garden fabric windcheater. In the summer, shirt and sleeveless pullover and shorts. And, confirming the working-class, decidedly low-caste image that cyclists have had to endure for so long, Robinson and his friends often wore a flat cap. The plateless cycling shoe made of perforated leather, cut below the ankle bone, its sole fairly supple, without stiffening, more resembled a Scottish dancing pump than a shoe per se shoe. In that cycling gear, on a jaunt, the muckers (pals) would occasionally play a kick-about game of football. Canoodling? Ah, but they were more reserved times, those. There was little to spare of time or opportunity for much of that lovey-dovey stuff. And perhaps not.

In 1950 (he thinks) the Huddersfield RC sent a bunch of their riders down to the concrete vélodrôme at Herne Hill for the Team Pursuit championship finals. It was Robinson's first trip to London. Since the Huddersfield crowd was known as road men, there were a lot of jibes from the hard-core southern trackies. 'All right lads? Worked out how you're going to stop without brakes?' Most of the Yorkshire men had never seen a banked track, so their showing – they got into the semi-finals – was a fair effort. Thereafter, they rode the circuits at Brands Hatch, in Kent (another motorbike venue), and at Bishop's Stortford. If it was the first time on a concrete track, the Huddersfield men were already familiar with grass tracks, the early proving ground of many racers of the era. They frequently rode across to the grass track at Roundhay for training stints and races and got a reputation for dusting up the local riders over five miles. One evening, before the start, a local grass track champion – one of the gold watch brigade as the Huddersfield men called them: accumulating wins through a season for the overall prize at its conclusion – expressed his umbrage at the interlopers who went off hell-for-leather from the start. 'Where's these guys who go from the gun at a five?'

'Not us. It's that big feller over there.'

The gun goes and the HRC hit the front, one after the other, belting it as hard as they could. As Robinson commented: 'They didn't see us for the rest of the race. And afterwards, we had to ride home in the dark, no lights. But we had a lot of fun, it was hard racing and good camaraderie, combining social and training, if you like. It's where I learnt track riding, at any rate.

One post-Tour criterium on a track in Britanny, I went down and Anquetil rode over me. I suppose you could call that a sort of privilege.'

As soon as he'd started racing, Robinson began to show well in a discipline he never really enjoyed, the time-trial. The continentals call it the race of truth – that gospel preached by the dyed-in-the-wool purists of the NCU – but it has never formed the staple of their racing, as in the UK. Their penchant had, from the beginning, been more for the duel, pitting the combined force of wits and brawn against an opponent. It stemmed from an innate thirst for competition which may be said to have begun with the ancient Greeks, for whom there was no human activity which could be separated from a wish to best a rival, whether in politics, on the battlefield or in the athletics stadium. The advent of the BLRC, which caused such conflict on the British domestic racing scene, arose out of mounting frustration at being denied the spur of this form of rivalry*. Initiated into racing in the test against the clock, Robinson's truer urge had been prompted by road racing. He was already showing singular prowess as a climber and developing the characteristics of an all-rounder, the classic rouleur: strong, fast, robust and clever. Second in a town circuit race in Dun Loaghaire in July 1950 (a prize of ten guineas**), a prime in the massed start race round Sutton Park a month later, fifth in the National Championships on the Isle of Man Clypse course, he capped his season with third place in the National Hill Climb race on Barber's Hill in Llangollen, followed by his first win in the Huddersfield RC Hill Climb to the top of Holme Moss.

The annual Huddersfield RC Hill Climb used the northern approach to what had become well-established as one of the noted landmarks in club racing. (Most clubs had their favourite ascent for the close of season lung-buster.) The village of Holmfirth – used as a location in the filming of *Last of the Summer Wine* – sits at the foot of steep banks which form either side of the Holme valley. The road out of the village keeps company with the river a mile or so into Holmbridge, approximately 623 feet (190m) above sea level. From there, skirting the Brownhill Reservoir, it climbs steadily towards the village of Holme. The road then sweeps round to the left and soon develops some hostile gradient, above 14% about a mile from the summit. The hill climb of three miles to 1,719ft (524m) opposite the radio transmitter, is timed from the shepherd's hut at the foot and, the first time I rode it with Robinson, he pointed the hut out to me as we went by at leisurely speed. 'What was your record?' I asked. 'Six minutes ten, I think.

---

* See *Appendix I*

** A guinea was 21/- in old money, originally a notional sum used in auctions where the auctioneer took a commission of 5%, ie one shilling in the pound, on a winning bid, to facilitate calculation.

I set it on an evening trial'* he said, his upper body bobbing slightly, pedals twiddling fluently. I glanced up at the climb ahead, long swooping bends, dry grass moorland to either side, a watery sun. 'Still is,' he said. 'What?' I said. 'It's not been broken, yet. Perhaps they don't bother.' And he laughed. He laughs readily. I watched as his bike pulled slowly away from mine, not that he seemed to be making much of an effort, just keeping the rhythm, turning the legs, steady pace, no abrupt changes in tempo. At a leisurely speed or not, I could only watch him go. Riding his home ground.

The following year, 1951, Robinson won the Team Valley massed start race over forty miles – first prize £3 and a prime which netted him two guineas. (A recently published index of money equivalence notes that the average weekly wage, then £7-8s, was worth £499 in today's monetary value.) Seventh in the amateur Manx Trophy, won by R.W. Bowes, Robinson took the Wagstaff Award – worth four guineas – and, a month later, the prize of a set of spoons plus £2-3s-6d for second place on the Hardway Course at Sutton Park. He won a major road race, in pelting rain, the 260-mile Dublin-Galway-Dublin, in August, his club Hill Climb over Holme Moss in October and, shortly afterwards, came second in the National Championships Hill Climb to the previous year's winner, R Stringwell. The course, up Saintbury Hill near Broadway in Gloucestershire, is still frequently used in hill climbs. It runs 1.3 miles, from a height of around 170 feet in the village up an extremely steep section onto a milder gradient and the top at 263 feet. The experience of the anti-gravity event is universal: a flat-out sprint up severe contours to rapid burn-out of lungs and legs, spent breath and flooding lactic acid – catchers wait to help spent riders off the machine. New Englanders call their end-of-season rides 'last gasp'. The ascription is apt for the British club hill climb folly.

On the reverse of the page where Robinson noted his results for 1951, he has totted up a list of smaller figures – 25, 50, 34 and so on – a number of figures over 100 and one of 1412. These he has totalled to 2962 and, underneath, '3000 miles', presumably the distance he'd ridden that year. On the inside cover of the folder, a piece of hardboard, his winnings '£24-7-0'.

Getting to races was, in some ways, simple: he and his fellow clubmen cycled to them wherever possible. To get to Ireland for the Dun Laoghaire Grand Prix on Saturday he had to finish up a job refurbishing an office in Bradford on Friday evening, and cycled off to Liverpool to catch the boat. Once landed in Ireland, a hunt for digs and, next morning, ready to ride. The man who beat him, Comerford, was a hulk of a man – 'he was that big, he could have put his hand on my head and squashed me into the ground' – and

---

* In fact, 6m 13s, set in the Festival of Britain Hill Climb, 1951.

went with Robinson when he broke clear then sat on his wheel, all the way to the finish. Robinson remonstrated, called him all manner of names, 'wheel-sucker' probably the mildest of them, but the man wouldn't budge and took the win.

For the races in Team Valley, they had to ride to Leeds and catch the Newcastle bus, wrapping the wheels up in a blanket and disguising the frame so they could get on. Until one of the men turned up with a bike, no cover, and tried to plead with the driver to let him on. That, says Robinson, was the end of their bus rides to Newcastle with bikes masquerading as oversize suitcases and the gormless creature who'd dished them got a right bashing for it.

The rides to the racing circuits were as much a part of the training as designated runs. To get to Sutton Park (which is still used as a bike-racing venue) entailed leaving work on a Saturday at noon, grabbing a sandwich and riding to Sheffield, a train if possible but, if not, riding on through Tamworth to Sutton Coldfield for an early start – the two-hour races had to be finished by 9.30pm – and then the ride home. In all, a round trip of 140 miles with the race in between.

3: CITIUS, FORTIUS, ALTIUS

'Faster, stronger, higher' (from 1924, the motto of
the Olympic Games)

Towards the end of the 1951 season, Robinson, by now a considerable force on the racing circuit, got sponsorship – a bike, nothing more – from the cycle shop of their club meets, Ellis Briggs of Shipley, which is still thriving. Opened in 1936 by two partners, Leonard Ellis and Thomas Briggs, the enterprise began to produce lightweight racing frames after the war and to back riders who, by riding their bikes, gave them useful publicity.

Three months later, on 3 January 1952, Robinson was ordered to report to the large army barracks at Strensall, north-east of York, to begin his National Service with the King's Own Light Infantry, motto *Cede nullis* 'Yield to none'. Originally the 51st regiment of foot, the KOYLI was one of the six Minden Regiments which won a famous victory during the Seven Years' War on 1 August 1759. Advancing across Minden Heath (between Osnabrück and Hannover in Germany), the soldiers picked wild roses – the white of Yorkshire's rose, coincidentally – to wear in their cap. They then attacked and defeated a force of French cavalry, far superior in numbers. In the quasi-tomfool tradition of the British army, it actually began as a monumental cock-up. Infantry never marched on cavalry. Perhaps they were picking the flowers out of a distracted, mind-numbing amazement that they were being required to do something so manifestly barmy. They did so on this occasion because of a mistaken order. A similar error, far more grievous in its consequences, sent the Light Brigade to its doom in the Crimean War, a century later.

Strensall served as a training depot for all the British Army's Light Infantry brigades – King's Own Yorkshire, Durham, Shropshire and Hereford, Somerset and Cornwall – lightly-armed regiments which originally acted as skirmishers and sharpshooters, a rapid-fire screen ahead of the more heavily-armed infantry. They famously quick-march on parade at 140 paces per minute, whereas the rest of the infantry marches at a standard regimental pace of 120.

Because Robinson was now a debentured tradesman, the Army registered him as Craftsman. Like all new squaddies, he underwent six weeks' basic training – drill (square bashing), weapons training, fitness and assault course, regimental history, elementary field tactics…the programme bound tight by that most cherished of army traditions: bullshit, namely spit and polish, accompanied by tirades of abusive contempt: 'Shine those buttons and boots 'til you can see your face in them, though who would want to see your ugly face, you horrible little man, apart from your mother, gawd bless her, beats me'…kit inspection carried out with a minute attention to detail bordering on the neurotic, and that catch-all directive which remains just, but only just, on the reasonable side of manic hyperbole: 'If it moves, salute it, if it doesn't move, whitewash it.'

He enjoyed the rigours of the discipline, excelled in the physical tests and passed out best recruit in his intake. It was a bit cold, sometimes, especially when the stove in the hut went out. It was hardly home comfort: bare board floor, iron bedsteads, lockers and a standing stove. The essential was to toe the line, the NCOs being quick to pounce and sharp to punish. 'You've to be smart enough to keep out of trouble,' as he puts it. This willingness to adapt to ironbound routine is a telling pointer to his ready ability to immerse himself in the exacting demands of continental racing. For the moment, the Regimental Sergeant Major must, initially, have been delighted with his star recruit, (not that he'd show it). For it was the RSM's ungrateful task to turn these raw, press-ganged apologies for soldiers into what passed for regular infantrymen, front-line fighting men worthy of the glorious battle honours of the regiment. Any remote sign of intelligence or aptitude in a recruit must have cheered his stony, cynical heart. Imagine, a senior warrant officer of his exalted standing reduced to playing nursemaid to a litter of wet-behind-the-ears civilian puppies.

However, there was a catch. Robinson was no ordinary recruit. Robinson had a let-out clause on routine duties which, in the RSM's jaundiced opinion, almost certainly ranked somewhere below that most miserable of temporary passports to idleness – and there is no more heinous sin in the military than idleness, from the idle playing (bum notes) in a bandsman to idle cleaning of a rifle – excused boots. Robinson had been singled out by the NCU as a possible selection for that year's Olympic Games in Helsinki. He was thus enrolled on full-time training as a cyclist and, therefore, not eligible for any posting overseas. The Korean War had broken out in June 1950, lasted three years and claimed the lives of thousands of American and British troops, many of these latter National Servicemen, some of them men who had joined at the same time as Robinson.

After a short break at the end of recruit training, he arrived back at barracks, with his Ellis Briggs bike. The Corporal of the guard snarled at him: 'You'll not be needing that', only for the Duty Officer to emerge from the guard house to inform Craftsman Robinson that he was required, the following weekend, (the first of a number of weekends of insolent leave to honour various invitations) to take himself off home to attend a cycling club function whereat he'd been invited to present the prizes. This thanks to his growing celebrity amongst the cycling fraternity of West Yorkshire and his engagement in the Army's cycling team. The Corporal was miffed, but

Corporals, when they are not hounding and harassing hapless junior ranks with the vindictive ferocity of a Jack Russell after a rat, which is rarely, have an ingrained predisposition to being miffed.

Captain Baughn, the officer in charge of the training for those enrolled in the Army Cycling Union and a former champion racer himself, had already contacted Robinson, before he arrived at Strensall. Baughn, an officer in the Catering Corps (motto 'We sustain'), was based at a Royal Artillery depot in Formby, Lancashire, just north of the Mersey estuary. Robinson joined two other cyclists already ensconced there, Peter Procter, a fellow Yorkshireman, whose name crops up prominently in Robinson's racing diary, and Les Wilmot, whose name does not, and with them began a full early-season routine of training on the road. 'Wilmot was a bit of a woodentop,' says Robinson, 'a loner, didn't mix. He could ride time-trials but wasn't at home on the road.' The road north led direct to the Lake District and the longer-distance sorties included rides from army camp to army camp: one to Heathfield camp near Honiton in Devon, approximately 315 miles, the second, a relatively short hop of 125 miles to Carlisle. Because of their status as army athletes, they did not have to attend parades.

Just as well, Robinson said: they were already misfits, but him being Light Infantry, the rest would never have been able to keep up with his pace.

He supplemented fitness conditioning with games of basketball and that cornerstone of army exercise, cross-country running. He was paid a wage of 25 shillings per week, of which five shillings were stopped and sent to his parents, as paltry compensation for the loss of his contribution to the household economy. One pound didn't go very far. As some gauge of its spending power, a night in a bed and breakfast cost five shillings.

The army supplied no equipment. The bike and vest came from Ellis Briggs. When I asked him where he got his tyres from, he said that although Dunlop were lavish in their distribution of free tubulars [hereafter 'tubs'], he would never ride them. 'Why not?' I asked. 'They were crap. I rode Pirelli 50s, bought them in the winter months and hung them up to cure.' The new tyres needed to be fitted onto an old rim, part-inflated and left for at least six months to allow the tread to harden. If they weren't properly cured, the tyres, still soft, would easily puncture.

Robinson wrote up three races he rode with the army Command team in the spring of '52.

Isle of Wight 1952

We stayed at RAF Honington on the way down. There was an army boxing team staying there, too, and we had steak for tea. A big treat, that. The weather was glorious, really hot. We rose at 7.30am and left Golden

Hill Fort* where we had accommodation, that is Pete, Les Bernard, Denis and myself. We had an army Troop Carrier to take us down to the start at Sandown. All the riders for three events were gathered at the start so there was quite a crowd. We got under way about 10h00 in brilliant sunshine. It looked quite good, but 150 starters was too many. It took me about eight miles to get to the front and then I had a little dabble with F.U. Mee of Coventry Meteor, [now defunct] but soon got caught. Up the hill, just after the finish line, Procter, Henley and B.J. King got clear. I was not feeling strong on the hill by any means. Vines, H.W. King, Pusey, Etherington and myself formed a group behind with Pusey and myself not working. Vines made one or two efforts to get clear but didn't succeed. Henley then came back to us, being very weak. It stayed this way until the Finish. I came sixth.

Observations: Race was four laps of 8½ miles. Very sporting. Not much flat, one good hill, finish could be improved. Never use little gear up the last hill.

Sherwood Forest, Nottingham, Easter Monday 1952

We travelled up in Captain Baughan's car after the race on the Isle of Wight. Arrived at the army camp near Bingham, twelve miles from the Forest, at 20h00. It took about an hour to get beds and then to the cookhouse where we were offered boiled sausages which, naturally, we refused. The breakfast was the same. We left camp at 10h30 on Monday, arrived at the Forest, got our bikes ready, hung around, met everybody and then went down to the NAAFI club** and had a good cooked dinner. (He added a gloss, during a conversation: 'There will have been beans. There were always beans at the NAAFI.') Then back to the Forest. The weather was very hot though a bit dull and sultry. Weather like this is just up my street. We lined up for the start at 15h00 and got up steam, all the big boys hung round the back somewhere. The first prime came up and I went right from the corner with Haskell fighting to get on my

---

* Constructed between 1863 and 1868, sixty metres above the north west coast of the Isle of Wight, near Freshwater, this unique hexagonal barrack building, the only one of its kind, had the height, strength and strategic position to help counter what was then perceived as a serious attack from the French navy's newly launched ironclad warship *La Gloire*.

** Navy Army and Air Force Institute, an organisation set up by the government in 1921 to run recreational establishments for other ranks in the British armed forces (officers were barred), and to sell goods to servicemen and their families. It runs clubs, bars, shops, supermarkets, launderettes, restaurants, cafés and other facilities on most British military bases as well as canteens on board Royal Navy ships.

wheel but even Haskell could not get me. It was a good effort, worth a quid anyway. Then H. Thomson, S. Jones and R. Parsonage got clear.

Haskell and I and G.W. were busy chasing with no help from anybody. We got within twenty seconds (they had 48 at one time) at the Finish. Parsonage won it with Stan Jones taking the sprint from the bunch. I came fifth.

Observations: Still not riding strong enough on the hills. Should have murdered myself to get clear.

Prizes: 15/- for fifth place, £1 for a prime.

That race took place on 14 April. The following Saturday, 19 April, Robinson reports on another massed start race, organised by Warwick Cycle Club.

Church Lawford

We started off intending to go from the gun as there were 150 starters, but a motorcycle marshall put a stop to that. We got under way, the usual 20 miles on or so with nobody succeeding in getting clear. Then Jim Turner and I went for a prime and found ourselves clear of the field, so we got stuck in and I kept away until H.W. King, B.J. King, Jones and Gravestock caught us. We got in with them and stuck it to the finish. The weather was good, fair wind blowing.

Procter punctured, Pusey came seventh, Robinson doesn't record where he came. A week later, they were back in Yorkshire. Interestingly, the race distance is set in kilometres but Robinson uses miles in his account.

Prizes: 4th place: one block value £2-4s, primes: one 3-inch GB extension (value £1), one pair of mudguards (value 15/-), valve Wilsons (value £1).

He seems not to have claimed these last two items.

Esholt Park, Bradford. 100km Saturday, 26 April

Weather was very good, fair wind blowing. We started off and thought that the course was very bad but got used to it eventually. Haskell got away very early and started piling up the points on the hill prime. Procter, Pusey and Hardcastle joined him and formed a group which worked steadily for about 17 miles but did not get more than one minutes advantage with Wilmot and I and the Huddersfield boys hanging back. Then they had a spill and got back with the bunch and Haskell was getting dropped at the same time, so I decided I had played about long enough blocking my efforts to chase so I left the group, passing Haskell and catching Procter and Hardcastle. We then worked together until the last lap when Hardcastle took us round. After trying to drop him on the hill we came down to the finishing straight which was hard. The form was Hardcastle, self and Procter. Hardcastle wound it up and Procter tried to get by on the outside but did not, so I squeezed round on the grass verge to win by ½ a wheel.

Observations: An exceptionally good team race was ridden by the Command blocking all efforts to catch anybody, in fact they dominated the race.

Robinson added that, as they came onto the finishing straight, Procter hollered at him: 'Go on Brian, go on.' 'But I was right on the edge of the road in the bloody gutter, so I nipped over onto a bit of rough stuff the other side of it and managed to get through. Peter's panic pushed me on a little bit harder than I'd have normally gone. That was a good result, it put us in Captain Baughn's good books.'

The long rides, bolstered by some weeks of intensive training with the Army, prepared Robinson for the Olympic road race in Helsinki. He, his brother Des and Les Ingman had been selected to ride in the road race. Procter and Wilmot had not.

The most significant disadvantage he faced in preparing for the Olympics was army food.

Des had already ventured to France to race and was drawing on personal experience of continental practice in the matter of diet and choice of food. Robinson had to rely on strictly hush-hush supplements from the cookhouse to make up for the inadequacies of what didn't even deserve the title 'menu'. (Getting adequate rest was also a bind: the Army frowned on any man taking to his bed during daylight hours. That was malingering, soldiers pretending to be ill.)

Des, to whom Robinson refers, in the way of Yorkshiremen, as 'our kid', was already an outstanding club cyclist and it was he who stirred his younger brother's nascent urge to sample racing on the continent. In 1950 (or '51, Robinson isn't sure), Des had been invited to attend an early-season training camp sponsored and run by Simplex, the French manufacturer of bicycle components, in Menton, on the Côte d'Azur, east of Nice. Bob Maitland also attended. Simplex, which introduced the first cable-shift derailleur in 1938, was keen to promote the efficiency of their gears, against the Italian Campagnolo, and to push their use by professional riders. They ran the camp for a number of years. On at least one occasion, the camp was managed by Charles Pélissier, youngest of the famous trio of cyclist brothers.* Simplex had more than once invited the NCU to send some riders to join the French

---

* Henri, the eldest, won the Giro di Lombardia three times, Paris-Roubaix twice, the Tour de France in 1924; Francis won Paris-Tours and Bordeaux-Paris and all three won a number of stages in the Tour – Charles was the first man to win eight stages in a single Tour, 1930.

gathering. The NCU, whether because they were ill-funded and could not finance the participation of British riders in events across the Channel, or because they continued to nurse a sniffy, stand-offish attitude to the continental racing scene, answered very few of such invitations, although plenty were issued. In Menton, Des got on particularly well with a veteran professional rider from Luxemburg, Jean 'Bim' Diederich – stage wins in the '50, '51 and '52 Tour de France and three days in yellow in 1951. It was such friendships, struck up during and after rides on strange roads in a foreign land, which augmented the sense of getting to the heart of the kind of racing of which the Robinson brothers had, so far, only dreamed. Des came back to Yorkshire full of it, brimming over with enthusiasm: the wild pleasure of the training in the hills and mountains of the Alpes Maritimes, the friendly rivalry in the bunch, riding with seasoned French riders who'd grown up in the culture of bike-racing on the road. *Contre-le-montre?* Okay, but it's not like the real thing. Here they were, English lads, fast racers but so uncouth in many ways, getting caught up in the great tradition of cycle-racing of which the Tour de France was the peak, but which embraced a plethora of lesser races, across France, Italy, Belgium, for professionals and independents alike. And, imagine, all this in January – warm sunshine, the Côte d'Azur, balmy breezes, the ultramarine waters of the Mediterranean. Winter? Only by the calendar. As well as a seductive account of that sunlit other-world of professional road riding, Des brought back copies of *Miroir Sprint*, the stylish magazine devoted to cycle racing. What a contrast with the parish magazine of time-trial results and backwater small talk they had to make do with in England. The pages of *Miroir* were filled with grittily shot, atmospheric photographs. The intelligent text (which the Robinson brothers couldn't yet decode) made home-grown journalism look distinctly mediocre, too. But, the pictures of cyclists scaling the monster climbs of the Alps and Pyrenees, the epic scale of the landscape, the roads lined with spectators, the sheer magnitude and popularity of cycle sport in France, fired Robinson with that precious stimulus to achievement, the thought: 'One day, I'm going to do that.' For, behind the romance of the photographs, he saw a franker reality: impressive as they were, selected to ride at this top level as they might be, these men on bikes were neither gods nor supermen, they were cyclists, as he was a cyclist. They might come from a different background, a different process might have made them what they were now, on the road, in that grainy photograph, but they'd started off with no more than he had: talent and drive.

When word got out that crack riders from the Army Cycling Union, professionals in all but name, were going to ride a 25 mile time-trial on Merseyside, the Liverpudlian clubmen had their dander up. The Wirral peninsula was, still is, a hotbed of racing, intense competition and innate pugnacity. The prospect of sticking it to a party of pampered professionals was blood to a shark, a hare to a lurcher, a doughnut to Billy Bunter. Robinson and company were slaughtered. Captain Baughn was furious. He railed at them: 'All this money, time and support invested in you and you post results that weren't even worth chalking up. On your bikes, the trucks are leaving without you.' They had, in army parlance, ridden idly. Useless, and undiplomatic, for Robinson to point out that they were in training for the Olympic road race and that, for his part, the time-trial was no real test – 25 miles? Barely long enough for him to get warmed up.

They got some road racing experience on aerodromes and other closed circuits – events which were not authorised, being contrary to strict adherence to NCU rules, yet supervised by NCU officials. (Such were the contradictions.) However, these races rarely exceeded 90 miles: the Olympic road race would be over a course of 120 miles. They needed much tougher conditioning and they got it in the south-west of France.

In late spring 1952, as a member of the joint NCU-Army team, Craftsman Robinson KOYLI rode the Route de France, precursor to the Tour de l'Avenir, ('Tour of the Future') for promising riders who might one day ride the Tour de France. The team – four riders from the army, including Bernard Pusey, with whom Robinson later rode the Tour de France, Wilmot and Procter, and four from the NCU, among them his brother Des – was managed by George Fleming of the Rugby CC. After the war, Fleming had been the first rider to go under two hours for a fifty mile time-trial and he'd won that open road Paris to London race, but this was the sum of his acquaintance with road racing. Of stage racing he, none of them, knew a thing.

As they prepared for the French trip, the Ellis Briggs people achieved their first major success in sponsorshop when Ken Russell, riding as a semi-professional/independent, won the fourteen-stage 1952 Tour of Britain, (sponsored by the *Daily Express* newspaper) despite having no team support. This long race was organised and run on a shoestring by the rebel BLRC, though how such a quarrelsome bunch of monomaniacs ever contrived to organise anything remains a mystery. The men who had started the League, an energetic clique of out-and-out enthusiasts, were succeeded by a series of committee-men who appear to have operated on a bloody-minded determination to do exactly as they pleased so long as it displeased everyone else.

Newhaven. The wind blowing a gale. The Channel running rough and high. Waiting for the ferry with the men in the combined Army-NCU team heading for the continent to ride the Route de France, the President of the NCU contemplated the heaving seas, the boat lurching nine feet up and down at the quayside and said: 'Well, lads, that'll save us some money – none of you will be wanting lunch once you get aboard in that lot.' So much for official exhortation. The NCU, though, were on a shoestring and the Army wasn't splashing money about. Robinson went down and had a sizeable lunch... rough crossing or not, he was ravenous.

At the start in Caen, the riders were issued with one pair of shorts and one wollen jersey apiece. (Professionals were using wool-mix, wool-polyester, because it was the best fabric on offer at the time to combat the incursion of dust and to manage sweat. The polyester gave the garment a shiny finish.) When the woollen jersey got soaked with rain or sweat, the colours ran, the soggy material drooped and stretched and weighed very heavy – an unwelcome extra load. They also ponged. Washing the garments out was one thing, getting them to dry overnight quite another. The race field included teams from France, Italy, Belgium, Holland, composed of road-wise men bristling with experience. Most of the continental riders and the French in particular, had followed a very structured path of road-racing from the junior level. Many of them had once been that folkloric wee boy standing agawp at the side of the road in a remote village in deepest rural France when the mythic heroes of the *Grande Boucle* rode by, unimaginable stars from a distant galaxy. And, as they were swallowed up in the dust of the horizon, like a mirage fading, the whippersnapper with patches on his short trousers was whispering to himself: 'One day, I'll ride the Tour.'

Joining the local club, winning races – and all across the hexagon there were races to be ridden – moving up the ranks, feeding the ambition, attracting notice, getting the contract...all directed towards participation in the great bike race, the legendary summit of any French bike rider's aspiration.

The Route de France was, said Robinson, a very intimidating baptism in the unforgiving discipline of continental stage racing. Not least, the lack of anything like adequate French meant that they were sometimes cut off from what was going on, such as the precise time of the day's *départ*. One morning, the team went into a shop to buy food, accompanied by the journalist Peter Bryan, interviewing them as they gathered up their provisions for lunch. They had, they thought, a clear thirty minutes before the start. Suddenly, they heard the gun, stuffed the food in their musettes*, raced out to mount their bikes and make chase, leaving Bryan behind to pay the bill. They hadn't been aware that the start had been brought forward.

On closed circuits at home, albeit on some chancy surfaces, there was very little in the way of the sort of impediments they faced on open French roads. Parked cars, narrow twisting main streets, often cobbled, through villages and towns, spectators hanging over garden fences, crowded into market squares, shop doorways, lining even remote outlying roads, and the roar of cheering and encouragement as they rode through. A constantly changing

---

* A small cotton bag with shoulder strap, originally the leather bellows sack of a *cornemuse*, bagpipe.

landscape might distract in quite the wrong way, too, take their mind off the job. It was all so strange and new. Unfamiliar with the routes and the roads, they had to rely on local knowledge from men they were racing against. Reading a race from the centre of the bunch was always problematic. Had an attack gone? The line of riders might suddenly attenuate and the speed mount, first indication of a chase, but the only intelligence they would have would be from the motorbike pillion man holding up the slate with numbers and times scrawled in chalk. When the day was hot and the roads were dry, dust added to the fogs of ignorance. And the sheer practicality of riding in such a mass of riders was something of a facer. Used to much smaller fields, Robinson and the others had to learn very swiftly how to ride elbow to elbow and wheel to wheel in a bunch hurtling along at speed, ever alert to a switch, a rider jiggling over a pothole, a sudden swerve to avoid another clot snatching at the handlebars and a barked 'Merde, alors', or a judicious shove to put the man back to rights.

The race started in Caen and headed south through the Cognac region to finish in Aurillac. On the anniversary of VE day (Victory in Europe – 8 May 1945 when the war in the west ended) they stayed in a hotel in the centre of a town in Cognac. Robinson and the rest got no sleep because of a night-long, rowdy celebration – the entire population was out in the town square, very rumbustiously *en fête*. The French need little excuse to take to the streets and make a noise, whether for a party or a protest.

There were other novelties to embrace besides riding in a large, jostling bunch. Wine, for instance. Robinson had never drunk wine before. *Vin de table* never laid claim to any great distinction and he says it tasted like vinegar. (He persisted, manfully, and managed to inure himself to the unaccustomed flavour and came, quite, to like it.) Troops demobbed after service on the continent of Europe certainly came home with a taste for the staple mealtime drink of France and Italy, but it was not only scarce in Britain, outside London and large cities, but also very pricey. Ardent sophisticates and tipplers resorted to homemade wine, all of it potent, much of it undrinkable. The skirting boards of middle-class living rooms were lined with glass demijohns full of cloudy liquid derived from anything from apples to parsnips, oak leaves and rhubarb, the plastic fermentation locks making a plop plop noise like frogs in a marsh.

As we sat one evening in the sitting room in Mirfield after roast chicken and all the trimmings (cooked by his wife, Audrey) and a passable Côte du Rhône (provided by me), Robinson told me he did remember a so-called wine drink called Keystone Burgundy being sold in chemists (much as the only available olive oil was sold as a pharmaceutical item, for earache, imagine). An advertising film for Keystone Burgundy tonic wine, made in 1951, showed a student leaving a college. Subtitles inform the viewer that he has passed his exams and, like his father, qualified as a doctor. He drives home and goes into his father's study where his father congratulates him and offers him a celebratory tipple of Keystone Burgundy from the bulbous, raindrop-shaped flask of a bottle. Ah, gentler, less vinous, less savorous times.

The race route took them into the Pyrenees. One aspect of racing in the mountains is rarely considered: the awesome sight of the cols themselves or, more often, of the huge massifs which loom on the horizon, beyond which, somewhere hidden, sits the unseen pass at unimaginable altitude. At the start of a climb up to the high ranges, all manner of doubts and uncertainties seep into the mind and trouble the legs. But, as scary as an intrusion upon the unknown may be, this is not time to be daunted: it is a time to take stock. You know that others have ridden here and that you are riding with others who will ride it this day. Therefore, you say to yourself, I will ride it, too. And so it begins and so you become acquainted with the peculiar sensation of riding to the tops of mountains, a feat so different from anything you have experienced. For it's not the steepness itself of the road, but the fact that the steepness goes on and on and on, over ten miles, twelve miles, sixteen kilometres, twenty kilometres, of nonstop climbing. This instructs caution. The one thing you must not do on a mountain is try to match a pace which is inherently beyond you. To do so is ruin. But, Robinson, remember, had twitted himself for not trying in a recent race on the Isle of Wight: 'Still not riding strong enough on the hills. Should have murdered myself to get clear'…this is someone who not only knew what all-out meant but could implement it.

As they rode towards the Tourmalet that day in 1952, Robinson says he looked up at the massive bulk which lay across their path, far far ahead, and saw, way up near the skyline, intermittent flashes of light. 'What's that?' Pusey asked him. 'I don't know, but it's a bloody long way up whatever it is.' He quizzed a French rider. The man replied in broken English: 'Tourmalet. Car mirrors. Windscreens. Sun.' As to the endless road winding up towards that distant epiphany of light, it was as steep as the learning curve on which these nervous debutants were embarked. 'I had,' he said, 'never seen mountains like that before. Holme Moss just fitted into a corner of those hills.' It was the photographic gallery of Miroir Sprint come to life, right in front of them, under their wheels.

Of that initiation he said: 'We were no more than hanging on, really. We didn't take any decisions in the race. It was a case of follow the rest, most of the time.'

With three stages left to ride, but the mountains in the way, Robinson lay fifth overall. The Pyrenean cols did for him. But, he made it. He absorbed the first, shocking tussle with those mountains in his legs and, more important, he had rooted the confrontation with them in his head. He'd faced them and not been beaten. The whole team, bar one man, Dick Henley, who crashed on the descent of the Col de Peyresourde and burst his spleen, finished the race. It was a considerable achievement for them all but a dire warning, had it been heeded, of just what lay in store for British riders coming to ride stage races on the continent.*

Robinson wrote a short paragraph after the race:

Conditions: First five days it was cold and raining though the sun often shone in spells. There was usually a fresh wind blowing up. We were issued with food, usually two fruit flans which were very good, bananas, oranges, rice pudding, hot soup and a ham roll which we ate at the start or threw away and also lump sugar and prunes. The second week was very hot. About 8 pints of water one day. The continentals spit out the water and also poured a lot over themselves. Toe straps made feet sore. A lot of the team had sores on toes. Bottoms took a big hammering. Whole body felt as though it had been hazed** with a stick. Everybody in the team was riding to the limit.

True, they had struggled, they'd taken a pasting, and they had had to cope with some fairly rudimentary accommodation. In one hotel where they stayed, the side wall plunged straight into the river flowing through the village. A balcony ran along this wall outside their room and, over a hole in the end of the balcony, sat a box, with a bum-sized hole cut in its cover…the loo. But, the queer sanitary arrangements, the lack of French and the abrupt lesson in stage racing apart, they came out hardened and raring to go.

Shortly afterwards, the two Robinson brothers were on the plane to Finland to take part in the Helsinki Olympics. It was the first time that brothers had competed in the same race in the same Olympic Games. The team went in two parties aboard the draughty old converted Avro York transport plane – its design based on that of the Lancaster bomber –through whose floor, somewhat alarmingly, they could see the ground far off while they were flying.

'We left home,' Robinson noted, 'to go to London. We spent the night at the Eccleston Hotel and were issued with sundry kit etc to put in our baggage. The following morning we left London, bound by coach for Bovington airport. Here we abandoned the coach for the canteen while waiting for the baggage and bicycles to be registered and stowed aboard the big 4-engined York aircraft that was to take us to the greatest sporting project in the world.

---

* The Dutchman Jan Nolten won the race, rode for his national team in that year's Tour de France and took the first of his two stage victories.

**'Haze' is a verb largely out of use, now, meaning 'to affright or scold', but in mid-Yorkshire dialect, it also means 'to beat'.

We stood around for a while and then the press photographer pounced on us and had us parading up and down like a kind of Horse Guards. Eventually we were all stowed aboard and the door was slammed for the last time in England for a few days. Most of us had no flying experience except maybe for the odd pleasure flights. We are now airborne and the English scenery was slipping away below. Everyone now relaxed and took a look around. There was only one female aboard and that was the air hostess.'

A total of sixty-nine teams participated in the XVth Olympiad in Helsinki – ten more than in 1948. Thirteen nations competed for the first time: the Bahamas, Gold Coast (now Ghana), Guatemala, Hong Kong, Indonesia, Israel, the Soviet Union, the (Communist) People's Republic of China (whose inclusion precipitated the withdrawal of the Republic of China, Formosa), Netherlands, Antilles, Nigeria, Thailand and Vietnam.

Rationing, of food, clothes and petrol, still obtained in postwar Britain – no lace or frills on ladies' knickers or turn-ups on gents' trousers, to save material. The black market and its shady operator the spiv – 'One who earns his living by not working' – flourished and a butcher in a country district might well pass extra cuts under the counter to favoured customers, but for most of the populace, privation was the order of the day.* Consequently, when the British Olympians first walked into the food hall, a large marquee in the Olympic village (an estate of apartments specially built for the Helsinki Games), their eyes popped out. There were countless tables spread with every imaginable sort of comestibles, some that they'd never seen before, a cornucopia of treats, a veritable banquet every day. The Arabian Nights tells of a ruler in Baghdad called Barmecide who put a succession of empty dishes before a beggar, pretending, by florid description and extravagant sniffing of aroma, that they were filled with a sumptuous repast. The beggar, perhaps knowing that dissent risked dire retribution, humorously accepted the fiction. But the feast on display in Helsinki was no fiction. Here were different kinds of bread – wheaten, rye, sour dough; various meats, sausages and ham; a variety of fish crowding the Scandinavian (originally Swedish) smörgåsbord; fruit cakes, sponge cakes, spice cakes and biscuits; all manner of fruit. 'Blueberries…I'd never seen blueberries before.' (When the first shipment of bananas arrived at Bristol docks after the war, the mayor laid on a civic reception for the unobtainable fruit about which a wartime song had been written – 'Yes, we have no bananas, we have no bananas today…') To young men and women long accustomed to a marked austerity of provision, this glorious abundance was quite simply stupefying. It was also the cyclists' downfall. They were there for a week, only, and, in that time, they gorged themselves. The temptation of ample grub to rumbling bellies proved too

---

* Sweets were reprieved in February 1953. The last items to come off ration, bacon and meat, were removed on 4 July 1954.

53

much and, on the day of the race, they had blunted their keen edge with a sudden spasm of easy living.

The race used a circuit similar to Windsor Park, round a narrow winding road. The Robinsons, stuffed with overeating as they were, nevertheless rode well and finished equal eighth in the bunch, which came in fifty yards down on the winner, André Noyelle of Belgium. The two brothers rode in tandem, Des calling out: 'Come on, sit on me wheel'. Robinson comments: 'It was bit and lump – he was lump and I was doing the bit.' (Placings had to be made by eye and were thus inaccurate, not that position in a bunch – containing, on this occasion, one Jacques Anquetil – mattered greatly.) Noyelle, who also won team gold for the same race, turned professional but never achieved much.

Robinson was sorry not to be able to see more of the other events, but he did spend one dreamy romantic day in the company of a young Finnish woman who was there as a spectator. She was a classic Scandinavian beauty, fine bones, lissome, fair-haired, and she spoke cultured English. For some time afterwards, Robinson, who readily admits his awkwardness with a pen, wrote letters to her. Of the pleasure in such ephemeral meetings, caught and never lost because never ended, they live in an eternal summer that will not fade.

That week as a British Olympian was, he says, a superb experience.

He coasted out the following year, the second of his National Service, riding a number of army events – such as an army time-trial near the Catterick depot in April. He won, took a prize of £1 and a future Tour de France team-mate, Stan Brittain – nephew of RSM Brittain who was reckoned to have the loudest voice in the British army – took 10/- for second place. The major outing was the fourteen-stage Tour of Britain, again sponsored by the *Daily Express*. The RSM waved him off with brisk words of warning: 'I tell you what, Robinson, you've had that much bloody time off, one way or another, and gawd knows how you get away with it, but I'm warning you: if you don't win this bloody race –and if you're to be believed, though who with an ounce of brain would believe you, you've done that much training for the bugger – I tell you, if you *don't* win it, you're on guard duty. Understand? Now get lost sharpish while I'm still in a benevolent mood.'

Robinson, riding for the Army, did well. He held the leader's jersey for a while and finished fourth behind the winner, Gordon Thomas. He'd taken the leader's jersey over from Dave 'Iron Man' Bedwell on the stage into Blackpool after the BSA riders had squeezed the Hercules man out. Two stages from the Finish he still held it, but Thomas told his BSA team-mate Maitland that it was time to squeeze him out as they had squeezed Bedwell.

'Today, first ten miles, either you or me in the ditch…we sort Robbo out.' There was local needle in it, as well. Thomas was a fellow Yorkshireman and no tyke gives way easily to another tyke. Maitland was from Solihull and the Midlands clubs were inveterate foes of the Huddersfield RC.

Thomas went off at a scorching pace, Maitland sat on Robinson's wheel. Suddenly, a small gap opened, Robinson didn't react instantly, the breach was made and Thomas was away, Maitland hanging on to Robinson's back tyre like a sheet anchor. He lost fifteen minutes. That crushing by the BSA coalition undoubtedly bit into his soul and probably hardened his personal ambition immovably.

After a celebratory dinner in London after the race on Saturday night, he trailed back to York and arrived in the late afternoon, knackered. The RSM greeted him. 'Fourth? *Fourth?* Guard duty. On the double.'

He eventually crawled into bed at some godforsaken hour and was still asleep at 9 o'clock next morning – in the room off the sports store where he slept on a pretence of security watch. Short of committing a nuisance on the middle of the parade square or turning up for muster in his cycling shorts, this was about as insubordinate as he could get…idle wasn't in it. Reveille, all ranks, sounded prompt every morning at 6.30 with a bugle call. The duty officer rousted him out and demanded an explanation for this untimely imitation of Rip Van Winkle. Robinson blearily explained. The duty officer went quiet, told Robinson to get himself dressed and at least looking like a soldier and walked off. The building next to the sports store housed the telephone exchange. A private in charge of transferring internal calls acted as a grapevine for what was going on inside the camp. As Robinson emerged into the light of day, the eavesdropper leaned out of the window and waved him over, excitedly. 'Come and listen to this, mate.' The Commanding Officer was on the phone to the RSM and the private and Robinson listened in on the most unholy dressing down of the RSM, followed by a studious protest by the RSM. Subject of the discourse: Craftsman Robinson 22623080 being detailed, unjustly, unnecessarily and against unit orders, for guard duty the night before.

Since the Army works on a principle not dissimilar, in some ways, to that of a card game, where some suits are immoveably superior to others, the RSM finally, and inevitably, got the worse of the encounter. The CO, an old school gentleman type, rounded off his objurgation thus: 'And that's it for you – first stop, Germany.' Hearing this, Robinson thought he was bound to get it in the neck, one last time, from a deeply disgruntled Warrant Officer Class One keen to land his full weight, boots and all, on the nasty little worm who'd dumped him in the doodah. However, when he saw the RSM next, the man was smiling, ear to ear. 'Sorry you've got to go off to Germany, Sarnt Major,' said Robinson, trying to sound more apologetic, which he was, than smug, which he didn't feel. The RSM laughed. 'Robinson, you've done me a favour, a right good turn. I'm bloody sick to the back teeth of this bloody place and I'm bloody glad to be out and join the battalion.' That is, be with some *real* soldiers.

'Actually I respected the RSM. He was a good soldier.'

That lunchtime, Robinson, in uniform, was marched into the CO's office, escorted by guards on Company Orders, a parade usually reserved for punishments. Heavy boots on the wooden floor, 'Craftsman Robinson… Halt.' Three sharp stamps of the shod feet: one, two, one/two. Silence. The CO looks up at Robinson and congratulates him on a fine ride in the Tour of Britain, credit to him, credit to the unit, credit to the Army.

On 26 October 1952, Robinson won the National Hill Climb championship on Mow Cop in Cheshire: he rode the 1070 yards, an average slope of 1 in 6.5, maximum gradient 1 in 4.5, in 3m 41.8s.

4: JOB'LL BE REIGHT

In 1953, Coronation Year, as Britain was still emerging from a long period of postwar doldrums, the warring regulators of cycle racing, NCU, BLRC, RTTC, signed an uneasy truce. On 7 March the international body, the Union Cycliste Internationale (UCI), voted at a meeting in San Sebastian to give temporary recognition to the BLRC, manifestly the only bunch of individuals interested in promoting road racing in the UK, even if the home federation regarded it as a rogue grouping. The UCI's directive amounted to a very public rebuke to an affiliated authority and, in April, the officers of the NCU grudgingly signed a tripartite agreement with the League and the RTTC, granting the League 'control of massed-start racing on open roads by Professionals, Independents, Aspirants and Amateurs'. The accord limited the number of events but it sanctioned the League's centre-piece Tour of Britain and some other events that the breakaway, outlawed BLRC men had run, with the cooperation of the police. Most importantly, it allowed British riders to race on the continent – hitherto, the NCU had banned any rider that did so. Thus, with the (unexpected) blessing of the NCU, Dave Bedwell headed for France. He rode the Route du Calvados in Hercules colours, won the first stage, came 3rd on stage 2 and 4th overall at the finish. On 30 August, he competed in the Worlds Road Race at Lugano, just across the Italian border in Switzerland. Riding the last 6km on a flat tyre, he became one of very few British riders ever to have finished the World's road race course. Fausto Coppi, on one of those days when he seemed to be far beyond the reach of any other rider, won by over seven minutes.

That evening, some members of the Hercules Road and Track-racing team management sat round a table in Nino's café near Lugano. It was a sun-soaked, hot summer evening, the wine flowed and with it animated talk about the recurring dream of building a team to compete in the Tour de France. Others joined the group, and past midnight two of them, Peter Bryan, that journalist with *Cycling Weekly* who had covered Robinson's first Route de France, and D.D. 'Mac' McLachlan, the Hercules PR manager, ambled round to the hotel where the celebrated cycling journalist Jock Wadley, reporting on the event for the *Daily Telegraph*, was in bed, fast asleep. They rang his room, called him down to reception, said it couldn't wait. He stumbled down in his pyjamas and, still half asleep, listened as they told him excitedly that the whole Hercules outfit was in agreement: a team for the Tour de France, now or never, worth a crack even if they knew they'd be up against it, but they were game…What do you think, Jock?

Wadley hadn't even had time to put his teeth in.

Seemingly unimpressed by Bedwell's brilliant showing against some of the best riders on the continent, the NCU suffered a fit of petulance. At a UCI congress in early 1954, they clawed back their jurisdiction over track and road races and issued a diktat requiring any British rider who wished to race abroad to hold an NCU licence. The League countered: they would issue their own international licences. After who knows what backroom finagling and collusion, the Minister of Transport weighed in behind the NCU, severely restricting the circumstances in which road racing would, thenceforward, be permitted in Britain. Thus, when the League sent six men to ride two of the great spring classics, the Liège–Bastogne–Liège and the Flèche Wallonne, on their own licence, not that of the NCU, the Belgian racing authorities refused them entry. Domestic politics had nullified the UCI ruling. The NCU and the RTTC pompously served further notice on the League that, because of its belligerent refusal to honour the spirit of the three-way agreement, any future application for international licences would have to go through the NCU. In the December issue of the BLRC's periodical *The Leaguer* a committee member, Chas Fearnley, wrote: 'There is a malignant ulcer prevalent in the cycling world and common to all three racing bodies in this country. It is the taint of vanity and culminates in clashes of personalities.' It was a brave, honest assessment of a very disagreeable truth. The fellowship of two wheels had been poisoned by the unseemly jealousies of definition.

Robinson was discharged from the army in December 1953 as 'Craftsman... UT', that is 'untrained'. The sergeant major squinted at this and growled. 'Bloody hell, Robinson, how did you get away with that?' 'Don't ask me,' he said.

He is, even now, somewhat bemused at how much he *did* get away with in the Army. 'The only time I went for a leave pass was when I was off for a race. I was never there most of the time, anyway, and I was the only one on the camp who had that. In fact it was a bit of a bind having to go in on Thursdays for pay parade, put on that itchy bloody uniform. Denims were better but parky in winter. And when you put the greatcoat on, too, you could hardly bloody move. How they ever fought a war in it I don't know.'

He rejoined his father in the workshop of H.F. Robinson and Son Ltd. The familiar smells of sawdust, wood, glue, coke in the stove, lubricating oil for the machines and the whetstones, the banter at the benches and the swish of planes, the thump of mallets at chisels, the steady rasp of the crosscut saw on grain. Robinson was keen to see the business expand into a full building firm – the experience he'd had at college and night school persuaded him that they would do better to diversify into bricks and mortar as well as carpentry and joinery. That way they could construct houses off their own bat. However, his father had worked for years in conjunction with an old builder friend of his and wouldn't hear of sidelining his brickie mate. It was a disappointment and, whether Robinson was conscious of it at the time, subliminally it was that decision of his father's which helped push him towards turning professional on the bike.

For the moment, this wasn't an option. He rode the programme of domestic races through 1954 as an independent, alongside his Ellis Briggs team-mate Ken Russell, but they found themselves constantly outweighed by the large professional, BSA and Hercules. In the flatter races, they had no chance of breaking clear, the opposition had too many riders and mounted enough power to close down any attempt at a break with ease. The only terrain on which Robinson, an exceptional climber, could worst them was his home turf, the withering high uplands of the Peak District and the Yorkshire Moors and Dales.

Six teams contested the 13-stage 1954 Tour of Britain, BSA and Hercules each with six riders, Robinson's Ellis Briggs with four. Robinson was well set for victory, even against a powerful BSA and Hercules opposition whose men were bent on spoiling the Ellis Briggs party. Smarting from Ken Russell's win in the second edition of the race, wearing the maroon and grey of Ellis Briggs, two years before, the big outfits were not going to let the prize slip again. In 1952, sixteen teams had competed, fourteen of them four or five riders strong, ranged against two one-man entrants: Romford CC and Russell for Ellis Briggs. For Russell to prevail against such heavy odds was quite something and here was another Ellis Briggs man showing them up. The heavy mob was not going to be shown up by a bumptious squirt a second time. They put their rivalry aside and went for Robinson with everything they'd got. He had no answer to the united force of their assault and he lost the lead on the final day.

Even so, he came second both in the mountains competition and overall to Eugène Tamburlini of France, riding for Peugeot.*

That startling result apart, it had been, in sum, a frustrating year and, towards the end of the season, Robinson made a make-or-break decision: either he landed a contract with one of the dominant set-ups or he would call it a day. Flogging himself to death with no real hope of a win had little attraction and he was ready to quit. Unless he got into a team he was 'done with this business'. Ellis Briggs had been good to him but they were very

---

* Born in 1930, Tamburlini began racing in 1948 and won a number of smaller races on the calendar but never cut it as a professional. Crossed in love, he put his head in a gas oven in 1959. On 25 January 1907, René Pothier, first home of a mere fourteen survivors of the seventy-five who had begun the 1906 Tour de France, hanged himself from the hook in his garage from which he suspended his bike. Another broken-hearted cyclist.

small fry and he had no relish for another season of being kicked about by the Hercules and BSA full-time professionals.

Hercules, in particular, was putting a lot of money into cycle sponsorship. They allotted sixpence of the profit they made on the sale of every bike to their publicity budget, part of which bankrolled the six-man team, including Dave 'Iron Man' Bedwell. (BSA, whose budget ran to only £7,000, were led by another top rider, Bob Maitland. According to Maitland, the Hercules sponsorship ran to around £100,000.) Since Hercules paid Bedwell just under £20 per week (around £1,000 per year and twice the wage of a manual worker)at a time when a standard sports bike was selling for £13 6s 6d, he was certainly being looked after in some comfort. For the outsiders, Robinson among them, the only cash reward that came from riding a bike was in prize money.

In late August, the manager of the BSA team, Syd Cozens, a pre-war track rider, a big pal of another track man, the Italian six-day rider Gino Bambagiotti, rang to offer Robinson a deal with BSA. Robinson said he'd think it over.The rumour that the Hercules people were aiming to get a team into the Tour de France had filtered through and pricked his interest.

Next day, lo, Hercules approached him with an offer of £80 per month, all his kit, staying in the best 4 star hotels when they travelled to races, and all expenses paid, which meant that his wages went straight into the bank...a first-rate deal. 'It was a gift from heaven for me, that.' He signed. Almost immediately, Cozens rang to exert pressure. Robinson said sorry, he'd just joined Hercules. Cozens lost his rag and slagged him off for his underhand dealing, his treachery. 'Bloody hell, I came to you first. Why didn't you wait to hear from me, you bugger?' A fortnight later, Cozens packed it in at BSA to become manager of the Hercules team.

GF   Cozens was a bit slippery, was he?

BR   He was a right scallywag. (Pause). He was a bike rider. (Laughs)

A word about that, and Robinson's assessment of Cozens was undoubtedly coloured by his dislike of the man. There is a hint of suspicion, too, of track men, known to be sneaky. However, a successful bike racer has to be shrewd, more sly than an outright burglar, but a consummate dodger, an adept in the artful practice of kiddology. Swift recourse to bluff. The face must be a mask and, emotion suppressed, give nothing away. One day on that occasion when I first met Robinson, in the Alps, skiing with what the ski liftmen referred to as 'le peloton Poulidor', he said to me of the former pros with whom he had ridden: 'If you've got a weakness, they'll find it out.' He laughed, not needing to add: '...and they'll exploit it.' It was just that trickster aspect of massed start racing which offended the pietistic Corinthians of the British amateur scene: in their prissy view, sharp wits vitiated the purity of true competition.

The following week, Cozens arrived at Hercules as manager. Robinson was wary. 'I didn't trust the four-eyed git, he was a bandit.* I knew I had to make a good showing, I needed to be first in this lot else I'd be out on my ear.' The choice of joining Hercules was a much better bet for a man of Robinson's ambition. BSA, whose team enjoyed scarcely a tenth the budget of Hercules, had neither the interest nor the resources to fund a shot at the Tour de France. The management at Hercules was already on the case. McLachlan said: 'This will be the greatest-ever test of British bicycles. A British win in the Tour, although only a dream at the moment, would have a terrific repercussion on the sales of British cycles throughout the world.'**

Robinson, newly signed, rode his first race for Hercules as a professional in the short-lived Tour of Europe, which left Paris on 21 September 1954, crossed five countries in thirteen stages, and covered 2,560km. He rode alongside Dave Bedwell, Derek Buttle and Fred Krebs.

He won the 190km sixth stage, Schwenningen to Augsburg, but got no prize money, (nor did anyone else), the race organiser being something of a fly-by-night who made off with the cash.

BR   What pushed me into the break was being switched into the gutter about 80km from the finish by a Colombian. It was bad riding on his part and I was that cross, I saw red. I got back out of the rut he'd dumped me in and flew past down the side of the road. No one followed and I just put my head down and went for it. Came into the finish on a track in teeming rain, over cobbles and tramlines, a bit hairy. The press recorded that 'Brian Robinson, the solitary pedaller, played the hare on the German roads.'

The day ended in tragedy. The young Swiss rider Jacquet collided with a car at the finish in Augsburg and was killed.

On the seventh stage, Augsburg to Innsbruck, 206km over two high passes in the Tyrolean Alps, the Fernpass and the Holzleiten, Krebs and Robinson – in cracking form after his victory – rode with great panache to chase down a breakaway group, having dropped the current race leader, and came in three minutes down. Robinson now lay 6th overall, Krebs 10th, Bedwell 14th, Buttle, 25th. The 8th stage, Innsbruck to Mantova in Italy, began with a 38km haul up and over the Brenner Pass. At 250km, Robinson punctured but raced back on. Since he was suffering severe discomfort in his knees, probably the result of too much racing, this was brave. On stage 9, 196km, Mantova to Bologna, the weather was appalling – driving icy rain. Robinson's knees

---

* An archaic word *cozen* means 'to cheat, to defraud...' secondary meaning 'to deceive, dupe, beguile...' Odd, that.

** Hercules was billed as 'The finest bicycle built today' although their top-end racing frames were actually built by a small constructor in the London area, not at the main factory in Aston.

began to hurt badly, the chill bored into his joints and, nearing the finish, he was forced to retire. So, too, did Bedwell with severe stomach pain. It was a huge disappointment. Krebs and Buttle rode on without them, via Como, Lugano, Montreux to Strasburg – a final stage of 344km. Krebs finished 5th overall, to the Italian Primo Volpi, and Buttle, described as a first-rate team-mate, who'd worked hard and selflessly for the others, came 27th of only thirty finishers from a field of seventy.

Early in 1955, Chas Messenger, international racing secretary of the League, who had had some experience of continental racing himself, asked a friend to get him a list of race organisers' names and addresses in France. A bit of smooth talking at the Paris offices of *L'Equipe*, the sports paper which sponsored the Tour de France, and, bingo, the precious information winged its way across the Channel to 'Mac' McClachlan. Pre-eminent was the need to prove to the Tour administration that a team had capable riders. Hercules did have a useful lever, of course: the first all-British team to ride the Grande Boucle would be great publicity, on which the financial viability of the race depended, after all. Robinson was aware of this ace up the sleeve. A ride in the Tour? It was, he told me, something that every bike rider in Britain dreamed about and here it had landed right at his feet. He was dead set on grabbing the opportunity with both hands to make the best of it.

The Hercules people rented a villa at Les Issambres on the coast of the French Riviera for their training camp. Robinson arrived full of zip, bubbling with enthusiasm for the fully professional life, determined to make a go of it. The other members of the Hercules team – Dave Bedwell, Derek Buttle, Fred Krebs, Clive Parker, Bernard Pusey, Denis Talbot – were more ambivalent. Over the four years that the team had been in existence, the luxury of a large budget with plenty of back-up in a cozy domestic racing season which they dominated – plus oodles of prize money – had made them a bit lazy and complacent, not best prepared for the shock of the hurly-burly of racing in France. Besides, to those of them who were married with children, the move to continental racing disrupted their altogether comfortable life-style back home. For a man like Robinson, 'more or less a bachelor at the time' as he put it, whatever *that* means, there was no such reluctance. His mind was made up: he wanted a life in pro cycling, specifically in stage-races, and here was the rare chance to learn and adapt. It helped that he got on well with the boss, Mac McClachlan, who splashed money around as if there were no tomorrow and drank as if today didn't count.

Villas and bungalows were relatively cheap to rent out of season. The weather on the Côte d'Azur is usually fine in January and the hinterland above the coast offers a vast network of excellent training routes on roads which were, in those days, more or less free of traffic. Many of the cols in the Alpes Maritimes, whilst not as grand in altitude as many of the High Alps further north, are steep and long, ideal for early-season conditioning. Next door to the Hercules bungalow stood a house occupied by the Bobet camp, headed by Louison and his brother Jean. Further along still, more stars of French cycling had gathered for the annual winter honing: Raphaël Geminiani, whose programme for the year included the Vuelta a España (in those days contested in early spring), the Giro d'Italia *and* the Tour de France; Tour stage-winners Jean Dotto (a fine climber), Jean Forestier, François Mahé and a man at the outset of an illustrious career, the ace rouleur, André Darrigade. The English never embarked on a ride with the French but they were soon sharing the roads with them. The younger Bobet, Jean, bespectacled, university-educated, fluent in English, was particularly friendly. His brother, already twice winner of the Tour de France (in '53 and '54) and reigning World Road champion, held himself more aloof. He was moody, could be extremely prickly before a race, at once arrogant yet prey to a scattering nervousness about his ability, a lack of self-confidence, curious in a man of his palmarès, an abiding neurosis complicated by a furious ambition, the *rage à vaincre* – 'I'm interested only in winning'. Nerves rattled him badly as he got ready to contest a possible third consecutive victory in the *Grande Boucle*. He was also plagued by a recurrent hardening of the tissue in his perineum which made riding extremely uncomfortable and painful.*

The Hercules men bought maps and set off to explore. Sunshine, peacock blue skies, warm air, the early scent of Mediterranean flora, the joy of being so far south in the unimaginable paradise of the Riviera, incurious and free, free simply to ride the bike. It was perfect. The coast road from nearby Sainte-Maxime as far east as Menton, just inside the Italian border is a rolling corniche with glorious views of the Baie des Anges. The undulations make for splendid stamina work, hills shallow enough for sprinting, steep enough to take a salutary toll on legs and lungs.

In his excellent memoir *Demain on roule*, Jean Bobet recalls the Englishmen:

> We occasionally met them on the twisting roads of the Var hinterland. In the back pocket of their jersey, the Michelin map which was both their passport and their open sesame to a region which was foreign to them, unknown territory. My team-mates mocked them more or less gently, but I guarded against the least superciliousness. Having studied the trade figures, I knew that Hercules manufactured five times as many bicycles as Mercier and that production of bicycles in England, overall, was ten times what it was in France. I was also

---

* After that year's Tour he had to have surgery on the wound which had turned septic. According to a medical report 'his flesh was full of holes. Dead tissue had to be removed to within several millimetres of vital organs'.

happy to offer my services as interpreter to this new colony, but my initiative proved unnecessary. A month after their arrival, their leader, a certain Brian Robinson, remarked, drily: "Hier on a pris la fringale. Aujourd'hui, on est rebecqueté."* They understood everything, these English, they spoke the slang.

Bobet exaggerates somewhat, out of politesse. Robinson alone, it seems, of the rosbifs was intent on learning French. The only real occasion for any parlez-vous was when the maid came to cook and serve their evening meal, so Robinson decided he would learn a new sentence in French every day.

Afternoons were free, for playing boules on the beach, pottering into Sainte-Maxime by bike or going round the crazy golf course in the garden of a bar in the village run by a recently-retired Tour rider, Apo Lazaridès, (10th in 1947, 9th in 1949) and his American wife. After a month of training, the racing began. The Hercules men were not assured of winning a place for a Great Britain team in the Tour: they had to prove their worth against riders who were. From the beginning of February to the middle of March, (typically 10 February to 15 March) the Riviera hummed with competition, massed-start road races over distances of 165km to 198km and two shorter distance events finishing atop Mont-Agel, which towers over Monaco at a height of 1,148 metres: the 12.5km out of Monaco itself and the longer 36.8km by way of the Basse Corniche from Nice. There were various Grands Prix: de Saint-Raphaël, de Nice, de Sigrand à Nice, d'Antibes, de Cannes, d'Aix Thermal, Catox in Marseille. Two major point-to-point races, the Genoa-Nice and the Marseille-Nice, preceded the first of the year's classic one-day races, the Milan-San Remo, (usually around 280km), nicknamed *La Primavera*, 'the Spring'. The jump from a race distance of less than 200km, the norm for the lesser events, to nearly 300km, calling for another two or two and a half hours in the saddle, marked the yawning gap between the norm of professional racing on the continent and what the British roadmen were used to.

The Hercules men were joined by Bob Maitland, formerly of BSA, and Tony Hoar in March. Shortly after Maitland arrived, it got out that the former leader of the BSA team managed by Cozens was being paid more money than the rest of the Hercules men. Robinson was incensed and, as Pusey told me, there was a 'bit of a shouting match'. Maitland's coziness with Cozens reinforced the feeling among the others that he was a bit distant from them, whether he espoused that himself or not.

Tony Hoar, 23 years old, a plumber from Hampshire, came to the team as a new professional. He'd signed for Hercules in February of that year after a

---

* 'Yesterday we got the bonk. Today, we got it sorted.'

solid ride in the Tour of Egypt,* for the NCU team, in January, against teams from Belgium, eastern Europe, Russia and the Mediterranean. His good showing attracted Hercules. He quit his job at the Admiralty (something he was already contemplating in favour of the bike) and went down to Les Issambres.

Maitland was now 31 years old and had a high and deserved reputation as a road racer and long-distance man in Britain, (he held the Land's End to London record). He'd ridden a lot of one-day events on the continent and the short Tour of Belgium stage race in 1953.

The Hercules team had a contract to ride the first major stage race of the year, the Paris-Nice. There'd been a late fall of snow in Paris – what the French call *la neige de coucou*, 'cuckoo snow' – and they set off in slush and bitter cold, wearing leggings. The event is aptly called 'the race to the sun'. Hoar and Pusey were actually eliminated, on time, but allowed to stay. Indeed, the French were doing all they could to encourage the newly-arrived British team. Jean Bobet won the race and Robinson came a very creditable 8th (Maitland was 12th). He said that he always rode well after a stage race and in the Flèche Wallonne, one of the Belgian spring classics, he proved that by coming fourth, behind the winner, Stan Ockers. Going over the Hautregard hill, the Belgian rider Henri Guldemont, said: 'We were all on the rivet and stamping on our pedals. Robinson came up to me and asked me if I needed a drink. I swear to you, I couldn't even unclench my teeth to reply. He seemed to be having no difficulty at all.'

They rode the Tour du Sud-Est, a seven-day stage race in late April through the country round Nîmes and Arles finishing in Marseille. Bedwell came second to Jacques Anquetil on the sixth stage into Fréjus and outsprinted him next day. Those riders in the team who were under 25 years of age rode the Tour of Holland in mid-season. Robinson wore the leader's jersey for one day and Hoar showed well in that race, won one stage and finished second on the last stage into Amsterdam. However, he riled some other men in the team by some outspoken and intemperate remarks during interviews he gave to Dutch journalists. While they were in the Netherlands, the older men, Maitland and Bedwell, were racing in Italy and France. In one race, the 300+km Grand Prix Pneumatique, in central France, Bedwell got into the winning break but punctured on the track at the finish. When Maitland, who'd punctured just as the break went clear, arrived, he found Bedwell in tears – he'd been sure of beating the eventual winner in a sprint. That disappointment proved fatal to his morale, says Maitland, and contributed to his poor showing in the Tour.

---

* This Tour was run by the British Army. Egypt was still partially subject to English control and there was a significant Army and RAF presence there, both of which held a series of races in Egypt at the time.

The pelotons in which they raced were large, comprising both professionals and independents, the latter riding on basic *à la musette* contracts* or none at all, scrapping for primes and prize money for a placing. (They hoped, of course, to attract the attention of semi-professional clubs as a step on the way to becoming professional.) This pointed up another major contrast with bike racing in Britain: the money.

The Sigrand company (a local chain of department stores still based on the Riviera) put up a lot of cash to back the race to which they gave their name; other local enterprises took the opportunity for publicity by sponsorship linked to advertising; newspapers, as ever, backed competition and all contributed to the distinction which had split professional sport on the continent from amateur in Britain. On the continent, cycle racing was a trade, un métier, and even a good independent could make an adequate living from earnings picked up in the long season of open races in France. It was, nonetheless, hard work and, if better paid than agricultural labouring or the slog in a factory, the rewards were always uncertain and often not much above subsistence level. For the Hercules men, this was not the case. The prize money they took was always a bonus, even if that was part of a commercial bargain: to promote and advertise the name of Hercules bicycles.

The publicity caravans, which attended even relatively minor races, as well as the Tour de France itself, did no more than emphasise the essential ingredient of all racing, the need for financial backing. It was Geminiani, second to Hugo Koblet in the Tour de France of 1951 (by a massive twenty-two minute margin), who convinced advertisers from a variety of trading marques that cycle sport offered a fantastic marketing window. Up to the early 1950s, racing jerseys were permitted to bear the names only of bike and tyre manufacturers and, by strict regulation, one name on the chest, one on the back, in letters of a controlled size. Once the tighter embargo on the sources of sponsorship was loosened, jerseys were emblazoned with a range of quite different brand names. Geminiani, riding with (and later managing) Jacques Anquetil, had secured sponsorship from the makers of Saint-Raphaël, an apéritif containing quinine, and the red, white and blue jersey they wore with the Saint-Raphaël name across the chest became famous. It was the vest Robinson himself later wore.

We are accustomed, these days, to top to toe advertising on cycling

---

* The *à la musette* contract was a basic ad hoc agreement between a rider and a sponsor who is paid (not much) by race organisers to find men to fill out their races, one-day or minor stage events. The riders, individually or riding as a scratch team, were allowed to keep whatever prizes they won but had the responsibility to get themselves to the start; the sponsor would pay for very few incidentals, if any. It was a bare minimum contract designed to give riders the chance to compete and be seen by better-funded teams and to help the sponsor looking for a directeur's role, to make contacts.

clothing, from socks to sunglasses. Even the yellow jersey, the golden fleece, is plastered with brand names. Until 1954, the *maillot jaune* worn by the winner (Louison Bobet that year) was blank, save for the initials HD, commemorating the father of the race, Henri Desgrange. The following year, it carried a strip of cloth with the name L. BOBET across the chest. (Bobet was contracted to Mercier Cycles, one of whose models carried his name. Hence the slogan.) As far as Desgrange's strait-laced opinions about the corruptions contingent on commercial intrusion in 'his' race, opinions to which his successor, Jacques Goddet had, for so long, cleaved, the writing was, finally, on the wool if not the wall.

The Hercules men rode the full programme of races on offer, apart from the Milan-San Remo, acclimatising to the nature of continental racing, and didn't really make a mark until they entered what turned out to be the only edition of the short-lived Route du Sud-Ouest, an eight-day stage race in May. If they were not outclassed physically, they did suffer from lack of tactical nous and a general sense of being rather in the dark. They didn't know the other riders, had no clue whom to watch, were caught up in a milieu altogether strange. One-day races were, by comparison, easy to read. The more complex stratagem that went into a longer campaign – economising of effort, judging which breaks to join and which to ignore, how best to marshall resources in different terrain, even feeling at ease in a peloton composed largely of strangers – was, for the moment, a closed book. However, Robinson, ever practical, insists that it was a necessary lesson and he applied himself to learning it. Moreover, he adds, it wasn't who you were but how you rode which determined how you were regarded. The bunch was, by and large, pretty good-tempered, aside from the odd oath or imprecation, if you inadvertently switched out of a pothole and barged into another rider.

The transition from amateur cycle racing to professional is always hard. Jean Bobet writes that to call it a step up is quite wrong: it's an entire storey above the amateur level. He also stresses the principal difference, something that other riders to whom I have spoken corroborate, and it is in rhythm. Whereas amateurs of that era tended to race at one speed throughout a race, the professionals changed pace frequently. The blasts of acceleration were abrupt and, to legs not used to such violent shifts in tempo, jolting, even crippling. The graph of energy expenditure in a pro race would show extreme and sudden peaks out of long troughs. Getting used to these fluctuations was central to making the grade on the continent. However, if from amateur to professional was a huge step, the Tour de France was something else entirely. It required an amalgam of experience, maturity, mental toughness and physical resilience which only complete immersion in continental racing could properly and adequately supply. French commentators were later kind enough about the gallant Brits – they didn't lack courage – but in their expert view, only Robinson had the wherewithal to stand any chance of finishing the Tour. That was largely because he had taken on this move to France in January as the start of a crash-course apprenticeship in the trade of riding the *Grande Boucle*.

As was evident, he began not only to feel at one with the style of racing, in the Route du Sud-Ouest he also began to show just what a fine rider he was: he went into the lead and wore the leader's jersey for a day before the continental opposition decided that the newcomer had tasted quite enough glory for the time being. This leap onto the pages of the sporting press, however, may well have been instrumental in alerting the organisation of the Tour because, shortly after the race ended, the entry of the Great Britain team in the Tour de France was confirmed. The Hercules men had proved that they could stay the distance and the final selection of the team lined up six of them – Bedwell, Hoar, Krebs, Maitland, Pusey and Robinson. Stan Jones, a solid team rider who had come from the first part of the season's domestic racing in Britain and quit work to train for three weeks, Ken Mitchell (of Wearwell Cycles) and Bevis Wood joined them. So, too, the Scot Ian Steel, winner of the 1951 Tour of Britain, the 1952 Peace Race, and the 1955 Trade Teams Tour of Britain, who actually rode for Viking Cycles. He and Mitchell had started that year's Vuelta a España in a team managed by Bob Thom, now enlisted as their Tour mechanic. Derek Buttle, the man who had first persuaded Hercules to enter cycle sponsorship, was a good rider but only a back-up man in the Hercules team.

The Austrian Fred Krebs was the only rider in the team with whom Robinson didn't get on. In fact, none of the other riders liked him. Maitland, himself not very popular with the others, is acerbic. Krebs, he told me, was a singularly selfish, awkward man, 'an upsetter'. Born in Vienna and working as an electronics engineer in Cambridge, Krebs was a stylish bike rider and an adept tactician. A strong climber, he had, in Robinson's view, a higher opinion of himself than he merited. Convinced of his own superiority, he didn't mix well and must have resented the fact that Robinson had established himself in the team as clear leader. His record and experience in stage racing, his results in the races they rode before the Tour, his clear superiority as a climber, confirmed that. He won the mountains prize in the Grand Prix de Cannes and in May alone he rode fourteen races and, apart from one 36th position, never dropped below 10th. He had demonstrated that most attractive trait in a racing cyclist, too, what the French call *fougue* – fire, spirit, vim. He was an attacker.

Although Maitland rode his BSA bike in the Tour painted and labelled with a Hercules decal, the other members of the team were mounted on Hercules bikes, with Cyclo gears from Hercules and GB brakes. They each wore the same Great Britain international jersey – white with a broad black hoop round the breast and union flags on each shoulder – but it takes more than a uniform jersey to establish cohesion.

The manager, Cozens, an abrasive individual, a former track rider, had a very limited experience of road racing and none at all of big stage races. According to Steel, (though uncorroborated by the others) by spring, relations with him had soured to the extent that the riders, now firmly welded as a racing unit, refused to let him come to races. They comandeered the car and drove themselves. It didn't augur well for his management of the great test to come. He did speak fluent French, learnt from his time racing on the continent, and he knew the scene – how to secure appearance money and so on – but he had no idea about tactics on the road. He was quite unable to read a race and wholly reliant on the riders, were he inclined to ask. He split the team into two squads, five apiece. The riders in each unit were ordered to devote themselves to their mutual fortunes: if one of the quintet needed help, one of or all the others had to help. Cozens hoped, thereby, better to accommodate a Tour regulation: the team cars could carry spare wheels but without tyres fitted. Each rider had to carry two spare road tyres (heavier than the track tyres they might otherwise have carried) and make the change of a punctured tub himself. Some riders carried a compression pump, with a cylinder of compressed air attached – this was heavier than the common push pump but it would inflate a tub very quickly and they offset the extra weight against the saving of time on the road.

Cozens' two-tier scheme was, says Maitland, the only way they had of meeting the Tour regulations.* No man who punctured or had mechanical problems could hope to get back to the fast-moving bunch on his own. (When a Spaniard punctured the whole team waited, if a Belgian got a flat he was left to it.) In the event, it put a heavy extra burden on the men who had constantly to bail out the puncture victims riding uncured tyres. Cozens didn't back the scheme wholeheartedly, either. On the road, when his riders were up against it, his catchall strategy tended to be 'Every man for himself'.

Robinson was suspicious of and unsympathetic towards Cozens, perhaps the most tepid expression of a deep antipathy. He was already emerging as a top-flight road racer with proven stamina for stage races, quick to recover and consistent, and the only member of the team totally committed to the goal of making a career as a professional bike rider, which meant in France. He was bent on riding the Tour in the manner that the Tour demanded, with total commitment and conviction, as a professional wedded to professional obligations. This tight mental focus effectively separated him from the others and he makes no apology for seeing the race as an exercise in personal survival. Nor did he disguise the fact at the time. He may have been the nominal leader but the team was not ranged round him. The central and superficially shared objective was to make it to Paris. The crucial factor that

---

* The grouping seems to have been: Hoar, Mitchell, Pusey, Robinson, Steel; Bedwell, Jones, Krebs, Maitland, Wood.

Robinson added to that objective, in his own determination to succeed, was to make it to Paris *whatever it took* in the way of personal sacrifice to his own ride.

Of the others, Steel was a first-rate rider, but from the Viking team, the other arch rival of the Hercules outfit, nor did he have any regard for Cozens. His record in stage-racing was outstanding. but his instinctive loyalty was to Viking, not Hercules and the notional unity of a 'Great Britain' team cut little ice. Krebs, the oddball, would have been a misfit in any team. Pusey, Bedwell, Wood and Mitchell, able riders each one, were ambivalent, hankering for the racing they knew best, at home. Bedwell, for instance, was a fine one-day rider but, as he said of himself, his speciality was sprinting and he was no more than a moderate climber. Maitland was a stalwart of the UK scene but ill-prepared for a three-week stage race.* Hoar was largely untested, and, whilst some of the men responded to his good-humour and laid back attitude, others found this unprofessional and tiresome. It was, however, a major error to bring in Jones, another BSA man. He was the kind of man who'd ride himself into the ground, a dependable team man, veteran of three Tours of Britain, but he'd been working full-time till only a few weeks before the race and was completely unprepared. To ask a rider to compete in the Tour de France without adequate build-up was idiotic. Did Hercules really believe that simply by throwing money at a race they could conquer it?

Considering that they were a bit of an assortment, a mongrel outfit, and the shaky foundation on which their entry into the Tour was based, the riders got on well, for the most part, but it wasn't close to the kind of solid, homogeneous unit needed even simply to complete so tough a race, especially at their first attempt. (To an extent, every team riding the Tour had to overcome a similar hurdle, since they all brought together riders from different trade teams, except that trade-team men knew the score and were race-hardened. The French, for example, unless despotically managed, tended to a positively Byzantine degree of internal discord and subversion.) Robinson was acutely aware, and candid, that the men fresh out from Britain were going to be up against it. 'They were on one leg, really,' he said. Used to riding at around 20mph they would find themselves having to sustain 25mph – from 32kph to 40kph. They were being pitched, unceremoniously, into a fierce level of competition for which they had not been schooled. When the hammer went down, they'd have no answer.

---

* In an interview with *Coureur* in 1957, Maitland freely admitted that he had left it too long before turning professional. Captain of the British road team at the London Olympics in 1948, he came second in the Manx International in 1952, a race billed as the final official Olympic trial, but wasn't selected to go to Helsinki. This rebuff drove him to quit the amateurs and join the newly-formed BSA team. He also said of Robinson that he was 'a born stage rider.'

Nevertheless, to begin with, before the Tour, there was no outright, flagrant dissent in the team, as has been described elsewhere. These men were cyclists, members of an indissoluble fraternity, their instinct was to cooperate. It was a basic impulse of pride. Once in the saddle, each man was primed to ride for the team, even if their acquaintance with the sometimes arcane requirements of racing in the continental peloton was callow indeed. Further, whilst Robinson now had enough French to converse at a basic level – to ask for help from French mechanics or other riders, for instance, and Maitland had French 'O' Level, none of the others in the team had any understanding or vocabulary of the language. They operated on a queer kind of macaronic, such as 'Give us a bollocks of wine.' Hercules ought to have foreseen the need for even a rudimentary grasp of the lingua franca of the peloton and it is a measure of just how bent on succeeding the man from Mirfield was, that he matched his exertions on the bike with determination to learn how to communicate with the foreigners he'd be riding with and against.

During their build-up for the Tour, Robinson came back to England to win the Tour of the Pennines, on the hilly terrain which was his sort of country, the familiar training ground round Saddleworth Moor to the west of Holme Moss. He also came fifth in the British road championship race.

5: TEN GREEN BOTTLES...
TOUR DE FRANCE 1955

In the July edition of *World Sports* W.J. Mills wrote: 'Don't dismiss the Tour de France (July 7-30) as "just a bicycle race". It's *the* cycle race of the year. As a journalist, I claim it makes the greatest sports story of the year, too. What other sporting event can make the front page of almost every Continental daily newspaper, day after day for a whole month?'

Here is a home-based journalist striving to sell the Tour to an audience whom he expects to be resistant to the idea that the race is something exceptional. It seems incredible. It does, however, point up just how wide the Channel was, figuratively, the divide between the domestic scene and that of the continent. It underlines, too, in what degree Robinson's pioneering career must stand.

France was so very far away, so very different, so very peculiar. The steam ferries that plied the choppy waters of the Channel took upwards of two hours or more to get from Dover to Calais. Britain still commanded an Empire, albeit creaky, Britannia ruled the waves and Europe was, to many sceptr'd islanders, impenetrably and irredeemably *foreign*. No matter that many of them had fought on its soil in a great war of liberation, 'over there', as a popular WWI song put it, was *weird*.

Mills gives some details of the magnitude of the event, sponsored at the time by *L'Equipe* and the now defunct *L'Aurore*. Cost of overall sponsorship amounted to approximately £100,000 of which the journals lost about a quarter in real terms, but recouped by the sale of advertising and entry to the publicity caravan. Local *syndicats d'initiatives* (chambers of commerce) paid up to £1,000 to host the race. (In those days, stage towns accommodated both *arrivée* and *départ*. There were no transfers.) Mills also notes that, at the time, Robinson was ranked 30th in the Trophée Desgrange-Colombo, (an unofficial season-long competition named after the founders of the Tour and the Giro, Henri and Emilio) based on an accumulation of points related to placings in races. This was roughly equivalent to the BBAR – 'Best British All-Rounder'. When I asked Robinson about this he was dismissive. The BBAR was based on *time-trial* results over a single season, he explained: '25, 50, 100 miles and 12-hour, though who the bloody hell wants to ride for twelve hours without getting paid?' and laughed.

Because coverage of the race itself in *Cycling* (later *Cycling Weekly*) was unavoidably delayed by nearly a week, Britain could not match the immediacy of Tour reports which, from its inception, had kept all France enthralled. July, at the start of the school holidays, was Tour month. Children were issued with school exercise books whose covers were illustrated with the route. They bought toy cyclists made of lead and painted in team colours. Pencil boxes, colouring books, board games, posters, postcards, popular songs, all bruited the *Grande Boucle*. Families gathered for picnics by the side of the route. The entourage following the race included fans from show business, notably the famous accordionist Yvette Horner, who serenaded the crowd round the route and in the *villes d'étape* on board a small lorry or in an open-top car.* The celebrated novelist Antoine Blondin, who rarely stepped outside the small enclave round Saint-Germain in Paris, quit the capital every year to indulge his passion for the Tour and submit reports to *L'Equipe* in his trademark florid prose.

The 1955 race (twenty-two stages and two rest days) set out from Le Havre on Thursday 7 July and the presentation of the teams took place in the vélodrôme on the Tuesday evening before. The announcer introduced the British riders: 'Pour la première fois, l'équipe Britannique' (*Cycling* reads *le premier fois...*) and the ten men wearing numbers 31 to 40 stepped forward onto the stage. When Robinson's name was read out, the crowd responded instantly. He was known. Not because he had made any fuss of self-promotion, never his way, but simply because the crowd was full of fans and his results in France had spoken for him. Bedwell had failed a pre-race medical examination (a problem with his heart) and been barred. Some hurried discussion ensued, arms were twisted – deprive a first-time British team of one of its main men? No. The examination was reviewed and Bedwell was in. Hoar was short of sleep because of conjunctivitis and Krebs' blood pressure was a bit high but they all reported fit to ride.

In an article based on an interview for Jock Wadley's *Coureur* magazine, after the '56 Tour, Robinson leads off with a statement that might surprise a contemporary reader: 'You will remember that in 1955 it was quite a simple matter for an English professional to get into the Tour – indeed, when it came to selection time, there were hardly enough riders available to fill the places.' (There was one Luxemburg-Mixed team and no fewer than five French regional teams.)

The team had had a final training stint for ten days at Poigny-la-Forêt, near Rambouillet, south-west of Paris, and then decamped to the Hotel Terminus in the centre of Le Havre, not far from the railway station and the docks, also occupied by the French national team.

---

* There were other brushes with showbiz. On one occasion, as he travelled to Britanny for the Tour de l'Ouest, in August after the Tour de France, Robinson stopped for coffee, met the singer Line Renaud, who was heading to the race to sing at a concert in the town square, and she gave him a lift in her chauffeur-driven motor…a lot more comfortable than the team wagon.

The Tour organisation doled out:

sun-goggles – big horrible things but they did the job – a couple of racing caps and lots of Aspro. They were one of the sponsors. I think there was a compressed air pump. [There was.] They gave us an aluminium suitcase for our kit – there was a fresh jersey every day, that was a luxury. We had to supply our own shorts, socks and shoes, of course. Into the case also went the issue tracksuit, a waterproof top – it all had to be signed for and paid for if it didn't come back. Plus our own washing gear, ordinary clothes to wear in the evenings, any other bits and pieces we had to carry. It was quite small, but regulation size so that all the cases could be stacked in the Tour lorry. The stars had everything carried for them. No standard-size metal case for them. We had a medical examination beforehand, a 30-minute workout session and measuring our heart rate before and after. [The race doctor, Pierre Dumas, introduced this precaution.]

Each team had three vehicles: the main team car, a drophead Peugeot 203 for the *directeur sportif*, with roof rack for spare bikes and wheels. The mechanics, Bob Thom, former racer and manager of the Viking team, and a Frenchman, Louis Debruycker, had a van, a *fourgonnette*, with L'EQUIPE painted on the side, to carry the luggage, massage tables, mechanics' stands and the bigger tool kit and so on. Robinson says of the soigneur, the Belgian Julian Schramme: 'He was brilliant, he really got your muscles sorted out. Schramme drove another car which either went ahead – it would have all the musettes in for the ravitaillement – or, if it was needed, say in the mountains, it acted as a second service vehicle, following the race.' He added: 'We were given a Tour handbook which contained details of each stage route – we tore that bit out and put it in a plastic wallet each day. We were on a wage of £4 per day, which was very good money, when the average weekly wage in the UK was around £5.'

Mills was not swept away in the euphoria whipped up round the mere presence of a British team in this 42nd Tour. Perhaps he had talked discreetly to harder-headed realists. 'I estimate' he wrote, 'that five will have retired before the halfway stage and that three, at the most, will finish the 4,345km course.'

Stage 1 Le Havre – Dieppe 102km

The sun shone on the seafront as the one hundred and thirty riders set off from Le Havre. Some 18km from Dieppe, Robinson punctured, Hoar waited for him, they bore down on a small group of five struggling to rejoin the main bunch, dropped them and swept up Pusey, who was struggling on his own. The trio raced on and arrived 5m 11s after the winner, Miguel Poblet, who had become the first Spaniard ever to wear the yellow jersey by outsprinting Louis Caput of France and Edgard Sorgeloos of Belgium. That afternoon, the British came ninth in a team time-trial on five-circuits of a 12km course round the town's main square. The Ile-de-France men won, in its team a man who became a friend and team-mate of Robinson's, Nicolas Barone.

Blondin devoted most of his second dispatch to the Brits and leads off with a momentous incident during the morning's opener:

> Off and on during the stage, there comes a pause in the tumult, a desert island in an expanse of sea, the vacuum beneath a bell and beneath this bell, a man flounders on his own in the silence. For some minutes he struggles as on a seesaw between the mass of the peloton grouped in convoy gnawing at his heels and the small handful of the day's aces whose glory shimmers in a halo of accompanying cars five hundred metres ahead of him.
>
> He already knows that he'll never catch them but nor does he want to return to the others so soon, to go back into the anonymity of the bunch. It is not for nothing that he wears a jersey bearing the colours of the Union Jack and that he has, this day, in front of an eager crowd, rendered illustrious the expression *filer à l'anglaise* ('to take French leave', abscond). For the first time, the dossard of a British rider features on the slate of honour of the Tour de France and his name attaches to one of its sudden changes of fortune. This man is Robinson; this desert island is a section of the route between Bruay and Lens; this historic day is Thursday.
>
> Directed by the former sprinter Sydney Cozens, whose scholarly spectacles, refined rotundity and meditative demeanour recall Mr Pickwick, the English team was welcomed at the start of the Tour with the affectionate curiosity with which one would greet a be-turbanned delegation from Pakistan turning up for the World Championships on postmen's bikes... These young men whose unfamiliar accent, a language familiar in other travel agencies, explodes in the heart of this peloton, resonating with Mediterranean exclamations and Flemish curses and who seem to have adorned their musettes with travellers' cheques, display all the characteristics of displaced persons. Jones would have done better to become a clergyman, Hoare [sic] to have returned to the pages of *David Copperfield*, from which he appears to have escaped, Pusey to have put his fox-like profile at the disposal of the shire hunt, Bedwell to pulling pints of beer as nutbrown as his tousled Cockney mop and Robinson himself to purchase a bowler hat and a midriff bulge before paying a visit to his money broker in the City.
>
> And yet, in less than three days these simplistic ideas find themselves turned upside down. On the seafront, under the foliage of trees swollen with rainwater, all along green pastures where heavy horses graze

with a noble indifference, so, too, across arid terrain which afford only shacks for dwellings, the English team has comported itself with a quite remarkable tact, discipline and practical know-how.

We have seen them picknicking with the other riders under a school's covered way, getting on happily with everyone, forgetting it was their tea time. We heard this praise from one hotelier in Dieppe: "It's the first time that I have had English guests who do not stand out because they're odd." Anyone who thought that the English gentlemen would be the first to pull out had better think again.

Stage 2 Dieppe – Roubaix 204km

Robinson never enjoyed racing in Belgium. At a little over ten stones in weight, he was too light to ride the cobbles. (His racing weight was 65kg and he's not much heavier now. After each Tour, he had added some two pounds of muscle weight.) The second stage to Roubaix was an added trial, therefore, and something of a shock to the Brits, some of them debutants in the cobbled Hell of the North. The weather was altogether Flandrian, too: wind and rain.

The large, domed boulder-like cobbles, the notorious *pavé* of northern France and Belgium, are variously described as babies' heads or bowler hats by riders who are familiar with the jarring sensation of racing across them. Bone- and bike-shaking, horribly treacherous when wet, in places badly broken and gappy, bordered by a trough of earth – in rain, a mud-filled trench – the *pavé* is beloved of the Flemings to whom they represent the real test of hard men, hated and dreaded by others for whom they constitute an absurd and parlous lottery. A high-speed prang on the cobbles can mean a season lost. The only way to ride them is on biggish gears to reduce the vibration and with nerves and reactions pinging at high alert. If a rider goes down under your wheels, as riders on the *pavé* frequently will, there is not much to be done, only to pray for an injury-free tumble. Graham Jones (an outstanding professional) gives a startlingly vivid impression of what riding the cobbles is like:

> The road breaks up into long cobbled sections, rough and uneven with frequent potholes. The bunch, over a hundred strong, looks for every tiny respite from the cobbles. You dive left onto a narrow sandy strip about six inches wide. Suddenly everyone is charging over to the other side of the road where there is a better strip of smooth track. The track finishes abruptly as you enter the outskirts of a small town. The twisting road offers numerous corners. You head into them at full tilt. You sprint out of them even faster. The town has trams (streetcars) and now everyone is trying to avoid getting their wheels into the tracks. Riders bunny hop sideways up on to the sidewalk. Back out of town

and the road opens up into a bleak, featureless countryside. Now the road is an endless strip of concrete slabs. About every ten seconds for the next twenty minutes the gap between each slab sends a sharp shudder up your forks and through your arms to rattle the teeth in your head. All this time a strong wind coming off the ocean is buffeting the peloton. Echelons form and no quarter is given in trying to secure a place in them. Those hanging on to the tail of an echelon will shortly lose contact. For the majority of the riders this infernal cocktail is not much more than an exercise in survival.' (*Cycling Revealed*)

Pusey, twice directed to wait for team-mates Robinson and Mitchell, who had punctured, rode into Roubaix exhausted, outside the time limit – that day set at 10% of the time, 5h 45m, of the day's winner, Frenchman Antonin Rolland. He was eliminated. Wood and Bedwell had gone down when Jean Bobet fell after the feeding station, Maitland fell some way on and damaged his gear. It was a rough blooding in the merciless pell-mell of the Tour. Robinson showed early in the stage when he joined Jean Stablinski in a chase after a breakaway of eight riders. Stablinski, the son of Polish immigrants, was an ex-miner who had worked in the pits of the coalfields through which they rode that day. He later suggested the inclusion in the Paris-Roubaix classic of what became a celebrated stretch of cobbles through the Arenberg forest. The pair of them was eventually swallowed up again by the peloton. In the rainbow jersey, Louison Bobet (who won the Paris-Roubaix in 1956) finished, all but anonymous, in the bunch. A marked man in the race – no rider had ever won three consecutive Tours – he was in a jittery state of tension, yelling obscenities at race officials and the drivers of following cars. It was not paranoia, either. The press fuelled speculation about a conspiracy: 'Everyone is against Bobet.' A French reporter divulged what the *directeur* of the Dutch team had told him: 'Louison is not going to win. He'll pack before the mountains. I've seen it in his eyes…A bad sign, a very bad sign.' Bobet was incensed. According to his manager, Marcel Bidot, he determined to get out into the open, clear of what felt like suffocation bound up close inside the peloton. Intent on shellacking the field and delivering a firm rejoinder to all the hostile talk about his weakness and lack of will, on stage three, he attacked from the very start.

Stage 3 Roubaix – Namur 210km
More cobbles to batter them, a succession of nasty Belgian hills, what the Flemish call 'bergs', and a finish on top of the final berg, up to the citadel of Namur… another brutal day's racing. Bobet took a number of top men with him when he broke clear but eventually led three riders, the only men who could hold his wheel, by four minutes, onto the Namur circuit. Hard

men of the stature of Poblet and the Belgian bruiser Rik Van Steenbergen had wilted, so, too, Charly Gaul. Jean Bobet, winner of that year's Paris-Nice, performed a magnificent job of support before he fell away, spent. (The *Cycling* journalist showed his naiveté in respect of team tactics – ride for your boss and, when you've nothing left, know that you bow to the universal law of survival: *sauve qui peut* – lamenting the fact that Louison had 'unsportingly' dropped his younger brother.) Hoar had tried to stay with the break but faltered. Robinson could not stay with them, either, but pursued hard to finish 25th, the highest British placing so far. Steel crashed and came in with Ferdi Kubler, the 1950 winner. Mitchell and Hoar arrived together, having stopped for a drink as the hills of the last section bruised them. Maitland, Jones and Krebs finished some way down, but Bedwell and Wood had lost so much ground, wrung out with the speed and the cobbles, that they knew they could never rejoin and abandoned. Jones, who had ridden selflessly to bring them back, remonstrated with them:

'You can't pack. This is the Tour de France.'

'Well we have' they said.

In an interview he gave to *Cycling* in 1993, Bedwell said:

I had punctured twice and was going nice and steady when I was talked into quitting by Bev Woods, who told me I was well outside the time limit. Actually, I was well inside. I didn't know until the next day that they would let everyone start, even those who had finished outside the time limit. I wasn't really interested in riding the Tour and I should have had the courage to say no. Another year, I would have been keen to ride. I had a medical test before the start and they said I had heart trouble, that didn't leave me with much morale for the race.

Stage 4 Namur – Metz 232km

Mitchell punctured, Robinson waited to relay him back, Steel and Hoar, parched in the heat of the sun, dropped off the back of the main field to search out drinks, and the British men lifted themselves above two French regional teams – Sud-Ouest and Ile de France – in the team rankings. *Cycling* applauds Jones 'who all along has proved himself the perfect *domestique*' thus introducing the readership to another racy French term.

Under their sponsorship contract, the Britons were required to use the Dunlop tyres about which Robinson was so scathing. Foreign riders routinely ignored such obligations: good equipment mattered more than brand names and Robinson took their lead. Since the Dunlops they were given came uncured, they were even less reliable but, Robinson had little truck with using a flat as an excuse. 'Maybe if you were in the lead it might count, but if you were already half an hour down, it made no odds unless you allowed it to. Question of mind over matter, if you like.'

Hoar, in an interview he gave in 2008, to Nigel Dick, a film-maker working on a feature about the *Lanterne Rouge*, gives this take on the puncture saga:

> The racing was overshadowed by the fact that we had a terrible crop of flats. The story was that Dunlop, one of our sponsors, said they would come up with a special tubular tyre for the tour. So they took a grass track casing, which was fairly large in section, and they put a road tread on it. But tubulars had to be matured for six to nine months or more for the rubber to toughen-up. Naturally we told them to make sure they were all mature. You know, it was the obvious thing. So, we had so many flats and riders having to wait for others in the team to catch up. That upset Ian Steel, who was a Viking rider, because he'd have to wait for a Hercules rider. So it wasn't exactly smooth sailing but the team manager told him he had to do it. One night, I recall, we sat in a hotel room discussing this and we took a tubular and cut it open. The date inside was just a few months earlier. So they weren't matured. We immediately stopped riding Dunlops and the manager went and got some Pirellis, which were mature. So we had no more flats to speak of. But it was really a factor.

What he doesn't say is that Robinson and Maitland were certainly not riding the issue Dunlops. Robinson used his favoured Pirellis from the start (bought from a shop in Italy just across the French border) and Maitland was using well-matured, special silk Dunlops with a narrow carcase and Six-Day treads. He didn't puncture once in the Tour.

Stage 5 Metz – Colmar 229km

The Col de la Charbonnière (961m) straddles a narrow, twisty road, fringed by woods, in the Vosges mountains. In the 1955 photograph it looks as if it had been a mountain path not long since widened and roughly surfaced by a regiment of military engineers and pioneers ahead of the army's main column. The gradient was not severe but the climb did come after a long stretch of what the French call *un pays très vallonné* – a taxing, nonstop succession of deep ups and downs, the sort of country Robinson was used to in the Dales. The French were riding solidly and, at the day's close, had five of their men in the top six overall, Rolland in yellow. The British all finished safely, but the Tour was beginning to show its teeth. This first day of uphill was no more then a gentle opener. It presaged much much worse.

Stage 6 Colmar – Zürich 195kms

The speed of the race on a course intermittently flat and rolling but at a steady climb into Switzerland, increased markedly. The current French road champion, Darrigade, outsprinted his partner in the break, the local man Kubler, by three lengths on the Zürich Oerlikon track, having ridden the stage at an average of around 43kph. Kubler, a few days' shy of his thirty-sixth birthday, winner of the 1950 Tour, was the oldest man in the race, but still touted by some as a potential winner. He'd driven the pace high, hitting the long cobbled ramp down through Stein, a few kilometres from home, doubly hard, keen, of course, to win on home soil. But, oh the bad luck he had been dealt so often of late, *pauvre Ferdi*. He saw the light of his once-bright flame dwindling in the dusk of age and reduced power... 'Poor Ferdi'. Beaten when he should have won.

The Swiss crowd, sympathising with the lachrymose Kubler, whistled, jeered and clattered cowbells at Darrigade as he made his lap of honour clutching the winner's bouquet.

Jones battered by the scarifying tempo – 'too fast for me' he said – came in just ahead of Jean Bobet, who had also had a terrible day, at the back of the field, over fourteen minutes down. Hoar had escaped early on in a group of six led by Jean Forestier, winner of that year's Paris-Roubaix. The break didn't survive, but Hoar's temerity showed the right spirit.

Stage 7 Zürich – Thonon-les-Bains 275km
Two kilometres out from Zürich, Jones punctured. Steel and Hoar waited for him but the previous day's ride had frazzled him and he was done. His morale blown, his legs enfeebled, he couldn't hold their wheel and, after 25km or so, he told them to leave him, he wasn't going to make it. A sad moment. Hoar and Steel, who by now had lost a lot of time, faced a long haul to get back. Ahead of them the bunch, containing Krebs, Mitchell, Robinson and Maitland.

At eighty kilometres an hour down the steep drop into Vevey on the shore of Lac Léman (Geneva), the bunch spread across the road, two Spanish riders crashed on a hairpin. Maitland tries to avoid them, slams on his brakes, a frightful squeal of over-heated pads, his wheel drifts in gravel, he can't hold the bike, hits a side wall and hurtles over the parapet. Luckily, there's no drop. He scrambles back over, badly shaken. Nearly sixty kilometres still left to ride. He remounts and, a short way on, the Hoar-Steel tandem catch him and they ride in together.

Cycling does not record Steel's withdrawal from the race after this stage and it is a melancholy story. He'd come to the Tour ultra fit and got on well with the other riders, but it was, he told me, a terrible mistake to put such a team into the race. Three of the men, him included, had been woefully short of racing miles. Cozens had tried to get Steel to join the Hercules team but Steel refused. The Viking people had been very good to him and he felt a powerful allegiance to them. He insists that his refusal angered Cozens and Cozens, for whom no one seems to have a good word – 'rogue' was Steel's contribution – set out to make life hard for Steel on the Tour. Steel liked the other riders, they all felt the innate bond of fellow cyclists riding for each other, but gradually the blatant lack of support and sympathy from Cozens ground his morale down, he lost interest and, when the mind has caved in there is little one can do physically. The wearying chase of Stage 7 flattened him and he went home. Interviewed by *Coureur* in 1958, Steel proffered no excuse for his abandon. He said that having fallen back early on the stage, he retired along with Hassenforder, Varnajo and Vitre. He also said that the lack of French isolated him, and the others, to such an extent that it was a major handicap. There was no chatting in the bunch for them and to the ordeal of just getting to the finish was added the misery of loneliness. About Robinson he was generous if not effusive: he admired his staying power but insisted that he was not an exceptional talent among British roadmen. Maybe not, but he did have something the others did not: the sense to know that he couldn't hope to beat the Tour de France, his best hope was to learn how not to be beaten by it. Including his one sentence of French per day.

The Tour organisation evinced little sympathy with riders who abandoned. Neither Jones nor Steel was allowed to stay overnight in Thonon (at the Tour's expense). They had to pack their bags and head straight back to wherever it was they'd come from. It was a limp conclusion to their great adventure.

Stage 8 Thonon-les-Bains –Briançon 253km
And now it really began. Col des Aravis 1486m…Col du Télégraphe 1566m…Col du Galibier 2642m. Taken individually, the Aravis and the Télégraphe are not that hard. Line them up ahead of the monster, the Giant of the Alps, the mountain which Desgrange classified as *grand cru* compared to the gnat's piss of the rest, they turn such a day as this into a merciless slog, potentially what the French with conscious flamboyance term 'a calvary'.

Robinson looked up as they approached the snow-capped ridges, a fretted line of mountain tops monstrously high marking the horizon, like a jerky graph of their suffering to come. He knew about the Galibier and the thought of riding it after those two other cols scared him. It wasn't just a matter of getting over them. With all day to do it they could certainly achieve that. It was the sickening dread of not being able to beat the time guillotine. The fear that this was the day that would beat them, that they would not be equal to the challenge.

They rode up the Galibier into snow and bitter cold. They saw other teams stopping by the cars to get a shot of chemical fuel and then speeding past them. The roads were wet with melting snow and the descent was doubly treacherous – streams of water and grit across the road, their hands freezing on the bars, which made braking difficult, plus the deadening chill in legs which can't turn the pedals to generate a calorie of warmth. And, whereas the first riders over the col could go down on a clear road, the riders at the back of the race had to contend with the following cars – up to a hundred of them, even in those days – some jockeying to get past to catch up with their men. The bikes were moving more quickly, however, on the straights between the hairpins. There was a strict code of courtesy to govern overtaking, but negotiating the congestion of extra traffic was vexatious. It made for added difficulty on what was already a tricky, if not outright dangerous, ride. The British men were not adept on alpine descents, either, ignorant of the skill in any circumstances and certainly not at race speed.

Today's riders are amply supplied with rain gear and warmers. Formerly, riders had much thinner, less close-cut protection for extremes of temperature. That day, on top of the Galibier, the snow still lay in huge banks to either side of the road. Down below in the valley, the temperatures were torrid, a burning sun, exposed roads, bare rock reflecting the infernal heat. The British wore no undervests – in fact, Robinson told me, on days of excessive heat, he'd have preferred not to have to wear a jersey at all, made of wool, remember, except that they needed the pockets to put their food in. When they stripped off the heavy jersey, sopping wet with sweat, to get into the bath, the skin round the chest covered by the black hoop, which drew the sun's radiation to it, had been tanned more deeply than the rest of the torso. Italian racing jerseys, made of merino wool, were far more comfortable.

Gaul, in his element and always a man for the cold weather, rode magnificently to take the stage victory by over thirteen minutes. Kubler led in Bobet. The British riders acquitted themselves with courage, despite a series of mishaps.

Hoar crashed on the descent of the Aravis, Krebs punctured on the Galibier, Maitland was still suffering from his contretemps the day before and all three had to battle hard to rejoin the back of the field. Mitchell, whose eyesight was not good and especially not in the dark, hit the side wall of the unlit tunnel which had been cut through the massif of the Galibier and through which, in those days, the Tour passed.* He was badly shaken and bruised, but they all came in inside the time limit, Robinson now 39m 45s down overall, and Hoar way back at 2h 12m 27s.

---

* Until 1979, the mountain's altitude was given as 2556m. When one of the supporting archways of the tunnel (built in the early years of the 20th century) collapsed, it was closed and the road extended upwards over the shoulder of the massif, an added kilometre of around 10% to 2645m. Lucien Van Impe was first over the new, super Galibier.

Stage 9 Briançon – Monaco 270km

The very tough first half of the stage, the ascent of the Col de Vars 2108m, around 50km into the stage, followed by the Col de la Cayolle 2326m, up a rugged, narrow canyon to a remote wilderness of rock and gaunt trees, made the second half of the stage – a downhill to the coast over the relatively shallow Col du Vasson 1668m, and the final 9.2km flip up from Nice to La Turbie (Col d'Eze) 512m – almost a relief. Riding southwards into the country which the Hercules men had explored on the training camp was a timely boost to the morale, too.

Maitland, alas, had not recovered from the miseries of the past two days. Crossing a low bridge not far from the start, he wobbled and crashed, Hoar went down with him. Maitland aggravated the bruising he'd sustained in Switzerland and, having grovelled to the top of the Cayolle, shunted along by the broom wagon, he abandoned. It was, he says, a matter of pride to reach the top of the mountain, even knowing that he was certainly dished on time and in no physical state to continue. Hoar was left to try to claw his way back to the main bunch on his own. Mitchell was riding with commendable aggression on the climb of the Vars but, heading for the first feed stop after the descent, his front changer broke and the chain shipped. Leaning down to get the chain back on, he caught his finger in the teeth of the chainwheel and ripped it open. Chain and chainwheel jammed up, Mitchell paddled the bike two-footed a kilometre along the road into Barcelonnette where the mechanic, Bob Thom, was waiting to sort him out.

Heavy rain began to fall, the road up to the Cayolle was awash with water, the air freezing, the sopping wet race jerseys added extra pounds to carry. At the finish in the Monaco stadium, Krebs (who'd been riding for two days with a saddle boil) came in 48m 5s down on the first nine finishers, Robinson at 49m 7s, Mitchell 55m 17s and Hoar, wasted by his long solo chase, 4m 24s outside the time limit imposed on mountain stages – namely 15% of the winner's time. However, anxious to give the badly depleted British team as much help as a certain elasticity in the application of the rules might allow, the commissaires reinstated Hoar on the grounds that he had been baulked by traffic. Robinson, containing his effort, was now eleventh overall, Hoar, last man, *lanterne rouge*.

There followed the Rest Day and the vinegar bath. Robinson described it to me: 'You dissolved two litres of wine vinegar and a kilo of sea salt in water, as hot as you could bear. An eight-minute soak – no longer – and the veins on your legs stood out corded, thick as chapel hat pegs. Driving out the toxins, it was a great relaxer' says Robinson. 'I always made sure to get from each finish to the hotel as quickly as possible and then straight onto the massage table. Those times on the table were always the best times on the Tour. You could talk things over with the soigneur and he acted as a sort of confidant, if you like, absorbing some of the day's hassle along with soothing the aching legs. A bit of light-hearted chat. It wasn't only that you had to recover physically, you had to recover mentally, too.'

Hoar, with whom Robinson shared a room, adopted a very different approach. He tended to dawdle around at the stage finish, amble off to the hotel up to an hour and a half later, and slump on the bed, completely spent. 'But he was a great joker,' says Robinson. 'He had a real zest for life.' What's also true is that his come-what-may attitude and genial disposition gave his more focused team-mate welcome, temporary distraction and moral support.

Stage 10 Monaco – Marseille 241km

The French riders called this 'the holiday stage', a ride along the coast road of the Côte d'Azur, the familiar ground of training-camp rides, then up and over the Massif de l'Esterel above Saint-Raphaël, to an altitude of a little over 300m, on through Les Issambres, whence the run-in to Marseille. The prime for the col (won by Darrigade): 50,000 francs, £50.

Mitchell had developed a saddle boil and, early in the stage, the mechanic cut a section out of his saddle to reduce the agony of the friction. That did not alleviate the pain itself and, although he rode for some distance with the '47 winner, Jean Robic (who later retired), Mitchell had to slog on most of the way alone, in blistering heat. Robinson joined a break that was soon caught and finished in the main bunch, with Bobet, and now lay 8th overall. The field was subdued, knowing what lay in wait the following day. Hoar was troubled by fluid on the knee but led in the finishing sprint of the autobus, the riders at the back cutting their effort to squeeze in just inside the time limit. By now there were but eighty-seven riders still in the race. The British team, reduced to four riders, Hoar, Krebs, Mitchell and Robinson, faced a grim battle. There was little question of mutual help. They were, effectively, each on his own. Better that one of them, at least, should make it to Paris than sacrifice that possibility by the roadside in a futile partnership of self-destruct.

Stage 11 Marseille – Avignon 198km

Mont Ventoux. The Giant of Provence. Robinson and company were not the only men never to have ridden this cruel mountain. Kubler was new to it, too, and when he set off on the lower slopes at a fiendish pace, Geminiani cautioned him: 'Careful, Ferdi, the Ventoux isn't like any other mountain.'

'And Ferdi is not like any other rider' he called back, insouciantly.

Those who knew it understood that the Ventoux was not to be toyed with. On its treeless upper slopes, overspread with a scree of bone-white, limestone shale, often roasted by sun and reflecting its pitiless glare, oxygen is thin, the air still and oven-hot, and lungs heave, breathless. Over 21 kilometres of ascent from Bédoin, the gradients vary but in places crank up to 14%. No one can ride a mountain for you, but Robinson, of course, sought counsel. The professionals who knew the Ventoux advised steady rhythm, riding the bends on the marginally shallower outside and no sudden changes of tempo.

This Monday, in the wicked cauldron heat of mid-July's canicule, the Dog Days, Bobet observed the advice closely. Riding alongside his team-mate Geminiani, he let Kubler go. Halfway up he was in third position at 1m 30s, reeled in and overtook Kubler to cross the summit alone with a fifty second advantage. In the space of ten kilometres, Kubler had lost twelve minutes. When Robinson, also riding at his own rhythm, caught up with the Swiss, the former champion was in a dreadful state, weaving across the road from side to side, moaning with pain and distress. As the Yorkshireman rode up to him, some three hundred metres from the pass, the Swiss croaked: 'Pushez Ferdi...pushez Ferdi...' Robinson isn't clear exactly what he said, but it was on the lines of 'Bugger that. Push yourself, what about me?'

Dense crowds, as ever, lined the route, pressing in on the riders, in places leaving them only a narrow passage to ride through. Spectators waited at the top with piles of newspapers to hand to the riders, now boiling hot and dripping with sweat. The paper, stuffed up the front of the jersey, helped mitigate the cool slap of the wind on their chest as they went down at speed. And at speed was the key.

Robinson had set off down the severe pitch of Ventoux's western face, the gradient exacerbated by extremely tight hairpins for the first kilometres, at a fairly cautious pace when the man Kubler shot past on what seemed a suicidal line: manic velocity, clipping the corners fine...Robinson didn't hesitate, he latched on. This was obviously a good wheel to follow, he'd beaten the man going up, he sure as hell wasn't going to be beaten by him going down, and there followed his first significant lesson in an essential tool of the trade: descending. The Tour itself was a massive lesson, separate elements of it never to be disregarded. On Ventoux that day he touched a fiery mystery and learnt how to detach himself from the objective fear of plummeting down mountainsides at a speed which would not only make up any time lost on the ascent but actually gain time. He had experience of hurtling down the fells in the Yorkshire Dales, but the mountains are a quite different proposition and he very soon became as good as any descender in continental racing. He still has that nerveless calm and balance. I have watched him, in awe, flying down the precipice of Mam Tor in the High Peak district with the nonchalance of that hard-gained capacity to give the work to the bike and leave anxiety in the tyre tracks.

Ventoux meted out some terrible punishment that day. Jean Bobet describes how he overtook a Belgian rider who was in tears, weaving across the road. A number of strong climbers –Stan Ockers, Gilbert Bauvin, Antonio

Gelabert – crumpled. Two men collapsed with borderline asphyxia. Richard Van Genechten toppled off his bike twice, was given oxygen and taken by ambulance to hospital. Ten kilometres from the summit, Jean Malléjac also collapsed. (A considerable rider, he'd come second overall to Bobet in 1953.) The journalist Jacques Augendre said that Malléjac had been zigzagging across the entire width of the road. Then he collapsed, one foot still in a toe-clip, the other pedalling at the air. Comatose at the side of the road, his eyes rolled back in their sockets, his face ghost white and slick with sweat, he lay prone, shivering, in a temperature of 35° C in the shade. Georges Pahnoud of the *Télégramme de Brest* reported how the race doctor, Dumas, who'd driven up in the Aspro van, 'had to force [Malléjac's] jaws apart to try to get him to drink. A quarter of an hour later, after he'd been given an injection of Solcamphor (a decongestant) and then oxygen, Malléjac regained consciousness. Inside the ambulance, heading for Avignon hospital, he kept lashing out, gesticulating, demanding his bike, trying to get out, back in the race.'

Robinson rode past Malléjac as Dumas, in shorts, crouched over him. Press photographers stood by. He did not know how serious the French rider's plight was, but the sight of a man clearly prostrate with exhaustion underlined just what this race sometimes meant: a ride to the limit of endurance.

We talked about this one morning in the kitchen in Mirfield, over yoghourt and fruit and fresh coffee. 'It was like ten green bottles, you wondered every day if it was going to be you next. But you had to look after yourself. All right, you might wait for a team-mate and ride him back on after a puncture, and he'd do the same for you, but otherwise, you had to concentrate completely on your own race, getting as much sleep as possible, for instance, any extra half an hour might just make the difference. Looking after your kit, everything, really, to make sure things were as good as they could be. And, on the road, especially in the mountains, you had to economise on effort. I soon learnt that you could make up a lot of time on descents, so I paced myself carefully on the climbs – I wasn't bothered about points or time, after all. Then, on the downhill, I could claw back minutes. In fact, that's the one great lesson I took from that Tour – I learnt how to descend.' It was something he also expressed at the time, with an emphasis that suggests it was the primary lesson he'd learnt.

Robinson and Hoar both made it to Avignon, but it was the end of the road for both Krebs and Mitchell. Since the British team had now but two riders, one of their mechanics, Bob Thom, had to withdraw from the race. Typically, Robinson's take on what must have been something of a challenge – eleven stages of the Tour still to ride and virtually no back-up for the pair of them – was unsentimental. There was a job that had to be done and they'd just have to get on with it, 'muck in'. Hoar's sunny temperament was an undoubted benefit even if his approach was, by contrast with his fellow survivor, almost lackadaisical. Robinson, himself, was on a mission: he'd lost just over fifty-five minutes on the stage and dropped way down from his 8th placing but he was still there.

[Malléjac insisted for the rest of his life that he had been given a drugged bottle from a soigneur, whom he didn't name, and said that although his belongings had reached the hospital intact, the bottle had been emptied. That evening Dumas, distraught by the experience of tending a man close to death sprawled on the stony blanket of the Ventoux, said that he was prepared to level a charge of attempted murder. He'd come to the Tour in 1952 to replace the original doctor and, at the time, had no acquaintance with the world of professional cycling. He was shocked. The soigneurs arrived for the season's racing after a winter at the Six-Day races – which were notorious for extreme levels of fatigue – with cases full of all manner of potions. Dumas called them fakirs. Riders took anything the soigneurs gave them, without question, as he himself said: 'Even bee stings and extract of toads' glands, medicine from the heart of Africa... they were like healers laying on hands or administering irradiating balms, plunging a rider's feet into unbelievable mixtures which could lead to eczema, so-called magnetised diets and everything else you could imagine. In the 1953 and '54 Tours de France, it was all magic, medicine and sorcery. After that, they started consulting Vidal, the French medicine directory.' (Council of Europe report.)

The French team manager of that era, Bidot, told an inquiry that 'three-quarters of riders were doped. I am well placed to know that since I visited their rooms each evening during the Tour. I always left frightened after these visits.'

The Bobet brothers, in conversation with Anquetil and Merckx after they'd retired, claimed never to have taken any dope when they were riding, only ever the little bottle that their soigneur and confidant, Raymond le Bert, gave them, although they didn't know what it contained. Merckx and Anquetil roared with laughter.]

Stage 12 Avignon – Millau 240km
The route crossed the Col du Minier 1264m and the Col de la Seyrède 1292m in the Cévennes, two climbs, one after the other, like peaks towering above a trough on a big dipper. Kubler, broken, had had enough and did not sign on for the start. Hoar was full of fight and spent some time in lone pursuit of a breakaway group. The effort did for him – he finished thirty-four minutes down on the winner, albeit he was awarded some points in the competition for combativity. Robinson had to chase, too, but only after being left stranded by a puncture. He ceded another twenty four minutes and now lay 40th overall.

Stage 13 Millau – Albi 205km

The Dutchman Daan de Groot took the best win of a fairly uneventful career this day. Nearly two hours' down overall, he was allowed to break away and to stay clear. The bunch was more intent on saving energy. They rode onto the motor-racing circuit at Albi twenty-one minutes behind him.

Stage 14 Albi – Narbonne 153km

Tony Hoar, the amiable rosbif, had become something of a popular turn with both the press and the public as lanterne rouge. The queer celebrity of the red lamp – what other race applauds the man who comes last? – kept him chipper and, more important, brought him some juicy contracts for the post-Tour round of criteriums, of which more later. He was dropped on the second category Col de la Fontasse and spent the rest of the day with a small group of riders who came in 17 minutes down. Robinson finished with the main field.

Stage 15 Narbonne – Ax-les-Thermes 151km

The Col de Portel 1432m lies on a long, narrow spine of mountain in the Ariège, to either side of which open glorious views – south to the High Pyrenees along the Spanish border, north across the plain towards Carcassonne. After a twisting climb out of the valley, through leafy glades, to the col, the road toboggans along and finally drops down a long slide into Foix. Here the riders turned south to Tarascon and thence along the beautiful rustic backwater ride of the Route des Corniches. From there they went over the Col de Chioula 1450m and down to the finish in Ax-les-Thermes, an old thermal spa town as the name indicates. Robinson, lagging behind wearily after the feed station (at 80km), somehow recruited his energy, chased and caught a small group of riders, but the pursuit had tired him. He fell away again, rode the final climb on his own and finished the stage alone. It wasn't just tiredness that slowed him: his right knee was swollen – a recurrent problem. Only seventy-four riders remained in the race and Robinson had moved up one place to 39th overall.

Rest Day

Robinson, either because of some food he'd eaten or from the effects of exposure to sun, the intermittent ordeal of chill to an overheated body and extreme physical stress, had an upset stomach but signed on next day, apparently recovered.

Stage 16 Ax-les-Thermes – Toulouse 123km

Flat roads, a pitiless sun, shimmering haze. Hoar, still mixing it occasionally, just missed out on a sprint prime in an intervening town but was still with the leading group when it rode onto the Toulouse track. He didn't have the legs to beat the veteran rouleur Van Steenbergen, but brimming with energy and the desire to be up at the front was ample evidence of his high spirits. Robinson, having no interest in sprint finishes and concerned to conserve as much strength and energy as possible, ahead of the Pyrenees, was content to sit the stage out in the bunch.

Stage 17 Toulouse – Saint-Gaudens 249km

If the Bosse du Hailla is no more than a molehill at 518m, the Col d'Aspin 1489m followed by the Col de Peyresourde 1569m gave Hoar his first sharp taste of the Pyrenean climbs to which Robinson had been introduced on the Route de France three years earlier. He'd clearly been steadying himself and concentrating his mind. He'd recovered completely from any ailment and rode with great verve. Only 4m 35s down on the leader over the Aspin, he forged on to the Peyresourde as other riders fell away, pressed on and came to the finish, on the motor-racing circuit at Saint-Gaudens, in fifteenth place. He moved up to 33rd overall. Interviewed at the finish, and reflecting on the one day of mountains which remained, he said: 'I'm confident of making it to Paris on Saturday and I'm going to have a real go if there's a chance, but I won't do anything silly.' Hoar, now 70th overall, kept his grip firmly on the lanterne rouge. Sixty riders had dropped out. That fact alone underscores the extraordinary achievement of these two Britons, riding pretty well as individuals.

Stage 18 Saint-Gaudens – Pau 206km

The route backtracked over the Bosse du Hailla and then headed for two monster climbs in what Tour mythology calls the Circle of Death: the Col du Tourmalet 2115m and Col d'Aubisque 1709m. Robinson could not (or decided he should not) stay with the group of ace climbers with whom he was riding on the ascent of the Tourmalet. To expend energy trying to match them went under the heading silly. He let them go and, on the descent, showed a new flair: down the twisting steep hairpinned descents of the mountain they call l'Incontournable, 'the unavoidable, intransigent', he caught up and rejoined the group which had crossed ahead of him. Hoar was a long way back. In fact, he eased up on the descent to wait for Henri Sitek with whom he had struck up a warm friendship. Sitek had earlier been his closest rival for the unlikely fame of lanterne rouge and although Hoar had this strange competition effectively sewn up, the pair of them had taken to riding together.

The weather broke and, in lashing rain, Hoar skidded and went down. Robinson vomited on the climb up to the Aubisque but kept going and in another huge effort, of will and power, he caught up with the group chasing the leading quartet – Bobet, Brankart, Gaul and Geminiani. He not only rejoined but contributed to what had already become a furious chase at high speed. It was a marvellous exploit and the French press and public were ecstatic that an English cyclist could show such class. (As Tony Hewson points out in his engaging memoir *In Pursuit of Stardom*, the very idea of *un coureur anglais* was still a quaint notion even four years after Robinson's début in France, although by then he had become a sort of honorary Frenchman.)

That day in the Pyrenees, he showed enormous courage to push himself almost certainly beyond a sensible limit without cracking. His name was constantly repeated in the commentary relayed by the loudspeakers on the Kleber-Colombes radio van. He finished in Pau a mere 2m 45s down on the winner, Jan Brankart, (second overall in Paris). It was, he said afterwards, the hardest day of his life. But there is evidence in that admission that he had confronted a very particular truth in those mountains: the truth of what it was going to take to make it as a professional in France. He had reached for and pushed himself up to a level of stress, on mind and body, which he had not previously attained. To go there and to come through without breaking – even if so depleted he could barely speak – gave him an insight into his own capacity and a confidence in it which nothing else could impart. The French ace, André Leducq, winner of the 1930 and '32 Tours, was there in Pau and he was full of praise for the English rider. 'Bravo,' he said to him. 'You climbed splendidly and descended like a devil. With such class and a good team to help you, you could finish in the first fifteen of the Tour next year.' As it was, he moved up to 28th overall. Hoar survived the fall and finished safely. Robinson had ridden himself into the Tour and, this day, had, indeed, had a real go. The journalists were impressed, calling him 'bon coureur, bon grimpeur, bon descendeur', good rider, good climber, good descender… ample plaudits. He was very tired, very relieved and disinclined to expatiate on his feelings. He had, after all, let the bike speak for him.

Paris was four days away.

He told the peerless Jock Wadley, covering the first of nineteen Tours (one unofficially): 'On the flat you can hang on to a rider who is two or three miles an hour faster because you are in his slipstream and economise on air. But uphill you are going much slower and must overcome the same gradient as the chap you are trying to follow. On a high mountain in rarefied air you can get in trouble trying to follow a wheel that is only half a mile faster.' The risk of blowing up was constant.

Stage 19 Pau – Bordeaux 195km
Sitek, a Pole by birth, riding with the Ouest regional team, set off by himself about 150km from the finish. His wife came from the area, he wanted to put on a show and the rest of the field wasn't much bothered. Even Hoar, nearly

an hour down on his buddy, had no fear of losing his prestigious station at the rear. Five riders eventually cut loose and chased Sitek down, he latched on and they all raced onto the Bordeaux track in front of a huge audience. Across the line, Sitek sat up and, as the others pelted on, he heard the bell… another lap to ride. He set off after them and managed to come in sixth, just ahead of a man to whom such finishes were so often a routine victory, Darrigade. Robinson came in with the main field, 5m 30s down.

Stage 20 Bordeaux – Poitiers 243km

It was holiday time. A long race against the clock on the morrow, the end of the Tour at hand, there was no call for heroics. Louison Bobet had matched the threat of Gaul and had over seven minutes in hand: he was on course to be the first rider to win three consecutive Tours, although the English journalist who claimed that he would 'go down in history as the greatest-ever French roadman' jumped the gun, somewhat. Jacques Anquetil, still only twenty one, had already taken two of an eventual nine wins in the Grand Prix des Nations and Bernard Hinault was nine months old.

Stage 21 Chatellrault – Tours 66km time-trial

The back-marker Hoar, leading the Tour out, as it were, set off first into a brisk headwind. Twenty-four kilometres into his ride he was caught and overtaken by the second man to leave, Pierre Ruby, whose finishing time of 1h 45m 32s on the cinder track in Tours topped the leader-board for nearly two hours and was eventually seventh best. By the time Robinson began his ride, the wind had stiffened. He began modestly, wound up as the crowds lining the route cheered and cheered, but dropped to 29th overall with a time of 1h 52m 43s, in 57th place. Van Genechten, who had, somehow, survived the ordeal on Ventoux, retired.

Stage 22 Tours – Paris (Parc des Princes) 229km

The noise in the Parc des Princes was deafening, the atmosphere vibrant with excitement, the joy among the 69 riders who made it to Paris boundless and palpable. MacClachlan was there to greet the two Hercules' men. He presented Hoar with a battery-powered red lamp, a British lanterne rouge for the man who had completed the French grand Tour. Rather intemperately, though, in the dizzy spirit of the moment, he said: 'We've broken through the Tour de France barrier.' An understandable outbreak of overweening optimism, maybe, but the implacable goddess Nemesis had her ear cocked. Cozens inadvertently revealed how ill-prepared the team had been: 'I'm a proud man. The boys did very well, learned a lot, *but it was tougher than we expected.* [my italics] Brian's Pyrenean effort was the best showing.' As for Robinson, he expressed his 'terrific relief at finishing. I'm so pleased. I don't feel tired any more. Tony and I are riding again tomorrow (Sunday) at Monthléry in a 100km race against a field including Bobet and Coppi.' When Hoar and Robinson rode round the open-air, pink concrete track on a lap of honour, the crowds gave them a raucous reception. 'Ro-ban-son' shifted easily enough into French but the lanterne rouge came out as 'O-arh, O-arh, O-arh.' Hoar himself was, as ever, buoyant: 'We know what we're up against, now…My best day was on the Ventoux, I think…We made a mistake by doing too much stage racing: today was my sixtieth day of stage riding this year.'

The page of *Cycling* which reports on the last day of the *Grande Boucle* – AN HISTORIC 'TOUR' – also carries a small ad informing readers that 'Oak Tea room, Tonbridge, Kent, popular among cyclists, will be closed for holidays from August 23 – September 3.'

Robinson's parents had come to Paris, invited by MacClachlan, to see their lad come in as part of the Great Bike Race. They were 'very chuffed' he says. With them was Shirley Fearnley, whom Robinson had met at a Harrogate Cycling Club annual dinner the previous winter. She, her sister and parents were all members, keen cyclists. Robinson thinks they dined at Maxim's in Paris that night, with his parents, Hoar and the Hercules management people. Wherever it was, a photograph shows him at the table with Shirley, he looking very dapper in a suit, tanned, lean, fit and very happy, she at his side.

Mrs Robinson, shoehorned into this strange culture, was not overly taken. The new liberal way of things – rock and roll had arrived and seemed to indicate a certain slippage in what she took to be normal manners – didn't much impress her. When her younger son later came back from France wearing a pair of the fashionable drainpipe trousers, affected by the younger set, she scowled and said: 'What's them?'

Reflecting on his feelings after the Tour he said: 'I had the impression of hardly sleeping a wink, the entire race. I was so revved up, I suppose, heart pounding away and some of the hotel rooms were that hot and airless. And if they were near the centre of town, there were people outside making a hell of a racket, all night long, or so it felt. I suppose I must have slept but I was that revved up I wasn't ever aware of it.' The noise of the race itself – crowds, cars, klaxons – was a major assault on the senses in itself and proved a considerable shock, a major problem. That the noise often continued late into the night, generated by people who didn't have to ride upwards of two hundred kilometres next day, compounded the exaggerations of fatigue the new men were experiencing. When I asked him about the other members of the team he reiterated his opinion that the men who'd come out from home to ride really 'didn't have a cat's chance in hell', but that he had been disappointed in the Hercules men who had had a decent preparation and ought to have made a better go of it.

Pusey expanded on his laconic reply when I asked him how he found racing on the continent – 'hard and fast'. He had no regret about not riding the Tour again, largely because unless you were with continental riders, the disadvantage was stark. Certain things went on in any race – not necessarily shady, but deals being struck – about which no rider new to the masonry would have a clue about. A whole world of experience to which the continental riders were brought up was denied to the Brits.

The Sunday race to which Robinson referred took place on the Autodrome de Monthléry, a motor-racing circuit about 25 miles from Paris. Special buses and trains brought crowds to the event.

First race, at 11 o'clock: the Grand Prix des Minimes, for juniors. Second race: the Grand Prix des Vétérans, followed by the Grand Prix Amateurs et Indépendants, at 1.30pm. A pause in the racing, picnics on the grass, before the start of the Grand Prix des Champions at 3pm. The field included the Bobet brothers, Fausto Coppi, Gaul, Geminiani, Darrigade, Anquetil, Lucien Lazaridès, Robic, Willy Kemp and…Hoar and Robinson, for a prize of 300,000 francs, with primes on certain laps.

The post-Tour criteriums, held all over France, went on for well over a month, into early September. Two rival agents, former bike riders, serviced all contracts for the circuit: Daniel Dousset* and Roger Piel. They controlled the programme of racing in about a hundred criteriums – whether on road circuits in towns or on tracks, over distances of between 50 and 120, even 140km – and Dousset, the doyen, had a stable of around fifty riders who would draw large crowds. The stars commanded big fees to ride, the lesser riders a mere fraction, but the sundry pickings were not bad – there was prize money for intermediate primes – and an essential supplement to what most of them got from their team sponsors. The agent approached riders during the Tour and offered contracts to ride at criteriums. These deals were finalised in Paris and the hectic roundabout of travel hither and thither began, to large towns, small towns, even villages, punctuated by the racing.

Robinson, the English révélation du Tour as the press hails any spunky newcomer, rode about twenty such races after the Tour. Hoar, too, on the queer celebrity of the lanterne rouge, landed a fat bunch of appearance deals. The coureurs anglais were a novelty, of course, and came relatively cheap. They certainly couldn't haggle for fees: they were told what they'd get. A Tour winner like Bobet could pretty well demand his fee (anything upwards of £600) and, in return for the support of his teammates during the Tour itself, he gave them a guarantee that they would take substantial fees to ride criteriums with him. The conduct of the races themselves was controlled by

---

* He later stood at the side of Milan's Vigorelli track shouting encouragement through a small aluminium megaphone to Roger Rivière when he set a new world hour record of 47.923km on 18 September 1957.

the top men in the field. The crowd had come to see them win and win they did. Men like Robinson might be allowed to snap up the intermediate primes but the final line had to be left to the champion. Bike riders are canny enough to stage a sprint which looks flat out but is regulated to half a wheel, and the important thing was to put on a show – startling turns of speed, jockeying for place, elbow to elbow duels…all part of the entertainment. Robinson's education in the ways and means of continental bike racing widened.

Immediately after the Tour, Dousset sent him to the hotel in Poigny-la-Forêt, (later used by the Saint-Raphaël team), L'Auberge des Trois Tilleuls, which his family owned – mother-in-law had the money – to rest and prepare for his first criterium, near the Bobet's home town of Saint-Méen-le-Grand in Brittany. A former Six-Day soigneur, Pierre Viel, ran the place as manager. He acted as a genial mentor to Robinson and gave the young Englishman sound advice: in preparation for the criteriums, he should ride out to a village some thirty kilometres from the hotel at a fairly leisurely speed then, on the way back, sprint to every kilometre marker (borne), a small rectangular stone with a yellow rounded cap, as soon as it was visible at the side of the road ahead, from about two hundred metres or so. Robinson also struck up a friendship with a Frenchman who'd just ridden his second, and last, Tour in the French Ouest regional team, Robert Varnajo. (Brother Des had met him at the Simplex training camp.) Varnajo, winner of the final stage in 1954, had decided to switch disciplines, from road racing to motor-paced racing on the track. (He went on to become national stayers champion three times.) A Breton, he knew the circuit the Englishman would be riding on and shared that most precious of resources with Robinson, local knowledge.

Refreshed and in roaring form at the end of the week, Robinson travelled to Brittany by train for his first criterium, riding alongside Louison Bobet in his pomp. There were rules as expressed in the French word *combine* meaning 'scheme, arrangement, trick' and, indeed, there was a slight nuance of trickery in the arrangement the professionals made amongst themselves for the round-the-town races. Having just finished the Tour, they had no desire to exhaust themselves further and they therefore controlled the speed insofar as they could. They had a tacit agreement to share out the winning of the primes, too, so that they all got a cut of the prizes on offer. The main man, Bobet, as Tour winner, resplendent in the all-wool yellow jersey (he wouldn't wear any synthetic material), didn't need to scrap for intermediate sprints but protocol demanded that he triumph at the last. Of course the local riders took every opportunity to out-sprint the elite men, to give them a good kicking, as much in the way of toppling the stars as of attracting the attention of team scouts.

The gun went and Robinson was flying, prime after prime, extra cash in his pocket to add to his £40 appearance money. As the race neared the finish, Bobet (on a £1,000 appearance fee) moved silkily through the bunch and appeared at Robinson's side. The admonition may well have been polite, the message was emphatic: 'C'est moi qui gagne.' I win. The implication, if not the explicit threat, was that if Robinson didn't pay heed, this would be the last criterium he rode that season. He bowed to the seigneurial nod and went on to ride those twenty criteriums before the end of August. He travelled by train, sought out a lift with another rider whenever possible, or, if there was nothing on offer, he used the Hercules team vehicle, a Vanguard estate handily decked out with racks on the roof but packing an extremely thirsty engine under the bonnet. It was a punishing schedule, there was no coordination in the programme and they often had to drive huge distances from one event to another, straight after a race. In August, when all France was on holiday, it was often hard to find digs and more than once he and his travelling companion had to sleep under the car. 'There were some bloody big ants, too,' he said.

At the beginning of September, he returned to Yorkshire. 'I'd done what I set out to do, so I came back home,' he said.

'You were pretty tired, I imagine?' I asked.

'Oh, jiggered.'

'And you went back to work in the family firm?'

'Oh, yes, our house wasn't the sort of place you sat around and twiddled your thumbs. You'd stick out like a sore one, a thumb, I mean. Everybody was busy so, yes, I just went back to work. I don't like to sit around idle anyway.'

Work included funeral arrangements and the laying out of the dead. Robinson père et fils saw to an average of one corpse per week, sometimes two. (Robinson laid out his first corpse when he was eighteen. I asked if he'd been reluctant. He shrugged: 'You did what your father told you. I never minded, only when it came to laying out father – which Des and I did. That wasn't very nice, but better us than someone else, a stranger.') Called to the house of the deceased, they climbed the stairs to the bedroom, cleaned the body, stopped up the orifices with material plugs, to obviate leakage. If it was a man, they shaved him. Then they dressed the corpse in Sunday best and carried it downstairs in a bag of heavy material on a stretcher to place in the coffin, either in the front room or the hallway. The coffins were made to size of oak or elm planks. In the guest bedroom at the house in Mirfield, where I've slept, stands a set of shelves which Robinson recently made in his workshop from old elm wood slabs left over from the days, long past, when the firm made coffins. The top shelf is very slightly bowed, as it had been in the drying rack of the wood store. He decided not to plane the gentle wave out, rather to keep the handsomely grained wood as it had been for so many years.

The additional work they had to put in for funerals was disruptive and being called out in the middle of the night, as they often were, made the working day very long and put a considerable added strain on them. Cremations were a bind, too – getting a certificate, as required at the time, was a real palaver. This reflects how recent the practice of cremation is in England. The Catholic church now does permit cremation but still doesn't encourage it. The Protestant churches admitted the practice some while ago (the first crematoria were built in the late 1870s) but in the 1950s, it was not at all common.

Des came back into the family building firm as a draughtsman when he was 25, but there really wasn't enough work for him in that capacity so he moved to a larger firm in Redcar as a draughtsman and, later, taught engineering. He carried on riding but developed a bad back and had to wear a steel corset. This put a stop to his racing.

MacClachlan's extravagant claim to have broken through the Tour de France barrier had, indeed, proved to be wild hyperbole. That winter, the Hercules racing team was disbanded, other marques also withdrew sponsorship, and Robinson and the others were ditched. It was a shabby end. Robinson felt that 'we proved we could do something' and it seems that the decision to pull the plug came from internal management. I asked him whether Hercules had sold more bikes because of their appearance in the Tour de France. He paused. Then he said, with a smile: 'They sold a hell of a lot in Egypt.'

Shirley and Brian were married in October 1955 and, that winter, lived with her parents in Leeds.

6: THAT'S A THREP IN'T STEANS*

The demise of the sponsorship was a bad blow. Everything that he'd achieved that year had given him good reason to believe that he could make a career on the continent. They do say, in the Ridings, 'Tha' can allus tell a Yorkshireman, but tha' can't tell 'im much' and Robinson wasn't going to give up on what he'd started. The following January, he, Shirley and Bernard Pusey set off for the south of France. The immediate objective was a ride in a criterium in Oran, Algeria (then a French colony), in mid-February, one of the big early-season races, secured for him by the agent, Dousset.

They drove down to Les Issambres and arrived at the bungalow they'd rented (for £30 per month) during a snowstorm. Next morning, they looked out on a vast, surrounding desert of snow, half a metre deep. It continued to snow, off and on, for a month. Locals said it was the first time it had snowed at all on the Côte d'Azur for thirty years. All the pros who had gathered for the January training were scuppered. It was bitingly cold, too, and the bungalow was not built for severe winter conditions. They seemed to spend most of the time beachcombing for driftwood to burn to supplement the meagre heating. Because most of the early races had to be cancelled, they were earning nothing and their money was slowly being eaten up. (Worst shock came at the end of their stay when they were handed a bill for coal - £5 per week. 'And Shirley thought coal was dear in Yorkshire.') He honoured the Oran contract, naturally, rode it with about fifty kilometres in his legs and didn't last long. Things were not looking good. Dousset had told Robinson that he'd been selected to ride in the Tour of Spain with the Swiss rider Hugo Koblet's team in late spring, but that was some way off. Dousset also told him that if he finished the Vuelta, he was guaranteed enough money to settle the debts accumulated over the enforced idleness of the winter. However, it was an anxious time. He would still have to finance the intervening period before heading off for Spain and his morale sank.

When the snow finally abated and the sun came out, they began to ride races but were unsponsored and still could not recoup enough money from prizes to cover costs. That a rider who had ridden the Tour was back in the millrace, as it were, scrapping for lean pickings, shows just how fraught was the competition for any sort of backing and gives some insight into the chancy nature of the independent's position. Then Georges Coupry, a former rider who had just got together a team sponsored by La Perle, offered to find them entry into races: all they had to do was turn up and ride. There

---

* Yorkshire: 'That's a kick in the shins.'

was no formal agreement, no contract, just that fairly loose bargain. Despite Robinson's aversion to the Belgian rough-riding, they drove up for the Hell of the North. Robinson smashed a wheel and retired. Louison Bobet won.

The Vuelta in late April was nearly a month away. Pusey, dispirited, had even less to go on. Robinson and Shirley discussed what they should do. They decided to drive back to England, sell the car – it was a bit battered by the time they reached Yorkshire – and, using the money from the sale, Robinson would finance his return trip by train ferry and train. It was make or break, one last go. Pusey stayed in England.

Decisions made, action taken, Robinson perked up. He remarked, at the time, that the prospect of a Tour cheered him greatly – he could get his own back on the one-day riders who had been thrashing him in Belgium. 'They'll be suffering at my hands after a few days' racing.'

Koblet, suave, debonair, movie-star good looks, nicknamed *Le Pédalleur de Charme* by Jacques Grello, a journalist with *Parisien Libéré*, had won the Tour de France by over twenty-two minutes from Geminiani in 1950. He was the first non-Italian to win the Giro d'Italia, that same year, but was by now way past his best. Ever surrounded by pretty women when he climbed off the bike, he had recently married the model Sonja Bühl and, according to Robinson, didn't really have his mind on the Vuelta. 'You have to keep your end up, one way or the other, and with Koblet in Spain it was definitely the other. He wasn't riding with any conviction, it was more or less a pushing job for me.' The team had no collective spirit and Koblet was notoriously close with cash. As Robinson said: 'Koblet made it clear that he wasn't going to share the prize money. So you thought, "Well, if you're not going to share the prize money, I'm not riding for you, I'll ride for myself".'* He was glad to be riding, however. 'Three weeks of being looked after, fed, watered and massaged – it was good for me. I didn't want a fortune, I just wanted to get by, live.'

Franco's Spain was impoverished, locked off from the rest of Europe, oppressed by El Caudillo's regime and his hated Guardia Civil, the military police. The race was badly organised, army jeeps ferrying kit tended to dump the bags at the stage finish line, often up to eight kilometres from the team hotel. The food the riders had to eat was mostly indifferent, always drenched in poor quality olive oil, seldom plentiful and, certainly on one occasion, tainted...Robinson came back with dysentery. He was passing blood and spent a month in the Lake District mooching about, as he put it, to recuperate. However, the Vuelta had shown him at a new level. He'd ridden exceptionally well, with very little support from the other riders in his team, and finished 8th only 20m 36s behind the winner, the Italian Angelo Conterno. Koblet had retired and Robinson was riding so strongly that he became team

---

* Cited in *Viva la Vuelta* by Lucy Fallon and Adrian Bell, Mousehold Press

leader in his absence. Lack of Spanish made no odds: the lingua franca was French and he spoke that passably well by now. One stage had taken them into Andorra where the roads were even worse than elsewhere in Spain – littered with gravel, poorly surfaced. They punctured frequently and spent a lot of time chasing to get back to the bunch. He remembers staying in a hotel in Aybar, a village in Navarre, north-eastern Spain, part of the Basque region. Two sisters ran the place and, conforming to Spanish practice, served the evening meal past nine o'clock, far later than elsewhere in Europe. (The riders had ordered it for 8.30pm.) The first course: a large plate of fried eggs and bread. Geminiani took one look, jumped up from the table, hurled the whole shebang at the wall and yelled: 'J'en ai marre de huevos' I'm sick of eggs, using the Spanish for 'eggs'. Robinson, recounting this, commented: 'He must have had a bad day.'

GF   Did you get on with Geminiani?

BR   On a surface level, but there was no depth to the friendship. He had a reputation as a bit of a twister, always plotting some big scheme.

Robinson's ride paid dividends. Koblet was so impressed with the Englishman that he recommended him to the Swiss Cilo team, co-sponsored by Saint-Raphaël, makers of the apéritif, for a ride in the Tour de Suisse in June. The three weeks of the Vuelta, despite the dysentery, had made him astonishingly fit and, as he says, he always rode well coming out of a stage race.

Cilo-Saint-Raphaël was managed by Raymond Louviot, a Frenchman born in Switzerland, nicknamed Laripette (slang for 'Parisian'). Louviot, a successful professional bike rider, had retired from racing some years before. Robinson, apart from a special daily prime on the Swiss grand tour, was still riding à la musette. Once more, he rode virtually on his own and came 9th, 23m 25s behind the Swiss winner, Rolf Graf.

From the very beginning of the season his mind had been set on the Tour de France, a hope jeopardised by his relative anonymity in the early round of racing. Because neither Luxemburg nor Switzerland had enough riders to make up separate teams, there had been some talk of the two small nations supplying five riders each to a combined team. The Swiss had entered a full team in the '55 Tour, but the mixed Luxemburg team, led by Charly Gaul, had included two Austrians, two Germans and two Australians. A similar grouping would be Robinson's best chance of a ride. Luckily, the Swiss-Luxemburg combine didn't happen. During both the tours in which he'd ridden, reporters from L'Equipe and Parisien Libéré had not only filed reports on the racing but confidential assessments of certain riders whom they deemed to be candidates for the Tour de France. Robinson had been singled out and, as a result of these glowing accounts of his riding, he was invited to join the Luxemburg mixed team. The invitation arrived ten days before the start of the race in Reims. He plainly needed nerves of steel both on and off the bike.

Tour de France 1956

Nicolas Frantz, the manager of the conjoint 'Luxemburg and the rest' team, which also included a Portugese and an Italian, had won the Tour in 1927 and '28 – his compatriot François Faber had been the first Luxemburger to win, in 1909. Two days before the start of the race, in Reims, the cathedral city where all the kings of France had been crowned, Robinson met Frantz as well as the mechanics, soigneurs, team-car driver and team-mates, against whom he'd raced and with whom he would now be racing. There followed a succession of routine checks and parades which reminded Robinson of being in the army: drawing his jersey and other bits of kit to pack into the aluminium case, official checking over of the bicycles, medical examination, presentation to the public, photographs, interviews, autograph signing and so on. Robinson fully expected there to be a team meeting on the eve of the race to discuss tactics and allocation of prize money. No meeting was called. The team, by virtue of Gaul's presence in it, was, de facto, going to be required to ride for him and all the French, Italian and Belgian papers were saying that the disparate bunch of men would, perforce, be united by orders to devote themselves to his cause, even if he hadn't asked them expressly to do so. An English journalist, picking up on what he chose to read as a sort of stitch-up, wrote, fatuously: 'Robinson must not win the Tour.'

Robinson says that there is no question that had a conference taken place and he'd been told to nurse Gaul from Reims to Paris, with the promise of a cut of the total prize money won by the team at the end of the race, 'then I would have obeyed those orders until I dropped'. He was fairly sure that Gaul could – ought to – win the Mountains' prize which was worth £1,000 at a stroke. (There were also daily primes, individual and team, and money for final placings.) However, when the matter of shares in a prize pot was brought up during a meal, the management dismissed it airily, there was plenty of time to talk about that later.

Effectively, this made Robinson a free agent. The year before, he had garnered a clutch of fairly lucrative contracts to ride criteriums because he'd been one of only two Englishmen to complete the Tour. This year, riding in the relative obscurity of a mixed team, he needed to put on a bit of a show to draw attention to himself. In no little way this aspect of the commercialism of bike riding on the continent, so completely at odds with the amateurism in Britain, even among the few professionals, was something Robinson had to, and did, embrace, along with the tougher exigencies of the racing itself.*

---

* In the middle ages, apprentices, mostly in the building trades, made a tour de France, to learn different skills and methods from local craftsmen.

One question: was he fit enough? He'd had a bad chest cold ever since the Tour de Suisse which had restricted his training and he was two kilos overweight. However, he was sleeping and eating better than he had for some time. Perhaps the enforced rest had done him good.*

Bobet was not riding. The scar in his perineum left after surgery the previous winter had opened up during the Vuelta and, part way through the Giro, he renounced, to the chagrin of the French manager, Marcel Bidot. Geminiani had had a minor operation and declared his participation only a week before the race. Robic was out, injured in a car crash. The French team was, therefore, weakened and in some disarray, with no clear leader. Many commentators looked to Gaul, who had ridden strongly in the '55 Tour (his second), and had recently won the Giro d'Italia, only the second non-Italian to do so, after Koblet in 1950, as well as his own home Tour de Luxembourg. The Belgians fielded a strong team based round Jean Brankart, second in 1955, Stan Ockers (reputedly something of a wheel-sucker) and Jean Adriaenssens. But, the race was as open as it had been for some time.

Stage 1 Reims – Liège 223km

They went off at a tremendous pace, 48kph, riders attacking incessantly. An hour in, the Italian Nello Lauredi, who'd worn yellow for four days in 1952, went off the front and Robinson followed. He'd never have tried such a thing the year before but, true to his determination to get noticed and confident in his power, he decided to have a go. The duo got stuck in, relaying each other, but they weren't able to shake off the bunch. Robinson looked round, saw them some way back, and then looked at Nello. 'Non,' he said. Lauredi responded: 'Non' and they sat up. Suddenly, however, seven reinforcements arrived, among them one of Robinson's team-mates, the Portugese Antonio Barbosa, and the French ace, Darrigade. For some distance they held no more than 200 metres on the chasing peloton, but when the Swiss rider, Fritz Schaer, bridged the gap to join them, the bunch seemed to lose heart, the break began to move clear and built a lead of nearly ten minutes. 'And it all seemed so easy,' Robinson told Wadley in the series of interviews they conducted during Robinson's week-long stay after the Tour in the hotel at Pouligny. 'I had somehow stumbled on one of those days which occasionally come to all racing men, a day when you can hardly feel the pedals. Such days are increasingly hard to find now I am a professional, but they used to come fairly often as an amateur.' That second sentence is telling, indicative of an essential difference.

---

* He wasn't the only English-speaker in the race. Seamus 'Shay' Elliott of Ireland was riding for the Ile-de-France regional team although still in considerable pain after a heavy crash on the track in Denmark. He lasted only a few days.

Gradually six of the breakaways fell off the fierce pace and, with eighty-three kilometres to ride, the three survivors hit the long pavé hill out of Dinant, in the Ardennes which Robinson knew from the Flèche Wallonne. Robinson attacked and Schaer was left struggling, back down the slope. Darrigade hung on. Gradually, Schaer worked his way back. Robinson was no sprinter and he longed for another hill, nicely placed before the finish, feeling sure he could get rid of Schaer altogether and maybe even Darrigade who, at the time, was not reckoned to be particularly resilient. Robinson did a deal with Schaer: if he promised not to sprint against them at the finish, Robinson would not try to drop him. Schaer agreed and then reneged. At the finish, the canny Darrigade won the sprint and took yellow, but Schaer found the legs to beat Robinson for second place and a thirty second time bonus. Robinson might have applied more pressure earlier to drop Schaer, but with some distance still to ride, three were a better bet to stay clear than two. As for Schaer, he was pretty well guaranteed third place as opposed to being swallowed up by the peloton.

Whatever the initial disappointment, this was, nonetheless, a terrific opener. Robinson took £60 for third position, the £100 prime de combativité, two £10 primes en route and a share in the day's £200 team prize, which the conglomerate Luxemburgs had won.

He was criticised for helping Schaer to a large time advantage (seven minutes) over his leader, Gaul, but Robinson had, in fact, been obeying orders, to prolong an attack that seemed likely to succeed. Moreover, now Gaul was out of the firing line and could ride a defensive race until the mountains. Still no team conference.

Stage 2 Liège – Lille 217km

Robinson reckoned that Darrigade would probably keep yellow at the end of the stage: all he need do was track him to keep his 3rd place overall. Again the pace was fast and, finding himself with Darrigade in a group at the front, minus Schaer, he realised that if only he could finish 31 seconds clear of the Swiss rider, he'd move into second place. Then he punctured. By the time he'd changed the tyre, Schaer was ahead on the road and only a furious chase brought him back. For that, he was awarded three more points in the combativity prize and preserved third overall.

'The Englishman Robinson, leader of the Luxemburgers, won the combativity prize in committing a gross error.' L'Equipe which also reported Darrigade as saying: 'Robinson is going to flabbergast us. He literally ambles and in the hills he had without doubt sworn to murder us.'

In room 21 of the Hôtel Vénitien, the murderer explained: 'I knew that last hill from the Flèche Wallonne but I was mistaken, thinking we were 40km from the finish. In fact, there were 70km still to ride. If I'd known,

I'd have waited a bit, but I don't regret a thing (je ne regrette rien) because I finished strongly and I didn't have a bad patch.'

Some of his so-called team-mates had been on hand when he punctured, but not one offered him his bike, to keep him ahead of Schaer and take second overall. They clearly thought his attack the day before was a flash in the pan and that his high placing wasn't worth defending. It became apparent that the mixed team was actually a tripartite, motley grouping: Gaul and his two compatriot Faema trade-team-mates, Marcel Ernzer and Willy Kemp; the Luxemburger Jempy Schmitz leading a second clique, comprising Aldo Bolzan, Nicholas Morn, Edmond Jacobs and Jean Schmit; and the Anglo-Portugese duo of Barbosa and Robinson. They still led the overall team competition but would never hold it with such divided loyalties at their heart. Since the team prize was worth £200 a day and £2,000 at the finish, it was worth fighting for. (In the absence of the quartet of grandees, Bobet, Kubler, Koblet, Coppi, there was no single team with a leader who could be counted on to bring in the cash. The prize pot was, therefore, open to general enterprise and cooperation.) Again, Robinson broached the subject of divvying up winnings at dinner. Ernzer riposted: he wasn't touching a franc, his job was to look after Gaul. Tempers rose. Robinson gave vent to a considerable frustration. Frantz soothed them, made the peace and promised that something would be done to resolve the situation right away.

Stage 3 Lille – Rouen 225km

Bob Thom was at the start to greet his man, wish him luck and urge him to hang on to his third place overall. He was but one of a milling mass of bystanders, fans, general public, ardent kids, ex-pros, journalists, to whom the riders were open for conversation, greeting, the signing of autographs. A friendly, easy-going holiday atmosphere such as might accompany any humble club event. None of the paranoid brouhaha that attends the event these days.

Once more they set off at cracking pace, but Robinson was denied. A break of twelve riders went clear, the favourites, Gaul, Ockers, Brankart *et al.*, sat in the bunch and did nothing to squash the escape, in which most of the teams were represented. Robinson could do nothing on his own. The breakaways finished fifteen minutes up and Robinson dropped to eighth place.

Rouen, morning: time-trial 15.075km

A two kilometre-long hill sprint immediately after the start lead onto a lap of the Les Essarts motor-racing circuit. A huge paying crowd gathered. First man off at 8am. Those waiting to go lounged in the sun until half an hour before their time, when the trainer told them to get on the bike and (as Robinson put it) 'excite ourselves', ie get the muscles working. Gaul, stung by derogatory remarks about him in the press, won and Robinson, 1m 44s slower, came 29th. He notes that none of his team rode light tyres but that he fitted Pirelli Media 280gm on the front and Pirelli Leggera 260gm on the back. His gears since the start were 52-47 x 14, 15, 17, 19 and 21. He retained the same ratios until the Pyrenees.

Stage 4, afternoon: Rouen – Caen 125km

After lunch in a big marquee, the riders set off again at 1.30pm. There had been a similar split stage in the Vuelta and Robinson was prepared: that afternoon ride which followed a time-trial had been 'anything but an amble in the hot sun…it was a blinder'. The same applied this day. The extreme heat made the roads heavy and sticky but, once more, the pace was hectic, driven by the French Ouest regional man Roger Hassenforder. (He was an inveterate joker and prankster, nicknamed *Boute-en-train*, life and soul of the party. Knowing how journos coveted the riders' musettes, he once delivered a bulging bag – its contents a dead cat – to a press car. Another time he attacked madly from the gun, disappeared up the road and, once he was out of sight, darted into an alleyway and watched the peloton hurtle past then hooked on at the back, laughing his head off.) That morning, his chain-wheel had come loose and dropped off after fifty metres. He scootered back to the start, the broken component in his hand. He had no spare bike and, because the commissaires wouldn't allow him to borrow one, he was disqualified and given last place. He was, consequently, fresh for the afternoon's action and broke away with around ten other riders. Robinson missed the move, thinking it was too early, and eventually went clear with Darrigade. They gradually scooped up other men who had tried but failed to bridge the gap and started to ride together. Such a group usually contains team-mates of riders in the break up the road so that its desire to work flat out is compromised. However, they did succeed this day and Robinson noted, for the first time, 'a chubby-faced rider in the violet and white jersey of the north-east Central team, no. 80 on the card, Roger Walkowiak'. Walko, as he was known, led their group in, 1m 45s behind the leaders. Hassenforder took the stage, the first of four victories in this race – the fourth of an eventual six Tours he started and the only one he finished.

At the *Arrivée*, Robinson made his way smartly to the Perrier mineral water van for the free handout of refreshing liquid. There was generally a crush of riders round it at every finish but not this day. The chasing bunch didn't arrive for nearly fifteen minutes and, as a result, Robinson had moved back to fourth place overall, Darrigade once more into yellow.

Stage 5 Caen – Saint Malo 189km

On the massage table that evening, the team soigneur treated a graze on Robinson's back – in the scramble to get under and through a level crossing gate as it fell shut, the lower edge of the descending metal bar caught Robinson across his spine. As they talked, in the way soigneurs and riders do, Robinson voiced his continuing disquiet at the lack of communication within the team, especially in the matter of prize money. The soigneur, Richardot, decided that the cash question ought to be settled, for the good of the team as a whole, and approached Frantz. Frantz was, according to Robinson, 'one of the real gentlemen of the cycling world'. An agreement was promptly drawn up: Gaul agreed that if he won the Tour he would not touch a franc of his winnings – his prize money would be shared out among the team members. (This was standard practice. A winner could earn as much as three or four times the £2,000 first place reward in post-Tour criteriums, for which he'd be paid upwards of £250 a ride.) A clause in the agreement said that Robinson would be permitted to keep his combativity prize – an individual effort, after all – and that if any team member shirked his duty to team orders, he would be excluded from the final shareout. The agreement, drawn up in German, was explained to Robinson in French, and he signed. Robinson sympathised rather with Gaul, an unassertive individual, who was leader of a team with neither unity of will nor purpose. He had observed how Bobet's men 'worked like slaves for their master and earned their money' whereas Gaul would, in some cases (no names mentioned), be giving away money for no services rendered at all.

Stage 6 Saint-Malo – Lorient 192km

Robinson's first day as an official team-mate of Gaul wasn't encouraging, he said. In fact, the Luxemburg man was 'riding like a novice…adopting the tactics which I have heard used to be employed by pre-war British riders in the World championships: sitting right on the tail of the bunch and then waking up to the fact that a big wide gap had opened in front of them'. In the middle of this stage that's exactly what did happen. Robinson had concluded that his best option was to keep an eye on the Belgian, Ockers, in the rainbow jersey of World road-race champion, who had 'a knack of sneaking off round tricky bends if he's not watched'. Frantz agreed. Sure enough, Ockers slipped away, Robinson pounced on his wheel immediately, but Gaul? Not paying attention, he lost three minutes before waking up to the need to chase after his English team man who was policing the danger man. Ahead of them, Darrigade had broken clear of a leading group of twenty-four riders to try for a solo stage win. He was caught, but increased his overall lead to five minutes – and this was the man who'd been described as a 'sit in and sprint boy…' Robinson was impressed.

Stage 7 Lorient – Angers 244km

If, on the first stage, he could hardly feel the pedals, this day, on a flat route, he found unrelievedly hard. For nearly a week they had been racing at speeds in excess of 40kph. Time to ease off, surely? Not a bit of it: hell for leather from the gun. An early break was clawed back, largely thanks to the efforts of Darrigade to protect the yellow jersey. Then another break went – what might be described as *the* break of the Tour. In it were Walkowiak, the eventual winner, and five others who finished the race in the top ten. Robinson's team-mate Barbosa was with them, but not Robinson. He later expressed annoyance that he had missed a break he could have stayed with. Tired legs and a less than sharp eye? Probably. He came in with the main bunch, which also contained Gaul and Brankart, the two pre-race favourites, 18m 46s down. Robinson dropped from 11th to 20th overall.

Stage 8 Angers – La Rochelle 180km

Robinson was in a quandary: having dreamed of being a domestique to a great continental team leader and wondering if he'd ever be able to keep up, he now found himself dillying around at the back of the bunch, wet-nursing a man who seemed, for the moment, to have no push in him, no combative instinct. Gaul might be an outstanding climber, but he couldn't afford to lose time willy-nilly on flat stages. It seemed very unlikely that he had any chance, now, of winning the Tour, even if the Mountains' prize, which he'd won in 1955, was still open. If Robinson continued to stay with the so-called 'Angel of the Mountains'*, he'd lose even more time himself before the Pyrenees and thereby jeopardise a good overall placing. It was imperative not to finish in obscurity way down the order. He decided to assert himself. Against a fierce crosswind, he fought hard to stay with a lead group and, as the wind veered to following when they approached the coast, the speed increased.

Robinson finished in seventh place and moved up to 19th overall. Had he stayed with Gaul he'd have dropped to 24th. Average speed for the day, 43.5kph.

Stage 9 La Rochelle – Bordeaux 219km

The peloton soon fragmented into twelve separate groups which eventually coalesced into two, Robinson in the second. They closed the gap and caught

---

* Geminiani described him as 'a murderous climber, always the same sustained rhythm, a little machine with a lower gear than the rest, turning his legs at a speed that would break your heart, tick tock, tick tock, tick tock.' The journalist Pierre About wrote that Gaul had 'irresistible sprightliness *[allegresse]*' and that he had 'the air of an angel for which nothing is difficult'.

the escape but Gaul, still loitering at the rear of the field, was dropped. When he did wake up to the danger, forty-five kilometres from the finish, he faced a hard chase not to lose too much time. This he did and the press applauded him for a fine, powerful show of riding, which demonstrated just what he was capable of, even if it wouldn't have been necessary, had he been paying due attention. Largely as a result of Gaul's dilatory tactics, the Luxemburg team was now two hours behind the leading French Ouest regional team.

Rest Day, Bordeaux

Breakfast in bed: ham and tomatoes, tea, bread and jam. After the vinegar bath, a pile of letters to reply to. Mobile laundries followed the Tour but there were always bits of clothing to wash out and hang from improvised lines strung across the bedroom. Lunch and a doze on the bed until 4pm when he went round to see the mechanics for a chat. At 6pm, a massage and then a stroll to the café run by Guy Lapébie,* a Bordelais himself, for champagne in company with Gaul, Ernzer, Kemp and the trainer, on hand to see that they drank no more than a single glass. [No outing on the bike, notice. It was, he admitted at the time, a costly mistake. Staying inactive, the body shuts down and, next day, Robinson's legs were 'heavy and lifeless'.]

Stage 10 Bordeaux – Bayonne 201km

They rode straight across the sandy, flat coastal Landes region into a thunderstorm. Darrigade, a local man, led the break, Robinson once again missed out, largely because of lethargy resulting from his error in not riding on the Rest Day. He dropped to 21st overall and, on the eve of the first stage into the Pyrenees, his leader, Gaul, was nearly fifty-four minutes adrift.

Stage 11 Bayonne – Pau 255km

Robinson switched his gear ratios to 52-47 x 14, 16, 19, 21, 23. Heading for the high Pyrenees he no longer felt intimidated, nor would he have the thankless and, so far, futile, job of trying to coax Gaul along. In the high mountains the Luxemburger came to life, and even Bobet, in 1955, had thought it folly to try to stay with Gaul in the Alps when he rode with such imperious style. Yet, this day, Gaul seemed unable to shrug off the apparent torpor that had so far dogged him. Had he simply been waiting to show his true strength, he would surely have crossed the Aubisque in the lead, leaving Robinson to sit on any rider in pursuit. In fact, he was outdistanced to the col by a quartet of strong men with whom he was riding, amongst them Ockers and Federico Bahamontes, the Spaniard who'd won the Mountains

---

* Guy Lapébie came third in the 1948 Tour, his brother Roger won in 1937.

prize in 1954. Gaul did rejoin, but he was not evincing anything like the superior form that had been expected of him. A shy, inward man, he had almost certainly been rattled by the adverse criticism in the press and lost nerve. The year before, when Robinson first encountered him, he'd been 'the most charming of companions' and he'd ridden with panache. The pre-Tour publicity which puffed him as a favourite seems to have unsettled him. Did he believe it and become proud or was he unnerved by the expectations that people openly had of him? Either way, he was not showing anything like the mastery of which he was capable in his favourite terrain. Robinson crossed the col in a thick fog – the dense, Pyrenean *mer de nuages* which smothers the mountains when warm air rising from the valleys merges with cooler temperatures on the mountain tops and condenses into a sometimes impenetrable mist. Get above the upper reaches of the fog and you look across a swirling sea of mist, often bathed in sunshine, mountain peaks sticking up like islands and atolls.

The descent, out of the enshrouding mist, gave him no problems, apart from the risk of slipping on some loose grit, and, having played no part in the chase after the lead group, containing Gaul, he sped away on a small hill short of Pau and took 14th place. This lifted him three places overall. Darrigade regained the yellow jersey. They'd ridden the stage at an average of nearly 40kph, despite crossing the Aubisque.

Stage 12 Pau – Bagnères-de-Luchon 126km

At the foot of the first of two mountains which lie quite close together, the Aspin and Peyresourde, Gaul was not only at the back of the main group but very quickly dropped from it. The tactic of working to get him into a good position for the climbs and then protect him from the chase was lost. All the way up the Aspin, Robinson expected to see Gaul coming up alongside him but, instead, he reached the col 35 seconds ahead of his leader. There, on a day of extreme heat, Robinson gratefully received, from a British clubman at the side of the road, a sponge loaded with water to squeeze over his neck. That heat seems to have been the cause for another mediocre performance by Gaul: he thrived in the cold and wet, but heat appeared to sap him, both bodily and mentally. It must be taken into account, too, that he had already won the Giro before coming to the Tour. The toll both stage races had taken on him, both physical and mental, must have been considerable.

On the ascent of the Peyresourde, Robinson hit his first bad patch of the Tour. This he attributed to working too hard on the earlier climb. Shed by the Ockers group, he watched a reanimated Gaul race past at high speed as he struggled on to the summit. He recovered sufficiently on the long, straight downhill into Luchon, one of the fastest descents in the Pyrenees, to make up some time and arrived 9m 47s behind the day's winner, Jean-Pierre Schmitz, who rode in on his own. Riders were still coming in half an hour later and Robinson jumped to 15th in the general classification.

Stage 13 Bagnères-de-Luchon – Toulouse 176km

From the west, the Col de Portet d'Aspet 1069m – some forty-five kilometres into the stage, past a minor col, the Ares, a placid climb through trees to 796m – is comparatively short, no more than five kilometres of real climbing, but horribly steep, up to 20%.. 'A reet brant hill' as they say in Yorkshire. Robinson found it the hardest climb in the whole Tour that year. He'd ridden it as an individual hill-climb time-trial during the Route de France in 1952 but on this occasion he struggled badly on his 47x23. For the readers of *Coureur*, who would appreciate the reference, he described the climb as 'Honister Pass with bends on it'.*

Gaul was first over, sprinting to take the points for the Mountains prize, and, as soon as he himself had crawled over the top, Robinson set off on what is another fast descent to rejoin. Misjudging a hairpin that seemed to spring out at him, he 'clattered down a gravel path into a farmyard'. Fortunately, he didn't come off or puncture. As a large group of riders at the head of the race went for the col on the final climb of the day, the Latrape, Robinson gave Gaul a Madison sling which sent him past Darrigade to score three more points in the Mountains prize. (He was now equal second, with Bahamontes, four points behind the French Sud-Ouest rider Valentin Huot.) Other riders were doing this all day in the mountains, he says. If anyone was caught, he'd be fined the equivalent of 5/- (twice the price of *Coureur* magazine). Persistent infringement might lead to disqualification.

Fifty riders contested the sprint on the Toulouse track, Robinson, his spirits high after three excellent days in the Pyrenees, attacked and came 13th.

Note: An incident on the Portet d'Aspet exacerbated the malaise in an already fractious and dissentient French national team, which, in Bobet's absence, lacked strong leadership. On the descent from the col, Gilbert Bauvin, who believed himself to be their best hope of a win in Paris, crashed and bent his forks. Bidot, the *directeur sportif*, who had just changed a wheel on the team car, sped up and set about repairing the damaged bike. As he did so, Darrigade, set on a win in Toulouse, and believing that he could win the Tour, albeit he was not so strong in the mountains, shot by without a word. He'd punctured some way back and had been left to change tyres without help. When Bidot drove up alongside him outside Toulouse to tell him he should have waited for Bauvin, Darrigade flung his punctured tyre

---

* Honister Pass, 358m, is a three-kilometre climb south from a height of 120m out of Keswick, at the head of Borrowdale in the Lake District.

at the car's windscreen. He felt that he had been betrayed. It didn't help that Bauvin, Walkowiak and Geminiani were all members of the same Saint-Raphaël–Geminiani trade team. Easy enough to see a cabal there.

Stage 14 Toulouse – Montpellier 231km

It was a day of fierce heat, the hot, dry Midi air sizzling with the stridulation of millions of cicadas, and many riders picked large cabbage leaves which they stuck under their hat to protect their neck from the flaying sun.

Robinson made a singular mistake on this stage and it probably cost him a finish in the top ten. He watched as a break of twelve riders, prompted by Raymond Elena of the French Sud-Est team, went clear. Hassenforder stirred a pursuit and, sensing that this was an important move, Robinson gave chase. Three other riders joined him and for some while they dangled some fifty metres behind Hassenforder and the same distance ahead of the peloton. Robinson decided that the move was doomed, that, sooner or later they'd be caught by the bunch, which would then hunt down Hassenforder. In fact, Hassenforder's group joined Elena's break and, at the finish, led in by the joker himself, they held an eighteen minute advantage over the main field. Had Robinson persisted in his effort to get onto the Hassenforder group, then he might have…ah, but who can tell?

Stage 15 Montpellier – Aix-en-Provence 204km

French journals and magazines printed a mid-Tour photograph of the peloton winding its way along the Provençal coast road, caption: *La promenade traditionelle au bord de la Méditérranée…*traditional promenade along the Mediterranean shoreline. In 1950, to the fury of the race directors, a number of riders dumped their bikes and plunged into the sea near Sainte-Maxime to cool off.

This stage was the closest the riders got to the sea but for ninety kilometres it was, indeed, a promenade. At a minor col, the leading riders in the Mountains competition sprinted for the points. Gaul, who needed more than a mere hill to stir him, finished seventh and Robinson, with the others, expected a regrouping on the descent. The Dutch, however, had evidently studied the route and spotted that the road changed direction sharply. They attacked into a cross-wind and established a *bordure* (file in echelon) across the road, the usual ploy to cope with the blustering, on- and offshore breezes with which they were so familiar in northern Europe. The usefulness of this manoeuvre is that, once an echelon has established itself fully, slantwise across the road, there is no room for any more riders and the only recourse is to form a second bordure behind. Robinson rode Gaul, who'd slipped back on the descent, up to the nearly full bordure and slung him into the one remaining vacant space. That left no room for him, he was stranded and, since the peloton had no interest in chasing, he had no choice but to fall back and rejoin. The promenade continued as the break gained time. Soon it had four minutes' advance. The Belgian team weren't pulling hard – they were all suffering from food poisoning (bad fish) – and the Dutch who'd stayed behind to protect the attack were slowing things down at the head of the bunch. Having missed a move the day before, Robinson knew he had to do something. He rode to the front, asked the Dutch, with whom he was on good terms, if they'd let him out of their prison camp (as he put it). They agreed, he started to pursue and, working happily again with four other riders, including Hassenforder, they recouped two minutes of the lead. The audacious Dutch ploy put their man, Wout Wagtmans, into yellow.

Aix-en-Provence, Rest Day

The team hotel was situated in a very lively quarter of town, the local residents and people who had flocked in to see the Tour arrive were in party mood: music, singing, laughter, loud conversation continued way into the night.

Robinson hardly slept. Breakfast in bed again – he notes that he didn't drink coffee during the race except from the hip flask. At about 4 o'clock, he went for a brisk ten miles to get a sweat on. The next night, the revellers had departed or quietened down and he slept soundly.

Stage 16 Aix-en-Provence – Gap 203km

No more than an approach to the Alps, this stage crossed three third-category climbs and most of the riders took it easy, mindful of the monsters that lay in wait over the next two days. A small group, including Barbosa, did break clear after only eight kilometres, hunting for a win when no one else was bothered. They were a minute clear over the first col Le Pointu at 50km and, beating along into a stone headwind, kept their lead through rocky and barren landscape towards the Mont du Forez and the Col de la Croix de l'Homme Mort 1213m...Dead Man's Cross. Nearing the col, Bahamontes suddenly attacked with a Spanish team-mate, Jesus Lorono (Mountains prize winner in 1953) and a French regional. None of his rivals, threatened as they were, made a move. The Bahamontes threesome caught the leaders on the descent of the col and, at the finish, Bahamontes was now only eighteen minutes down on the overall leader. The journalists castigated his rivals for letting so dangerous a man take back time on them. Robinson says that they neglected to state what was clear to him: Bahamontes had more punch than the majority of riders that day. One senses, again, his frustration at Gaul's lack of mettle, his failure to transfer the self-belief he felt in the high mountains to the cauldron of the flat.

Stage 17 Gap- Turin 234km

The riders faced the Col d'Izoard 2360m, Mont Genèvre 1854m and the ski station of Sestriere 2030m, which lies on the Franco-Italian border. Robinson felt much calmer about these High Alps than he had when he was a novice the year before. His form had been consistently good since the start of the race and he was confident. He knew, too, that if he ate and drank wisely, there was no question of suddenly losing form in a stage race. This says as much for his constitution and powers of recovery as about his growing experience. Determined to get some time in hand before the climbing began, he attacked early on with a small posse of others who had the same idea, including Barone, and the *lanterne rouge*, Raymond Chaussabel. They built a small lead and, as they approached the first lifts of the Izoard, suddenly, the regional Huot, now leading the Mountains prize, went past. No sign of either Gaul or Bahamontes, who must have seen him, their immediate rival, going away. This was odd.

Robinson, now on 45x25 settled into his rhythm as Huot sped off alone. 'I took it very steadily,' he told Wadley 'knowing that a minute gained on the Izoard [ie by forcing the pace beyond what was comfortable] might well mean five minutes or more lost on the next two cols.'

As he expected, the big hitters of the peloton began to arrive and go past, among them Bahamontes, Ockers, the astonishing Walkowiak and Gaul, turning the small gear he preferred, with smooth fluency at a gliding speed. The photographs of the climb up through the Casse Déserte of that formidable col show a road that would have been classified *Unsuitable for motor vehicles* in England: a narrow, unmade track hacked up the mountainside, its surface of compacted stone gravel, littered with loose chippings and large crumbs of broken rock. Fans line the route, some in walking boots, others in cycling shorts and maillots, some in fore and aft Martini paper hats, women in cardboard and gel sunglasses, dispensed by the publicity caravan. The sun is nearly overhead, the shadows on the stones attenuated.

Sticking firmly to his own pace, Robinson nonetheless crossed with a following group, a little more than two minutes behind Gaul – and, waiting to hand him a drink, as they had promised in a telegram, several members of the Yorkshire Century club. He rode on, by himself, quicker on the descent than the others, down the long drop through trees and onto the open acres beyond, into and through Briançon, thence over the Col de Montgenèvre, the main route into Italy. On the climb up to the pass at Sestriere, he caught up with a small group containing Ockers and a number of Italians, including Gastone Nencini. The *tifosi* were out in force, letting rip with a boisterous chorus of *Forza...forza* for their heroes. Ahead, Gaul was over four minutes up, to Robinson's delight, Huot and Bahamontes somewhere in between. Frantz had told Gaul that he needed to put some time into Ockers, who was breathing down his neck, so he was on the rivet into the force of a headwind. On the long slide down the chute of slackening contours into Turin, Robinson was powerless to put much of a brake on the group, which included Wagtmans, even as they caught Huot and Bahamontes, who were driving on hard to prevent Gaul taking a solo win. They did overtake Gaul and the whole group, now sixteen-strong, surged onto the 'hard tennis court track' in Turin, watched by a crowd of 80,000 Italians. In the sprint for the line, Robinson came sixth, but the cheering, whistling, screaming and hollering of the huge crowd rose crescendo to an exuberant fortissimo as their man, the local boy, born in the city, Nino Defilippis, took the win.

Robinson imputed his strong performance this day to the experience and the conditioning he had brought away from the Vuelta and the Tour de Suisse. 'At times,' he told Wadley, 'the going had been wickedly hard, but I knew that on general form everybody else would be suffering, too.' He jumped four places overall.

Stage 18 Turin – Grenoble 250km

At last Gaul showed his true class: he won the stage and was now within strike of Huot's lead in the Mountains prize. The Luxemburg team's aggregate of finishing times also won them the stage prime of £200.

Robinson, as ever, rode at his own pace over the Mont Cenis pass 2083m, a long drag of a climb out of Italy to a plateau road skirting the lake which fills a hollow scooped out of the mass of rock forming the massif of the mountain. He rated the next climb, the Col de la Croix de Fer 2087m, named for one of the wayside crosses made of ornate wrought iron which stand by many roads in rural France along the old pilgrim routes, as one of the severest obstacles in the Tour. It wasn't only the gradient, a final 7.5km of relentless 8-10%, but the appalling uneven, stony, loose surface which tugged and nagged at the tyres. His rear tub went flat on the descent and, being on his own, no team car in sight, he replaced it with one of the spares every rider carried in a figure of eight under his arms and across his back or strapped under the saddle. A few bursts with the compressed air pump and he was off again. Almost at once, his front tyre went down. Another hasty change with the help of the pressure pump. He lost, in all, no more than about two and a half minutes – which would have been a disaster if it happened in a 40kph flat stage, but on a descent, not so serious. He gradually caught the others by whom he'd been left when he had the flats. Yet, as he was changing his second tub, his team-mate Jempy Schmitz rode up and said he'd wait to help him rejoin. It was, Robinson says, the only time during the entire Tour that any of his team-mates gave or even offered him any assistance. Once the two of them got going, Schmitz, alas, couldn't hold Robinson's wheel and eventually finished the stage eleven minutes behind him.

On the last col, the Luitel 1235m, a tough twelve kilometre climb that winds up on a tight, narrow, twisting road out of Uriage-les-Bains, much of the way at around 9%, through closed woodland to a broader road near Chamrousse, Robinson was going very strongly. He passed the yellow jersey, Wagtmans, struggling to hang on. He overtook, one by one, a number of known riders, including Gilbert Bauvin, the French national, and then another French national, René Privat. Some way on, he caught the Italian hard man, Nencini, and was, at that point, (although he didn't know it at the time), fifth on the road. This was remarkable. Suddenly, an Italian spectator dashed out into the road and started pushing Nencini for a hundred metres. Robinson, right behind him, was furious. As he came up alongside Nencini and his pedestrian outboard motor, he took a swipe at the man with his fist. The Italian, mortified, at once transferred his charitable energies and tried to push Robinson – *buona fede* – but the effort of shoving Nencini up the steep slope had winded him. He stumbled, fell and took Robinson with him. His only crash of the Tour, going uphill. The well-intentioned Italian immediately helped him up again but the idiotic misadventure cost him nearly two minutes and a deadly loss of rhythm.

Ahead of him, Gaul led the race, clear of Ockers, (2m 15s), Bahamontes (6m 10s), Walkowiak (6m 35s), Van Genechten (7m 30s) and Nencini (7m 50s). In the final kilometre of the climb, Robinson joined Bauvin, now in some straits, and Privat, both men showing the strain. Over the top, they began to recover and although Robinson tried to slow their chase, for his team leader, Bauvin was desperate not to lose any more time to the young usurper, Walkowiak. (Their rivalry was complicated by the fact that Bauvin and Walkowiak, close friends and team-mates outside the Tour, were snared in bitter opposition within it.) However, Walkowiak, who had stuck fast to Gaul for most of the day and went with him over the Croix de Fer, lost contact only on the Luitel, arrived in Grenoble two minutes ahead of Bauvin and took over the yellow jersey. Had it not been for the stupid prang on that climb, Robinson would almost certainly have come in with Nencini – from the top of the col it was an easy descent to the finish – who arrived two minutes' ahead of him. As it was, he moved up two places overall to 13th. He considers that stage, Turin – Grenoble, to have been the best of his '56 Tour and perhaps of his whole career.

As for Walko, his courage in following Gaul when his rivals for yellow hung back, won him the Tour.

Stage 19 Grenoble – Saint-Etienne 173km

When Walkowiak went down in a crash at the foot of the Col de l'Oeillon 1233m, towards the finish of the stage, Bauvin immediately attacked, so incensed were the French team that they were being made fools of by this provincial whipper-snappper. Yet Bidot, who had ridden the Tour in the '30s, in effect rebuked the supine hauteur of the French team he managed. He had spotted Walko on an alpine stage in the Circuit des Six Provinces in 1951 and admired him. 'This lad reminds me of Bobet,' he said. 'The resemblance is striking: same comportment on the bike, same strength in his back, same style in the mountains.'

Walkowiak managed to catch Bauvin, whilst Gaul was out on his own, chasing Ockers, in the lead, and snapping up Mountains points to put him in the lead in that competition. They came in first and second. Robinson improved one more place on general classification to 12th having buckled on the climbs, somewhat, after the all-out effort of the previous day.

Stage 20 Saint-Etienne – Lyon time-trial 73km

The fatigue dogged him still and he had a bad day. He didn't like contre la montre, anyway, and, by his lights, had never performed well in the discipline, except in the two tours before this Tour de France. Those results had persuaded him that he might show well in the grand tour. Sadly, not.

Thinking that the road was fast, he fitted light 180gm tubs. By the time he started, 2.40pm, the sun had been fierce for some while and the roads were sticky. He sat on the bike, Frantz standing beside him, holding him steady, by the saddle. The time counted down, he set out, trailed by the official Tour white Peugeot 203 team car, his name on a large banderole across the radiator. The first twenty-one kilometres were all uphill and he punctured twice. At the top of the climb, his time was already 4m 3s down on that of Ockers, for example. He made up some of the deficit on the second part of the course but finished in fiftieth place. He had simply not felt up to the mark.

Stage 21 Lyon – Montluçon 237km

There were two cols left, the minor bump over Feurs 330m, and the Col du Beaulouis 824m, neither of any great difficulty, the second no more than a long, sapping uphill slog. The day was boiling hot. Robinson led Gaul out for the sprint to the summit at Feurs and, in the pause as they all gathered breath, Hassenforder attacked. He'd already won three stages and, for a week, had been predicting that he would win the final gallop round the Parc des Princes. Here he was, going a day early. The other riders saw nothing more of him all day except from the blackboards displayed by a motorbike marshall with the time of his growing lead scrawled in white chalk. Having got Gaul over the Col du Beaulouis to win maximum points and secure the Mountains prize, Robinson could relax, as did everybody else, while the clown prince, Hassenforder, built a lead of twenty-two minutes.

The heat was relentless, Robinson was dry with thirst. He and a few other riders made a hurried stop to snatch a drink at a refreshment table set up in a village. Then he remounted, rode fifty metres up the road and realised he'd taken the wrong bike – he'd pinched Darrigade's machine.

The pace livened up as it always did towards the end but Hassenforder still took a splendid solo win, 8m 8s in the lead. Walkowiak rode into his home town in yellow…a glorious moment for a man who was, barring accident, heading for victory having come, in the eyes of many, out of nowhere. Bauvin might well attack on the final stage and attack hard – hadn't Robic snatched his win from Brambilla on the last day in 1947 with a dramatic final push on the open road?

Stage 22 Montluçon – Paris 331km

Over two hundred miles of racing from the town whose museum contains a remarkable collection of hurdy-gurdies to what Robinson called 'the magical vision of the Parc des Princes'. (In 1952, the final stage ran to 354km.) They were out of bed at 5 o'clock for a 7.15 start. At breakfast Robinson was given strict orders to beat Gaul at all costs. The pair of them lay equal thirteenth overall and the Luxemburger wanted to be fourteenth, ie not unlucky thirteenth.

The press hyped the possibility of a classic duel between Bauvin and Walkowiak. It didn't happen. They kept riding to the front of the bunch on call to oblige journalists and be photographed together. The pace didn't rise much above 35kph until about forty kilometres from Paris when a break, including Nencini, went clear. Bauvin was, inevitably, criticised for not attacking, but the 'third thief', the Belgian Adriaenssens, was hovering, two minutes down on Bauvin, and it was in the interests of both Frenchmen to contain him. Walkowiak was censured, too: he'd won the Tour without taking a single stage. His victory, deserved as it might be, lacked flourish, and the French public were hot on flourish, a show of class to gild the triumph. (Unkindly, certain sniffy members of the the press later described any lacklustre performance as being à la Walko.)

On the last hill of the Tour, which Robinson knew well – it was on his training ground out of Poigny-la-Forêt – Ockers attacked. Robinson jumped, too, along with Darrigade and eleven others and they were soon clear. They hurtled under the five kilometre banner, across the Pont de Sèvres, past lines of cheering spectators, which sent a shiver down Robinson's spine. He looked up, the 5km sign, and, as they sped underneath it, a spoke in his wheel snapped with a violent twang…his first mechnical trouble in the whole Tour. As he waited for a wheel change, eighty riders flew past. By the time he was back on the bike, the race was over. He rode out of the darkness of the tunnel into the blinding glare of the sun, the massive crowd a blur in the haze, a dense pack of riders and officials, photographers and journalists, milling about in front of him. He had to ride the statutory final lap of the great stadium on his own, feeling rather disconsolate…the elation of an arrival in style entirely squashed. He had also, involuntarily, dropped a place and Gaul kept thirteenth. Nothing to be said but get on with signing autographs and confirming a goodly budget of criterium contracts. There to greet him somewhere in the crowd were Shirley, Milly and Henry and, at trackside, the four times World sprint champion, Reg Harris, in company with the current French sprint champion, Roger Gaignard. Louison Bobet came up to congratulate him. 'Bravo Brian,' he said. 'Next year I hope to ride the Tour again and you will be on my danger list.' This was not just empty flattery. There is no doubt that if Robinson had the support of a team, he would be in contention for a very high placing. To come 14th (in truth 13th) effectively as a solo rider was really quite amazing. He did believe that had the team made a unanimous deal to support the indecisive Gaul, the Mountains prize winner would surely have done better overall, might even have won. Throw in a calculation of prize money based on stage victories and days in the yellow jersey (£200 for that), and the team would have won a lot more than the £3,160 they did net. (When Merckx rode on after cracking his jawbone in 1975 it was partly to assure his team's overall winnings.) On the other hand, had Robinson sacrificed himself completely for his leader, he would have come much lower down in the order and passed into extremely unprofitable obscurity.

Robinson made a summation of much that he had learnt in his burgeoning career on the continent:

Gears: Experience had taught him to gear lower. It was, still is, a foible of British clubmen to go for the macho big gear (and the over-high saddle) and Robinson, in his Tour of Britain days, would routinely change up to a 104 inch top gear at any excuse. By contrast, the only time the French riders used such a high ratio was when they had a strong following wind or on a fast, straight descent. For training, he now habitually used a sixty-six for as much as 250km at around 26kph.

Saddle position*: Louviot had advised him to change position after the Vuelta. He put the saddle forward 2.5cm and reduced the handlebar extension by the same amount. 'With the change came the discovery of what I believe to be one of the secrets of all the big names in the road cycling world –the

---

* All riders treasured their own saddle – almost always a custom-shaped leather Brookes – and fitted it to whatever bike they rode. 'You never let it out of your sight' says Robinson. When the hide had stretched a bit, pros would remove the rivets and tighten the saddle on its frame and punch new holes for the rivets. Robinson's Tour bike, to which he attached no sentimental value, with the cherished saddle, was stolen from his house when he and Audrey moved to where they live now.

ability to relax when riding. Not just to relax when the pace is slow but even during a chase.'

A third innovation: the combined saddle-clip and pin, manufactured by Campagnolo. This allowed for precise and minute adjustment of the saddle height and guarded against a common breakage, that of the saddle clip.

Fourth novelty: handlebar control for gears, the levers protruding from the bar ends. Disliking them at first, he was now a convert. It allowed a rider to change gear in an easy movement whilst on the drops.

Food

The old wisdom was ride lots in training and eat lots. French slang for the 'bonk' is the 'wolf' and wolfing grub is what you did to keep it at bay.

A grocer's bill for one team to be handed to the Tour organisers during the 1947 race lists jam, eating chocolate, coffee, tea, block sugar, Dutch cheese and quick snacks for seven while they waited. Jean Robic won that year, his regional team's diet supplemented, in the pinch of post-war shortages, with oodles of butter and eggs donated by supporters in Brittany. Images of early Tours emphasise the scavenging aspect of feeding: Colle and Parel sitting on café steps, a stein of lager apiece, 1921...Brackeveld lounging in a field scoffing rolls, 1922...a begrimed Jacquinot at a restaurant table (bike leaning against it – caution against sabotage) tucking into soup, bread and wine to hand, 1920s...Fachleitner peels off, in torrid heat, the '47 Tour, to eat his sandwiches in an apple tree's shade...

By the 1950s, diet was more regulated and teams better drilled for supply. Coppi, the data and statistics man with petrol in his veins, had led the way, insisting on a certain austerity in the quantities of what was served – he scrutinized every aspect of racing, from gear ratios to the constituency of the pasta sauce. Robinson outlined what the Luxemburg team ate on and off the road:

Breakfast: (Served at least two hours before the stage start, to allow the body to digest the food and convert it into a source of energy.)

Thick vegetable soup – the hearty *garbure* which was the staple of peasant fare – with added wheat germ and a nutritional supplement called Vita Levure, containing important amino acids. (Nowadays used to fatten cattle.)

Two slices of cold ham and tomato salad with olive oil.

Rare-cooked beef steak.

Green salad of lettuce and dandelion leaves.

Creamed rice.

Fruit compote – generally apples or pears. They were forbidden to eat strawberries or apricots. As to why, maybe because apricots were considered to have aphrodisiac properties. Titania, in *Midsummer Night's Dream*, bids her fairy helpers induce love in Bottom, the weaver, now transformed with ass's head with whom she is besotted:

> Feed him with apricocks and dewberries,
> With purple grapes, green figs, and mulberries.
> Steal honey-bags for him from the bumble-bees,
> And with the wings of painted butterflies
> Fan the moonbeams from his sleeping eyes.   *MND III I 159*

Apricots are also considered sovereign for constipation. Randy riders making extra loo stops? Bad idea. As for strawberries, they can produce an allergic reaction which causes respiratory problems.

Weak tea – half tea, half milk.

One digestive tablet.

Musettes

They were given one musette at the start of a stage, a second during the race and, if the stage was particularly long, a third. The food was standard for all teams and supplied by the Tour organisation:

Leg of chicken.

Two white bread ham sandwiches. (White bread has much less fibre than wholemeal.)

Two white bread jam sandwiches.

Four 5cm square rice cakes.

Two fruit tartlets.

Three peaches.

Two very large bananas. (Robinson comments that they were 'whoppers'.)

Two packets of dried prunes.

One orange.

Twenty pieces of white sugar. (Robinson always replaced them with brown lump sugar.)

In exceptional circumstances, on a cold day, they were given one piece of chocolate.

Drink

At the start of a stage, one bottle of lemon cordial and one bottle of Milkor sweetened with twenty lumps of sugar. (Milkor was a malt extract vitamin drink containing chopped up fruit and Robinson said that it was 'pleasant and easy to take at speed, especially in hot weather'.)

At the first feed station, the same mixture in the two bidons. If there was a second feed station, they'd contain the lemon drink only. Some of the Luxemburg team preferred to have beer. Robinson carried a hip flask containing strong, well-sugared black coffee, the only coffee he drank during the race. Although they did consume caffeine tablets (for a stimulating hit) liquid coffee lies quite heavy in the stomach and he often thought better of the hip flask, too. 'I'd often flush it out with about 10km to go,' he told me, with a laugh. 'In fact, you might as well have chucked it over the hedge.'

He always put some grapes in his pocket, to refresh his mouth.

Arrival

A small bottle of Perrier water at the finish, '...two if you could grab another'.

At the hotel, lemon tea and biscottes, (twice-baked slices of bread).

In the bedroom: a jug containing a litre of milk. This allays hunger, lines the stomach but does not affect the appetite. This was optional and they were advised to lay off dairy products if they took a chill – to cut down on the build-up of catarrh.

Two hours later, after a massage:

Dinner

Garbure

Hors d'oeuvres of grated raw carrot, diced beetroot, tomato salad, green beans.

Fish (when freshly available, at a stage town near the sea or a teeming river, for example) or ham.

Veal or calf's liver or chicken.

Cooked vegetables – beans, carrots, potatoes (which Robinson generally eschewed, having gorged on hors d'oeuvres.)

Green salad.

Sweetened yoghourt.

Fruit salad.

Red wine with sugar of glucose added (which aids digestion) and Vittel water.

(He notes that this main meal, paid for by the Tour, cost 1,500 francs, ie 30/-, a considerable sum of money. The top quality lightweight 240gm Pirelli Leggerissimo road tubulars he favoured cost 70/- in England at the time.)

Note: Eggs were taboo. The French thought that they were bad for the liver, the liver being somewhat of an obsession with them. When the soigneurs got to the hotel, many hours ahead of the riders, they'd go through the menu with the owner and remove omelettes, egg mayonnaise and any other egg-based items on the list. Olives, pickles, sauces, gravy and pork were also banned. (But not the cold cut of the pig, ham, observe.)

They were discouraged from using salt which causes water retention and, thereby, raises the blood pressure.

Robinson spent the first week after the Tour in the hotel in Poigny-la-Forêt, training and giving Jock Wadley his account of the Tour. Then, leaving most of his gear behind, he loaded his bike into a taxi - front wheel removed, a plastic bag tied round the saddle to protect it - and the single suitcase out of which he would be living for the next six weeks of travelling by rail and car on another Tour de France, of road and track contracts. This day, first stop the Gare d'Austerlitz to catch a train taking him back to Montluçon, whence he'd find some way of getting to a small village in the country wilds, Sazeray, for the first criterium, 120km. Result: 1. Louison Bobet, 3h 6m 25s 2. (at one length) Brian Robinson ahead of five French riders, three of whom had just finished the Tour, another who had abandoned and another who never rode the Tour. Minutes back down the field came Barone, Dotto, Geminiani…

Robinson returned to England and, that winter, he and Shirley lived in a caravan in the family firm's yard. As he put it, he came back to what he'd been doing before life as a pro, work and club runs. Later in the following year, 1957, he bought a building plot by the hilly road out of Mirfield – there were only four houses there at the time – and, that summer, the foundations and masonry work was done and his father put on the roof. Robinson had some trouble with the planning because the design was French: the plot, cut into the slope, a double garage and utility room on ground level, stairs to the living quarters in the upper floor.

7: BREAKING EVEN…1957

Robinson and I bought small dictaphone machines so that he could record his recollections and send me the tapes. When I told him, on the phone, that I'd got my machine but that they'd given me the wrong batteries, he said that he'd got his machine, too, but hadn't thought about batteries. In a subsequent e-mail, putting more questions to him, I signed off:

'Have you got the batteries? It won't work wi'out 'em, tha knowst.'

He replied:

'Dear Graeme,

Ea lad tha naws nowt reight abaht Yorkies. Stick to la petite pomme de terre chaude! Hercs bikes were hand built by some small constructer in London area….'

In the course of his talks with Wadley in the hotel in the forest of Rambouillet, Robinson said that the Tour de France was his prime objective for 1957 but he also confided that, 'Although primarily a stage-rider, I have an ambition to do well in an early season classic, particularly Milan-San Remo.'

The first of the springtime one-day classics, *La Primavera* (Italian for spring) covers around three hundred kilometres across the flat fast roads of the Lombardy plain, over the Passo del Turchino into Liguria – a climb that can hand out a real savaging – down to the coast. The final one hundred and forty kilometres or so along the littoral of the Mediterranean throw in three significant minor hurdles, the celebrated Capi, which hoist the road away from the sea: the Capo Mele, south of Alassio, 74m high, 2.14km long, an average slope of 5.5%; the Capo Cervo, 75m, 1.4km long, maximum gradient 6%; the Capo Berta, into Imperia, 138 m high, three kilometres long, around 8%. In 1960, the race planners added the famous Poggio (in Italian 'hill') on which sits the town of that name, three point seven kilometres long, 144 metres of height gained at around 3.9% (maximum 7%) just east of the finish.* The humpback of the climb up into Cipressa, 233m high, 5.6 km long, at around 4.2% (maximum 6%) was included for the first time in 1982. There is no way to ride this succession of prominences but at a sprint.

Robinson now had a new jersey, emblazoned with the names of two sponsors of a team, managed by Louviot: the apéritif *St-Raphaël* and

---

* In the north-westerly Italian province of Liguria alone there are four locales named Poggio, another called Poggio Favaro as well as a Poggialto and a Poggi but, to the racing cyclist and the clued-up amateur aficionado both, there is only one worth mention: the Poggio of *La Primavera*.

Geminiani bikes. Geminiani was still riding and, entrepreneur and wheeler-dealer that he was, he'd set up sponsorship deals through the branding of bikes with his name. Which of two possible marques, possibly both, manufactured the cream Geminiani bikes was not certain. The apéritif *St-Raphaël* encapsulates three classic elements beloved of the French: alcohol, (good for the morale) salubrious ingredients (good for the health), and a penchant for mystification and gastronomic jiggery-pokery in the form of a secret recipe from sacred sources. The story goes that in 1830, one Doctor Juppet was trying to develop a drink containing quinine – curative qualities coupled with good taste. Quinine, brought back to Europe from South America by Jesuit missionaries in the early seventeenth century, has noted qualities as a tonic, febrifuge and antiperiodic and has long been used as a primary anti-malarial drug. Dr Juppet, straining his eyes in long hours of experiment, was losing his sight and then, hop-là, he remembered the story of the pious Jew Tobit, blinded by sparrows which 'muted warm dung in his eyes'. The archangel Raphaël sent a large fish which Tobit's son caught and, when the gall of the fish was applied to Tobit's eyes, he was cured of his blindness. Dr Juppet called the drink he came up with after the good angel and, lo, his own failing sight was restored. Thus, by the by, in not dissimilar circumstances – the kindness of visitant angels to mere mortals who showed reverence, not knowing the identity of those to whom they showed it – did the recipe for Yorkshire pudding reputedly reach earth.

The St-Raphaël–Geminiani sponsorship brought Robinson a monthly wage, enough for subsistence, at least, and the first minimal security he had known as a professional bike rider.

He and Shirley drove their car and caravan down to Cros de Cagnes, between Nice and Cannes, on the Côte d'Azur, in January and he embarked on his third training camp. A good friend of Wadley's, René de Latour, a journalist, wrote of the couple: 'They are as happy as two birds in a tree and already Brian is riding great. He should soon be doing well.' A photograph in *Coureur* shows Robinson coming out of the sea after a dip in a small cove, bordered by a reef of rough limestone. The caption notes the fine all-round development of his body. Robinson glosses the remark: 'Strengthen the arms, they are as important as the legs for mountain-climbing.' Although he had done some weight training as an eighteen-year old – under the tutelage of a weight lifter – he owed this latter development of his upper body to a winter's labouring. In addition to the routine joinery work, he had built a shed for his father from the ground up: digging the foundation trenches, mixing the concrete for the footings and then erecting the structure itself. An unconventional approach to all-round fitness, maybe, but most efficacious as the belting start to his season attests. Of his core strength, he says that it was in his legs, which are long for his body weight of 10.5 stones.

Two weeks later, Latour's assessment proved accurate: Robinson got his first big win on the continent. On 4 March, he took a truly outstanding victory in the Grand Prix de la Ville de Nice. In the photograph, he stands by his bike, wearing the jersey of his newly named and sponsored team, having just ridden a lap of honour. A silk sash of the City of Nice across his chest, he cradles a large bouquet of flowers wrapped in cellophane and he's being congratulated by Latour and Louison Bobet, who finished second, 50 seconds behind the Englishman. 'Congratulations, Mister Robinson,' says Bobet, in English, continuing, in French 'the only words of English I know. I willingly dedicate them to you.'

The Saturday before, 2 March, they'd ridden the relatively flat 196km Gênes-Nice (Genoa- Nice). Anquetil, having been worsted by Bobet in that race, elected to return to Paris to see a boxing match rather than ride the Nice course. The GP de Nice, the oldest cycle race in the region – dating from 1923 – was far lumpier. It ran 170km from Nice along the coast to Cannes, across the foothills of the Alpes Maritimes, via Grasse, back down towards the coast, over the Grande Corniche into Monaco and back to Nice.

The Mont des Mules, some 300m above sea level, dominates Beausoleil, the old town of Monaco. It was just the sort of short, steep hill which suited Robinson and he attacked. Two kilometres from La Turbie, and the start of the long drop over the Col d'Eze along the Grande Corniche, he was clear. Behind him, Seamus 'Shay' Elliott, in a rival team, led the chase to catch him, but his Saint-Raphaël team-mate, Gilbert Bauvin, blocked the pursuers, aided by Roger Rivière. Bobet was in the hunt, too, but well-marked and still tired from his recent win. However, he it was who led the gallop in the final stretch along the seafront Promenade des Anglais.

Just over a week later, Robinson lined up with his team-mates in what was now the co-sponsored Geminiani-Dunlop-Saint-Raphaël team, including Bauvin and Barone, on another Promenade des Anglais...in Massy-Palaiseau, an outlying banlieue to the south-west of Paris, not far from Versailles, at the start of the Paris-Nice. Acknowledging the Englishman's recent show of cracking form, L'Equipe said that Elliott, Planckaert, Robinson and Schepens 'carry the hopes (secret) of their *directeurs sportifs*'.

The fourth stage, Saint-Etienne to Alès, hit the famous Col de la République just after the start. Anquetil, together with Robinson's team-mates Mahé, Malléjac and Barone, attacked and relayed at tempo. A bit further on, Robinson got clear with a few others to join the break. One hundred and twenty kilometres from the start (one hunded and sixteen to ride) Barone went clear, Robinson and three others chased and caught him, Robinson escaped at 193km on a hill into Saint-Marcel in the Ardèche gorge. Barone checked any pursuit and then, sensing that the rest had had enough for the day, he broke free on his own and caught up with his team-mate and friend. They rode bit and bit, establishing an unassailable six minute lead by the time they reached the finish, to ensure a one-two victory for the team. Thus began the run-in, each for himself. There was no pact: Barone took the right side of the road, Robinson the left. Barone had few illusions about beating Robinson – he was too strong, he'd dropped everyone in the GP de Nice. The *Equipe* interview records Barone's take: 'Four hundred metres from the line, I found myself on Robinson's wheel and I had no idea how the sprint would go. Then Brian committed a gross error: he changed gear.' In the days of friction levers, the chain rattling on the cogs – especially if it was a muffed change and the teeth of the cog didn't engage instantly and sweetly – was frequently used as a prompt to attack. Barone duly accelerated and dug in, all out. His initial surge gave him a lead of several lengths. It was just enough. He hung on and took the victory on the line by no more than half a wheel. (Typically, Robinson himself offers no excuse.) *Equipe* was full of praise for the pair: theirs was one of the most significant victories of the Paris-Nice, 'may the gods be blessed'. Robinson was third on the next stage, and finished eighth overall behind the winner, Anquetil.

Two days after the Paris-Nice arrived on the Côte d'Azur, Robinson lined up with two hundred and twenty-two other riders at the start of the *Primavera* in Milan. The early Italian classic tended to be won by rouleurs, those men who can ride the flat, climb and hold a forcing pace tirelessly through an entire race. Latterly, more sprinters have mounted the podium, but that is a function of how racing has changed not the basic character of the Milan-San Remo. The massive field was an Italian thing: most races elsewhere on the continent were restricted to an entry of around one hundred and fifty. This added to the problems the riders faced: squeezing such a large peloton through the narrow streets of small towns and villages *en route* was a rude hazard and, when riders got shelled out merely because there was no space on the congested road, it was often the end for them. Rarely did any more than half the start field make it to the coast.

Two years after his debut in France, Robinson was not only a sharp racer, he had learnt the essential wiles of the trade. He freely admitted that he had ridden his first Tour as an amateur, attacking three or four times, sapping his strength, instead of making one big powerful effort. He was, in his words, never short of having a go. But that was small beer tactically. He had become craftier, he could read a race, now, as much by instinct and feel as by keeping his wits about him. He was about to learn another hard lesson about *le métier*: stepping aside on team orders.

Shirley drove him across in the car, they checked into the hotel and, next morning, knowing that there would be a crush to use the loos, he said to his wife: 'Nip out and tell me when it's free, would you?' Shirley went along the corridor to post guard. She approached the door of the *gabinetto*. It was open. She pushed it wide and there, on the pot, sat the Belgian, Fred de Bruyne, a man destined to play a singular role in the events of the day. He smiled, she smiled, closed the door and stood by, waiting for the flush and the all-clear.

GF   Can you remember where the race started (at 9.45am on 19 March)?

BR   It was in a suburb of the city, somewhere, not far from the centre, a big, wide, draughty street and it was damned cold. We had arm warmers on, like, and the noise was incredible – police klaxons, car horns, the crowd, a real hullabaloo, even as we went out from the neutralised zone to the off. One of the things was that the following cars were so far behind that you needed luck not to puncture. A flat would have been it.

GF   It was a huge field, wasn't it, 223 riders?

BR   Biggest I'd ever ridden in. Bobet and Anquetil, they were favourites, I suppose. Them and all the big names.

GF   What of the *tifosi*?

BR   Very noisy and sometimes very dangerous. They were all over the place.

GF   Any sense of hostility from them towards the foreign riders?

BR   Not that I was aware. I didn't really take much of the race in until the top of the one big climb, over the Turchino. The field got shaken up a bit, early attacks that came to nothing, but it meant some guys got shunted off the back. After all the racing that I'd done to that point, I knew most of the French and Belgian riders, if not the Italians. That meant I could spot who the danger men were – I could recognise riders from about three hundred metres, so you knew which moves to react to and which would come to nothing. Then Nicky Barone went clear and kept a lead. He'd been away for some time and a small group of us caught him on that col, the Turchino – it was a very narrow road. Big disappointment for him, of course, when we hooked on. We rode off down to the coast and I was beginning to get the feeling that I could do something. We hit the three Capi and I decided to have a bang on the last one, the Berta.

There were just under twenty-nine kilometres still to ride. Robinson was in a group containing the day's clear danger men: the Spaniard, Miguel Poblet, and the Belgians Julien Schepens, Joseph Planckaert and Fred de Bruyne. De Bruyne had won the Primavera the previous year and his palmarès eventually included three Liège-Bastogne-Liège victories, two in Paris-Nice, one Paris-Roubaix and Ronde van Vlanderen. Planckaert was a solid performer, the young Schepens, a very nippy sprinter who'd lately beaten Bobet in the third stage of the Paris- Nice and Poblet, the current Spanish road champion, was steadily forging an illustrious career. This was exalted company and the smart money would probably have been on Poblet, but Robinson felt it was his day. The pithy phrase used by Bobet in the criterium – *C'est moi qui gagne* – is also used by riders who feel certain, barring accident or act of God, of a physical and mental peak: today *I* win. Robinson knew he was completely on song. He was keenly aware, too, that being up against rated sprinters, he had no chance if it went to the line. Poblet, for example, was possessed of what one journalist called 'a murderous speed'. The last Capo was the obvious place for a man of Robinson's climbing strength and explosive power to attack, and he attacked. The others reeled him in. Unfazed, he attacked again, as fiercely as the first time and only de Bruyne and Planckaert could stay with him. His best chance was to try to burn them off and that was his adamant intention. Behind him, in the bunch, Poblet and Schepens were stirring: the Englishman looked dangerous. They set off in pursuit even as Louviot drove past in the team car to speak to his man, now leading the dash into San Remo. Earlier in the day, he'd told Robinson that if he found himself anywhere near Poblet towards the finish of the race, it was incumbent on him to ride for the Spaniard. Poblet was not only riding one of the Rapha-Geminiani bikes, Louviot was also trying to induce him to join the team. Robinson found himself caught in the squeeze. Through the open window of the car, Louviot cautioned his man: 'Remember what I told you…' As countless men of rare talent riding in a team alongside a proven star have discovered, their own scent of victory can never override the obligations of team service. He had no choice but to sit up and allow Poblet back on for the run-in. It was a bitter moment. Robinson says of that race, that had he won it, he'd have been made for the rest of his career. What a difference it would have made, instantly, to his contract for that season alone.

On the Via Roma, flanked by a huge press of spectators, Poblet became the first Spaniard to win the Italian spring classic, (on his 29th birthday), de Bruyne, who'd beaten Robinson into the loo that morning, beat him to the line that afternoon and he came third. It was, nevertheless, a brilliant ride. Foremost a stage-rider, he became the first Briton to stand on the podium of a major continental one-day race, but…Oh, but no buts. There is no place for speculation, repining, regret or *what if…*? beyond the acrid curse that escapes the lips in the immediate nausea of the disappointment. As the saying goes: 'Thought followed the muck cart and took it for a wedding.'

The *Equipe* coverage of the race allows Robinson very little credit. In fact, the reporter writes that when the small group caught Barone 'the race was all but over. All that remained for us was to get to the finish on the Via Roma, black with crowds, to watch a comfortable victory by the Spaniard.' He did have the grace to remark on Robinson's fulgurant attack on the first of the Capi: 'he had never justified his forename so emphatically'. The play is on Brian and *bruyant* (pronounced as the French pronounce the English name) which means 'with éclat, resounding, thunderous, making a noise'.

On that post factum hack sloppiness, Robinson is as close to acerbic as he ever gets.

BR   Have you ever followed the Milan-San Remo?

GF   No.

BR   It's chaos. The roads are so narrow, we'd just come off the mountains and there's no way the following cars could have been anywhere near us. Nowadays journalists can see it on television, but at that time, what happened at the front of a race, especially that one, was anyone's guess. They couldn't have seen anything, they were far too far behind.

Poblet was, however, agreeably sensible of his debt to the Englishman and he got him a ride in an important race in Barcelona, the Criterium des Ases (Aces), the weekend afterwards. Robinson went to stay with Poblet at his house near the sea in Barcelona and, when they went out training together in the week before the criterium, with other local riders, so well-known was Poblet that the police cheerily stopped traffic for them and passers-by waved and cheered. Robinson and Poblet got on very well – there was no hint of friction and the Englishman had no idea what business agreement the Spaniard had with Louviot.

The race used the Montjuich open-air circuit which was big and fast and, as Robinson put it to me, 'I was flying.' *El Mundo Deportivo*, a Spanish sports paper published in Barcelona, reported on the race on 3 April 1957:

Barcelona cycling fans, who can distinguish between the good and the ordinary, turned up in hordes at the Exhibition circuit to watch the Criterium. A number of outstanding international stars had been signed up ad hoc for the programme, among them Baldini, Gaul, Robinson, Barbosa, Olsen, Hassenforder, Walkowiak, Caput, Boher, Bover, Bahamontes, Bertrán, Mas, Mostajo, Corrales and Mazo, together with Poblet, to race over twenty laps, with a sprint prime every two laps.

The race was a brilliant success. And that success, it must be pointed out in capital letters, was thanks to Miguel Poblet, Bahamontes and the Englishman Robinson. We might also include Miguel Boyer and the Portuguese rider Barbosa. For an hour and a half these five supplied all the glories of an exceptional race – the emotion of the sprint and the excitement of the chase.

On the fourth lap, Robinson escaped with such power and so elusive was he that he even confused the judges, who thought he was still on the third lap. On the fifth lap, Robinson recorded a time of 4'18', which proved to be the best lap-time of the afternoon, and earned him a magnificent trophy. Then on the sixth lap, Poblet shot out of the sleeping peloton like an arrow, and with him went

Bahamontes. The pair soon caught up with the Englishman and this trio continued at the front. The primes and the sprints were dramatic, highly emotional, all three riders giving everything they had.

Olsen abandoned on the fourth lap, indisposed. Gaul punctured on lap 11 and fell even further behind. From time to time a reaction from Hassenforder or Caput or Baldini forced the pace of the pursuit, but the three leaders continued to gain time, and points. On lap 15 Boyer and Barbosa escaped from the peloton and started closing on the leading trio. On lap 17 they caught them. The main peloton fell further and further behind.

Poblet was still ahead in the points classification going into the final lap which carried double points, as well as a prime worth three thousand pesetas. The sprint was stupendous, the points went to Poblet, Boyer and Robinson.

The final classification:
1. Poblet (1h 32m 57s), 27 points
2. Robinson, 14 points
3. Bahamontes, 12 points.

GF   What happened to the 'magnificent trophy'?
BR   I've no idea. It was only a tinpot something or other bit of kitsch.

Back across country to Luxemburg, capital of the Duchy, for the Grand Prix de la Forteresse, an eccentric time-trial/mass start evening medley race. The fortress in question had been rebuilt under the supervision of Louis XIV's celebrated military engineer, Vauban, after he had overseen its capture by siege in the late 17th century. The Vélo Club Les Cyclistes 1909 inaugurated the race in four stages: two open races of 2km, twice up and down the 700 metre-long steep incline from the lower city to the fish market in the high city, site of the fortress. These races sandwiched two individual time-trials up the hill. The total distance to be raced, 5.4km, overall classification to be judged on the accumulated time of each rider on each lap. Competing with the professionals – among them Bahamontes, Barbosa, Gaul (the local man), Jempy Schmitz, Ernzer and Robinson himself – were the best of Luxemburg's amateurs.

Gaul, smarting from his defeat in the 25.5km Mont Faron hill-climb, outside Toulon on 3 March, due to a mechanical failure, was doubly intent on a win in front of his home crowd on terrain which suited him perfectly. Bahamontes had beaten the record to win on Faron and he and Gaul had fought hard for the last three Tour's Grand Prix des Montagnes. The papers talked up a ding-dong fight between the two mountain men. Added spice would come from the duel between Barbosa and Robinson 'the two best Luxemburgers' with reference to their inclusion in the Luxemburg combine of the Tour. On 12 April, the headline of the report read: 'Neither Gaul nor Bahamontes but ROBINSON WINNER OF THE GP FORTERESSE.'

After the offices closed for the day, a huge crowd gathered on the slopes of the Grund and Brettenweg, lined with old houses, expecting Gaul to win, but they didn't get the result they expected. Even before the start, Bahamontes was dished: his smallest gear ratio of 46x21 was simply too big for the 16% of the Brettenweg. Gaul, on the other hand, rode smoothly on his 46x25 and was catapulted by cheering supporters to easy victories in the first ride against the clock and the next two stages, on line and second time-trial. But, on the final open race, he punctured two hundred metres from the line and had to pull out. 'Thus the brilliant and consistent Brian Robinson, twice third and once second in the first three laps and winner of the last with some metres lead, took the win in this hard hill race.'

Robinson and Elliott went clear together in the Het Volk, which, with Gent-Wevelgem formed the Weekend Ardennais, that came two days after la Flèche Wallonne. Although they were caught just before the finish, their escape netted them all the town and hill primes while they were out in front, a good haul of some £150 apiece and shares in a washing machine. At the end of the week's races, Robinson was named King of the Flemish Mountains and won the often grudging respect of the hard-core Belgian fans: he and Elliott had become danger men to the local stars. The uplands which rise out of the flat plain of Flanders in the area called Heuvelland, 'hilly land', are short, steep and none much higher than 150 metres. Wags refer to them as the Belgian version of Switzerland, Flemish Alps. However, their cobbled surface, the extreme gradients – generally in excess of 12% – and the punishing speed at which races hit them can, in the parlance, break the legs of many lesser men. Robinson's prowess on them is not to be underrated.

Although Hercules had pulled out of sponsorship, they were still avidly milking their participation in the '55 Tour. Their *Tour de France Equipe* bike, 'the most successful road-racing machine Britain has ever produced' was retailing at £28 5s 6d cash. The advert reads: *'If legs could only speak... They'd say 'Give me a TOUR de FRANCE EQUIPE machine every time'.*

It was the triumph of wishful thinking over humbling reality.

Robinson was still uncertain of a ride in that year's Tour, even if his manager Louviot was full of praise. He told Wadley that 'under his direction and with nine of his Geminiani team-mates...the Englishman could finish in the first five'. It was a pleasing thought but no more than that. For, despite his high placing in 1956, the uneasy experience of that race had not encouraged him. Were he to ride in such a disparate team again, subservient, or not, to the mercurial Gaul, his own ambitions would be hostage to the indefinable whims of nine other riders. He might rely on support from Shay Elliott, but the 23-year old Irishman was not very keen to ride the Tour yet. Therefore, when he signed up for the mammoth Bordeaux-Paris, the 'Derby of the Road', in May, Robinson told Wadley that if he did well in it he might do better to concentrate on the criteriums staged by towns hosting the *Arrivée* of the Tour rather than riding the *Grande Boucle* itself. They'd use the same track or circuit as the *Arrivée* and put on races before and after the Tour came in. Robinson was well enough known, now, to secure fair start money, the podium placing in Milan-San Remo had given him more cachet and the prime requisite for a bike rider was to make money in the saddle by fastening his name on leader boards. At the outset of Anquetil's career, the journalist Alex Virot gave the teenager from Normandy some shrewd advice: 'Young man, if you set out to make money, you will lose races. If you set out to win races you will make money.' Robinson's hunger for primes in criteriums, his constant determination to 'have a go', his persistent desire for better and better rides, his willingness to learn, all indicate that he had taken this shrewd counsel to heart.

The Bordeaux-Paris, approximately 550km, was first contested in 1891 and won by an Englishman, George Pilkington Mills, who completed the then 600km course, paced by a relay of other hired cyclists, in just over twenty-four hours. From 1931, the pacing was done by motorbikes (for a time cars) and, eventually, by the famous 98cc Dernys, which were developed for pacing on the track. The Dernys joined about halfway along the route, in Poitiers or Châtellerault. Riders left Bordeaux at 2 o'clock in the morning. The last professional edition of the race – won by Herman van Springel of Belgium no fewer than seven times – was held in 1988.

The race was, primarily, a test of stamina and mental solidity, but, as in everything to do with bike racing, there were contingent imponderables: in the case of Bordeaux-Paris, the relationship between rider and Derny driver. If there were not full complicity, the pacing was virtually nullified – the riders who paid the most got the best, that is most cooperative and pliant drivers. Robinson did a lot of heavy training behind a Derny the week before the race. Because a rider is not only pulling very hard but getting forward in the saddle to make as much use of the draughting as possible, he adopted a position similar to the modern time-trialling posture, forward thrust on the tri-bars. In the course of that week's rigorous preparation, Robinson, for the first and only time in his career, developed the curse of bike riders: saddle boils. The chafing of shorts on the tender flesh of the perineum, working sweat and any attendant dirt into the ever sorer skin, produced multi-headed, purulent abcesses, whose immediate source is a bacterial colonisation (mostly from staphylococci) of hair follicles, that is the small lymphatic glands, or sacs, out of which grow the hair.

BR   I calmed them down for the start of the race, by massaging them heavily to break them up and discharge the pus. It was bloody painful. In fact, that's what I'm having to do with this injury in my leg right now. Then we used a cocaine pomade, Mercuricaine or some such.

GF   Did you make it to the finish?

BR   Oh, yes. It was bloody hard, of course, behind the Derny, leaning right forward in the saddle. In road-racing, you can ride on the tops for hours until you have to get down to it – is that where that expression comes from?* – but when you are pulling that hard, behind the motors at maximum, there's no resting place to be had. There were only about ten or maybe sixteen riders in the race all told and when we got to the Parc des Princes, where the race finished, the gates were shut, so we didn't make it in.

And so, the Tour it was.

The July 1957 edition of *Coureur*, carries a short article about The Peace Race, inaugurated in 1948 as a stage race, linking Prague and Warsaw, for amateurs. Post-war Europe had been divided by a demarcation line between the eastern Communist bloc and the free West. In a speech in Missouri, USA, 1946, Winston Churchill spoke of the divide across Europe:

> From Stettin in the Baltic to Trieste in the Adriatic, an "iron curtain" has descended across the Continent. Behind that line lie all the capitals of the ancient states of Central and Eastern Europe. Warsaw, Berlin, Prague, Vienna, Budapest, Belgrade, Bucharest and Sofia; all these famous cities and the populations around them lie in what I must call the Soviet sphere, and all are subject, in one form or another, not only to Soviet influence, but to a very high and in some cases increasing measure of control from Moscow.'

The so-called Tour de France of the East was intended as a gesture of solidarity across doctrinal ideology and politics between nations on either side of this iron curtain. It was strictly amateur – Soviet riders were not allowed to be professional. Ian Steel won the 1952 edition, newly-expanded to include Berlin, and in 1957, Stan Brittain of Britain came second. (The significance of the event weakened after the fall of the Berlin Wall and the last Peace Race was staged in 2006.) *Coureur* heralded Brittain's achievement:

> Among the followers of the race was M. Jean Garnault, organiser-in-chief of the Tour de France and for ever on the lookout for new talent. He was openly impressed by the workmanlike display of Brittain and his team-mates and on such evidence is hopeful that within a few

---

* US colloquial and military (from 1910) meaning 'to go to sleep'.

years Brian Robinson will at last have the effective national team support he now lacks.

Aside from the fact that the Tour de France organisers were always scouting for men to ride their race, the most interesting word in this passage is 'workmanlike'. Robinson would have approved. The French phrase is *faire le métier*, learn the trade, do the job, and it has always been applied to professional bike-racing, just as boxers heading for the ring speak of 'going to work'. Every rider, of whatever talent, had to work at it, some more than others, but work, graft, apprenticed toil, was the essential and imperative ethic. It included knowing how to race as well as the basic requirement of riding fast and for long periods. That came with training, the expertise came from study, in the saddle and in the analysis of mistakes made. Robinson adds another dimension: the satisfaction. 'I've had that all my life, even just growing a cabbage. If you don't get satisfaction out of your work it must be very hard.'

Louison Bobet, who'd missed the 1956 race, announced that he intended to ride. Bidot began to shape a team round him as leader, backed by Geminiani. Almost at once, Darrigade, whose antagonism towards Bobet had deepened in the year since the supposed treachery of the '56 Tour, declared for Anquetil, his friend and Helyett team-mate, twenty-two years old, already winner of three Grand Prix des Nations (the major professional time-trial). Clearly, the young Norman was a potential Tour winner, but the idea that he would slip docilely into a team led by Bobet was fanciful and Darrigade, in particular, was keen to stress the point. He said that he would rather ride in a regional team than alongside Bobet and Geminiani. A little more than a month before the Tour was due to depart from Nantes, Bobet, riding in the Giro, sent word that he would not, after all, be there. He wasn't sufficiently recovered to ride two major tours, he wanted to do what normal people did in their summer holidays, for a change, swim in the sea, spend time with his children…This statement was widely, and with some justice, interpreted as cynical. Bobet's lieutenant Geminiani, also riding the Giro, immediately announced that he wouldn't be riding, either. The journalist who scribbled down his statement described him, 'naked as a worm, striding up and down the hotel room'. "If Louison is renouncing, I am, too. We've been on the treadmill for ten years. Time for others to do as much. Me, I'll ride the Tour in a regional team, yes, smoking my pipe, the most relaxed Tour I ever rode and I'll still be smoking my pipe, on a bench in the town square, when I'm ninety."

Bidot readjusted: he brought back Walkowiak, the '56 winner, who, plainly, could not have been expected to work for Bobet. He also selected Anquetil and Darrigade. Almost immediately Bobet, as if in a fit of pique, now said that he might ride the Tour, after all. The French have a phrase for it: *un panier de crabes*…a basketful of crabs.

As for Robinson, he rejoined virtually the same Luxemburg-Portugese-English (him) team led by Gaul, with two changes, only, of personnel. Shay Elliott was not riding. Wadley's editorial in the August issue of *Coureur* spells out the underlying problem of such mongrel combines:

> As Brian Robinson says, the international and inter-regional system is not entirely satisfactory. Quite apart from the cases of men like Gaul…and Robinson himself, who cannot get full national team support, there is a growing reluctance on the part of concerns sponsoring teams to release their men for the Tour. [For]…a rider is duty bound, on occasions, to sacrifice his own chances in favour of a man riding for a firm which is his own employer's biggest rival in a dwindling market.

The solution was to introduce trade–sponsored teams, as in Italy. However, the Tour bosses, true to the profound distaste of Desgrange for rampant commercialism and his entrenched aversion to any manufacturer exerting a stranglehold to crush the purist sporting integrity out of 'his' race, were against this. There was even talk of ditching the Tour de France for a grand Tour of Europe. As if.

Robinson came to the Tour after a hectic first part of the season catapulted by his excellent early showing. After a hatful of Belgian one-day races and the springtime three-stage Tour de Picardie, he came much to the fore in the Tour du Luxembourg, taking fourth overall and three podium places. He did express some disquiet about his form before the main Tour and Jock Wadley divined that he was in two minds about whether to ride or not. The prospect of, once more, being in thrall to a leader who neither raced as if he wanted to win nor paid much attention to the welfare of the team as a whole had little appeal. Stars like Gaul might have the luxury of disinterest in such lowly matters as day-to-day prize money, but for the lesser riders, whose sole means of livelihood was to translate hard work, opportunism and a cunning use of talent into cash, they were paramount. If trade marques were not to take over the team entry, perhaps Robinson's best solution was to take out residency in France, as his friend Shay Elliott had done the year before, and thus qualify for a French regional team. He might not be able to claim leadership status but he would, at least, be teamed up with men who knew the value of cooperation on the road. There was, too, the option of missing the great French Tour in favour of the Giro d'Italia. In sum, Robinson's experience as an odd-jobber in a mishmash of a team had undermined his confidence in the Tour as an essential portion of his annual economy.

Stage 1 Nantes-Granville 200km

The heat was intense and remained so for the three opening stages. Pierre Chany, in *L'Equipe*, spoke of the '*Tour crématoire*', the crematorium Tour. The tar melted and the stars wilted. Gaul, perhaps smarting at his poor showing in the recent Giro – he came fourth – and aware that his dilatory tactics in 1956 had served him extremely ill, set off with unwonted determination and finished about one and a half minutes behind the first winner, Darrigade. Robinson, though, was already in a sorry way: he came in ten minutes back, 113th in the field of 120 riders, at the tail of the last bunch to finish. Jacques Goddet, *directeur* of the Tour, voiced his disappointment: 'Robinson was in a grievous state'. It says something for the splash his early season results had made that his form should give pause. He didn't actually feel bad but, for no obvious reason, there was no life in his legs, he couldn't raise any speed and it was beyond him to follow any wheels. He slogged through the stage and began to feel anxious about the following day.

Stage 2 Granville – Caen 226km

In Bidot's memorable words 'Gaul fell like a fly', completely shrivelled by the heat. Robinson had recovered himself – inexplicably, but happily – and noted Gaul toiling at the back of the field, his old haunt. He and three other team men – Ernzer, Morn and Kemp – dutifully went back to rally him just before the feed station in Cherbourg, where the road swung south back down the Cotentin peninsula. It was immediately apparent that their leader was cooked and Robinson faced a hard choice: if he stayed with Gaul, he himself would be finished. The tug of this ill-defined loyalty was slight. Self-sacrifice for no good purpose was idiotic. He knew that unless he got in with some kind of bunch in pursuit of the main peloton, he would be out of the race. He set off alone. The team car drove up alongside. Frantz, the *directeur*, told Robinson to wait for Gaul. He ignored him and pushed on. He eventually joined a straggling group who had been delayed by punctures or by water stops – riders were peeling off in all directions to fill their bidons – and they managed to get back to the main bunch. At the finish, he learned that Gaul had succumbed and climbed into the sag wagon. Ernzer, Kemp and Morn had also quit. Thirty minutes down on the winner they knew they had no chance of beating the time limit. In the team hotel that evening, supper passed in near silence. Gaul himself ventured nothing; Frantz never talked much anyway. He'd told Gaul to stick a cabbage leaf under his hat as protection against the severe heat, but Gaul scoffed at what he took to be an absurdly antiquated idea. The fact that most of the riders were sporting vegetable neck flaps did not persuade him and Frantz was convinced that he'd suffered accordingly.

That day, Bahamontes, who surely was used to riding in the blazing sun, collapsed at the side of the road and refused to ride on. His *directeur*, Luis Puig, pleaded and pleaded with him and, at last, he agreed to remount.

Stage 3a. 15km team pursuit, six laps of the La Prairie motor circuit.
3b. 135km to Rouen

Their team depleted by almost half, the Luxemburg combine started at 9.45am, first off, against the ten-strong Belgian team and, remarkably, conceded only 40 seconds. In the afternoon, two hundred metres from the finish, ten minutes down, as the winner, Anquetil, was completing a lap of honour in front of his home crowd, Robinson's front tyre went flat.

Stage 4 Rouen – Roubaix 232km

The more you drink the more you want to drink, said Robinson. Driest is fastest, was Anquetil's dictum. 'The trouble with the tropics is / The dire necessity for fizz' wrote Hilaire Belloc. In blazing heat, thirst is a cruel foe and lack of water makes eating difficult. Once again, the piratical scavenging for liquids. Robinson ducked into a café to grab a couple of beers for himself and his particular buddy, Jempy Schmitz, then stopped at a drinking fountain in Abbeville to refill his bidons with water. Suddenly, a group of following riders came round the corner very wide and clipped the Englishman as he stood by the fountain. He went down in a general pile up and fell on his wrist. His team-mates Schmitz and Aldo Bolzan had also gone down. Robinson got to his feet – the frame of his bike was bent and useless. He took his spare from the mechanic and set off again on his own. Schmitz and Bolzan were both out. He rode some distance alone until Jan Diederich arrived to help, sent back by Frantz, who seems to have nursed no resentment about Robinson's earlier refusal to do the same for Gaul. The pair managed to join the next big group on the road, but Robinson's wrist had begun to ache badly, he could hardly pull on the bars and there was pavé ahead, out of Arras. It was still scorching hot as Robinson, in some pain now, time-trialled the remaining thirty kilometres into Roubaix, intermittently doused with cooling spray by spectators who had run hosepipes out of their houses.

In the hotel the race doctor Dumas came to examine Robinson's wrist and arranged for an X-ray the following morning. There was no break but the joint was wrenched, severely contused and inflamed. He began the stage but was in such distress, unable either to pull on the bars or work the brake, that it was clear his Tour was over. He rode nine kilometres and climbed off.

The rest of the year garnered sparse pickings. He rode the Tour de l'Ouest, a seven-day stage race in Normandy and Britanny rated by the French as third in importance after the Tour de France and the Dauphiné-Libéré. He came fourth overall, third on the fourth stage, and then the races dried up. All the post-Tour criteriums were either finished or fully signed up and there was nothing to do after riding a few scattered events but go back to England for the winter. That off-season, he went swimming once a week, joined the Huddersfield for club runs but did little else and, when he arrived for a weekend's riding in Derbyshire on 5 January, his friends were amazed at his lack of form: he could barely climb the stairs without wheezing.

He and Shirley lived in the new house, albeit it wasn't yet finished. There was no surplus in the bank. At the season's end, he had no more than broken even.

Perhaps that explains the resort to a fee for product promotion. In one issue of that year's *Sporting Cyclist*, Robinson features in an advertisement for Dextrose Glucose tablets. His puff reads: 'Extra energy makes the difference. Hard work getting in trim for championship racing means about three hundred miles really hard training every week to get you in peak condition.'

GF   Did you use them?

BR   No.

8: LE PLUS SCHITT DE L'ETAPE

A journalist writing in *L'Equipe* said of Robinson in 1958: 'Brian is out of the ordinary in that he regrets nothing. Not even the fracture of his wrist which forced him to abandon in '57. He has said that, having finished 14th in the '56 Tour, he thinks he can achieve his goal and finish in the top ten this year.'

Speaking to that same reporter, Robinson said that he had decided to base his season round the Tour.

'And Bordeaux-Paris?'

'That was a little supplement. I like its ambiance a lot.'

He put aside the major setback of 1957. No point in chewing on gristle that has no flavour in it. As Mark Twain's Connecticut Yankee at the court of King Arthur opines: 'A man has no business to be depressed by a disappointment, anyway; he ought to make up his mind to get even.'

He arrived at the training camp on 16 February to be told he was racing next day, an event starting at Saint Raphaël. He lasted sixty kilometres and doddled back to the start, a fair training ride. Next day: the Grand Prix de Monaco. On the second lap he shot off the back on the big hill. A couple of days rest and a long ride, 160km, into Italy and back. Next day, off at 8am to meet up with some of the Mercier men and began to feel in better shape over the climbs. 'But French riders do not like to lash themselves more than necessary during training.' Another gentle ride along the coast for fifty kilometres, enjoying the sun and the sea breeze and on Sunday, back to work: 170 kilometres out of Fréjus, over lots of steady climbs in a 69-inch gear. Warm weather to restore the spirits. Not so for the GP Sigrand de Nice, the last race in February: rain, snow and wind. Robinson did not start. He was, however, back in fettle for the first stage races of the year.

He came 19th overall, second on one stage and Mountains' Prize in the Paris-Nice, fifth in the Tour du Sud-Est, one stage win and one second, 12th in the Het Volk and, at the end of May, at 2.30am he lined up with fourteen other riders by a roundabout on the Quatre Pavillons Zone Industrielle in the eastern suburbs of Bordeaux. A crowd of some 2,000 spectators had gathered to see the start of the 560km race. The night was chilly, a strong wind blew from the south-west. The street lights cast an eerie glow, the fifteen riders wore woollen leg and arm-warmers, like Six-Day riders of the era. In the field, Darrigade, Walkowiak, Van Est (winner in '50 and '52, second in '51, '53 and '54), Dupont (second in '57), Cieleska (third in '56). The presence of the French stars Darrigade and Dupont (a team-mate of Robinson's) prompted the *Equipe* writer to call this a 'modern-style Bordeaux-Paris'.

First prize: one million francs. (£7,000).

The weather forecast predicted: rain showers, favourable wind.

And they were off.

Dawn came up as they approached Barbezieux-Saint-Hilaire, 77km, and with it a slight rise in temperature. They discarded the warmers, took on some food, and, hands off the bars, indulged in a swift wash and brush-up with wet flannel, sponge and towel. Bouvet, Cieleska (French with a Polish father) and Walkowiak fired the first ranging shot at around 230km, on the Côte de Saint-Maurice, a hill some way out of Châtellerault. They gained some ground and Walkowiak then went clear with a small advantage. In Châtellerault, the Dernys peeled off, one by one, from the side of the road and the riders tucked in behind. Three hundred and twenty kilometres to ride.

Emile Masson, the winner of the 1946 edition (he and his father, Emile, winner in 1923, each rode the race seven times) said that 'the buzzing whirr, like snoring, of the small motors made up the music of this unique race'.

In turn, Bouvet, then Cieleska followed by Robinson stirred the chase after Walkowiak and, at 340km, they formed a small group, including Dupont, in the lead. Five kilometres on, the whole field regrouped even as Forlini, trailing behind, quit.

In such a long race, riders are prey to a succession of mental swings which may, or may not, reflect the dips and surges of physical strain. The temptation to attack, to get away, to cut loose, countered by the feeling that this is not the time, caution…caution…a lulling of concentration as the thought process gets drawn into the incessant drone of the Derny motor, the wandering attention which picks at an errant desire for rest…no, stop that, focus, focus…and, when an attack goes, should one follow? Let it go? Bide one's time? Patience against impatience, except that this may be the key break. In a small field, the to-ing and fro-ing is immediately apparent, the chances of alliance reduce the closer to home you get, the need for vigilance remains constant but more and more difficult as fatigue seeps deeper into the system. As Masson put it, the Dernys have the effect, like a haemorrhage, slowly but surely to drain the riders of their vital reserves. In effect, he is describing what marathon runners call 'the wall' a mixture of fatigue and low blood sugar, in French, 'le loup'. This sudden depletion of strength and will can strike without warning and, in the Bordeaux-Paris, even as late as the Vallée de Chevreuse, within forty kilometres of the finish. That happened to Masson when he was in the lead in 1946. His mind caved in, he succumbed to the dismay which an attack of the wolf brings with it: he was never going to ride this awful race again…*if I'm caught, I quit, second place doesn't interest me.* Tears coursed down his dust-caked cheeks. The thought of another hill trashed any remaining shred of willpower. Then, by whatever curious alchemy, aided by a bidon of beer containing twenty sugar lumps, the attack of what mediaeval monks called 'accidie', utter despair and spiritual vacancy, dissipated. He revived and won.

Hills may hurt but they can also stir boldness, offering an ideal opportunity for a rider to take the rest by surprise and challenge their desire to respond. Morvan took his chance and, by Vendôme, 377km, he had built a lead of 2m 16s on Bouvet, 3m 15s on Cieleska and 5m 30s on the bunch, in which Robinson was riding. Privat tried to get away from the peloton but failed even as Darrigade and Bouvet were falling away, Bouvet paying dear for his expended effort, Darrigade seized up with cramp. They both abandoned.

The Eure-et-Loir département is the grain bowl of France, a vast tableland of cereal crops. On a tor rising out of this great plain the Druids first built a sanctuary, then the Romans, a temple dedicated to their Dea Mater (the Mother goddess). From the late tenth century it was the site of a church and, finally, the base of the cathedral of Chartres. There it stands, a mediaeval evocation of the terrestrial Civitas Dei. As the road from the south dips and rises, bends and swerves towards it across the open expanse of farmland, its towers and pinnacles tapering into the sky, it reinforces the original intention of its architect: to stun, to make a bold, unequivocal, material statement of the transcendent glory it represented and embodied. This was the house of God, his presence realised in stone on earth, the majesty of his being reflected in the blaze of light transferred through the cathedral's windows. Chartres says this all, on its hill: man built this magnificent edifice in praise of the supernal God and in recognition of his own miserable frailty. A paradox, if you like. An impressive silhouette against the sky in any mood, without question.

From Chartres, the road swings east across the billard table of the region between the Seine and the Loire rivers, known as the Beauce, towards Dourdan. Here Cieleska cut free and caught and dropped Morvan. That's the fix: you go when you're feeling good, yet with no certainty that the power you feel now is going to last. But if you feel it, you do it, no matter what. As Morvan felt the exuberant effort of his attack die under his wheels, Cieleska was taking his own chance too, but, confident in his strength, he gradually drew further and further ahead into the Vallée de Chevreuse and its tiresome hills. Their celebrity in the Derby of the road comes at a high ransom. An enthusiastic crowd had gathered, though, and cheered him on. Ah, welcome noise, that, a surge of adrenalin, victory, surely. Now Robinson decided it was his time. He began to pull away, accompanied by the Belgian Hoevenaers. Cieleska was riding with impressive strength but Morvan was snapping close behind and Robinson was coming on strongly further back. 'The elegant Brian' they called him, just as Barone had been called the most elegant rider in the '57 Tour de France. So very important, in France, to cut a debonair dash.

At Limours, 61km to go, Robinson was four minutes down. Hoevenaers now went clear.

The route led them past Versailles, up the famous Côte de Picardie – no more than a kilometre of mild gradient but, at 540km, a cruel last-minute grind before the final drop through Ville d'Avray towards the Seine over the Pont de Sèvres. From there it was a short pull onto the pink concrete piste of the Parc des Princes vélodrôme, where a huge crowd was waiting to see the race come in that first day of June. All afternoon they'd been entertained by various events on the famous track, including a Franco-Belgian omnium pairing, Van Steenbergen and Vlayen, against Anquetil and Rivière, riding together for the first time.

As they approached Versailles, Pino Cerami, born in Italy, but recently a naturalised Belgian, flew past 'like a meteor', a stock simile in French cyclo-journalism. He overtook first Robinson then Hoevenaers then Morvan to finish 1m 45s down on Cieleska, who crossed the line at 5.24 pm.

Robinson's fifth place (just over nine minutes' down) netted him 100,000 francs, £700, some compensation for the barren account of 1957. Shirley was in Paris with some girlfriends to meet him and they all went off for supper and, as Robinson put it, they 'did the Java that night'.

GF   That's a new expression to me.

BR   I got it from detective fiction, it's all I read.

GF   I read it, too, but I never saw it except as slang for coffee. Or tea.

BR   Over to you on that one.

GF   (So far, nothing.)

The Derny riders, known as *entraineurs* in French, literally 'leaders, carriers' as of a river in spate carrying logs or debris along with the current, were described, in the slang, as 'mother hens' tending their chicks, the riders. Good Derny men would observe their charges continually and adapt to shifts in the wind or irregularities in the road surface, moving to a more suitable position on their saddle, puffing out their coat sleeves and body to deliver a better wind shield, their feet planted on the pedals, sticking out to the side like the waddling feet of a duck, for even that additional block of draught. It was a particular skill and could save a following rider tiny discomforts and stresses to make the race that bit more manageable and conserve small increments of vital energy.

GF   Did you go through a bad patch during the race?

BR   Well, the distance didn't bother me, though I was glad it wasn't any further. The night ride was fine, no problems there, I enjoyed it. Occasionally your mind does ramble and you have to jerk it back. It's a bit like sunstroke, lack of blood in your head, I suppose, hallucinations, like.

May Day, 2010.

Robinson and his wife Audrey had just come home from a three-day get-together in the Peak District with his cycling friends of long date. There was no riding, just good company, jovial meals, lots of conversation and the pleasure of an enduring companionship fostered in the saddle and confirmed out of the saddle. He came in from the garden to answer the phone.

BR   I'm just putting polythene round the plum trees. We had a frost last night. It's bloody cold up here. What's it like down there?

GF   Bloody cold. What happened to spring?

BR   It must have sprung off somewhere else.

GF   How's the injury?

BR   Comes and goes. I did forty miles with the usual crew this morning and it was fine.

GF   What rides do you do with them?

BR   We have a choice of three. Up the Dales goes to Grassington through Skipton to Wharfedale, that's our favourite, but it's a hard ride and I haven't done that so much lately. Not with the bad leg. South Yorkshire goes through a lot of pit villages, no mines left, of course, so they've mostly turned into dormitory towns. And the Mast Run, which goes round the two radio masts, Holme Moss and Hemley Moor, for brunch or breakfast. I've had the bonk a couple of times lately, sorted out with a Mars bar – clears it in about ten minutes but it's very sweet, I couldn't eat one any other time.

GF   Could you tell me about your friendship with Elliott? You knew him well?

BR   I'm not sure that I knew him well. He was a deep character and I never got down to the real depth of him. I probably got to know him as well as anybody did, but I doubt that even his family knew him, really. There was always a bit of restraint, reserve, if you like, with him. He never volunteered much of himself. When we raced together it was mutual help, of course, never any question about that. We travelled together, shared a room, it was friendship, no more. Not that sort of friendship where you fit like a glove, though. You'd meet, you were friends, then go your own way. There was never any socialising.

Seamus 'Shay' Elliott, stocky and thickset in build, more like a Flemish flahute (roadman) than a lithe stage racer, had joined the amateur ACBB (Athletic Club de Boulogne-Billancourt) in south-west Paris in 1955. His performance on the Tourmalet in the 1954 Route de France, said one of the journals, had marked him out as someone 'soaked with class'. Since the ACBB was closed to non-French sportsman (until 1977) Elliott took out residency papers for France and, in 1956, signed for the professional Helyett-Félix Potin team, for whom Anquetil and Darrigade, amongst others, rode. (Helyett made bicycles, Félix Potin was a chain of grocery stores.) He lived in a cottage in Le Perreux-sur-Marne on one bank of the river which flows into the Seine just outside Paris to the east. Across the water, in the bankside premises used by a local branch of the Kayak Club de France, the Robinsons parked their caravan. One of the soigneurs knew the club president and he agreed to let Robinson occupy a plot of ground. (This was probably illegal, but the club wasn't much used during the week, the caravan was out of sight and the premises were enclosed behind a fence and a large gate, so it was secure.) Just along the river, in a house in Bry itself, Jean Bobet, and not far away, the *soigneur* who had looked after Robinson for some time, Richardot.

Their training runs took them eastwards, in a radius of around 100km, along the valley of the Marne into Champagne – Epernay, Reims, Laon, Soissons – or on a more southerly sweep into the upper valley of the Seine, Melun, Fontainebleau, Provins. A few of the Derny riders lived in Melun and, occasionally, they got free training rides behind the motors on the flat roads of the river basin.

Shirley was pregnant with their second child, their first was six months old. Her willingness to manage the isolation – she spoke little French – was a vital support to Robinson. From January to late September, their ménage, intermittent domestic interludes punctuating the relentless round of professional duty, (she took him to and from the northern races), thrived in no small part because of their shared devotion to the cause. In Bry, after the morning training run, they'd go for a walk, do some shopping in the local Félix Potin, rarely stop for a drink in the bar – no alcohol except at supper-time. They ate a lot of salad and, generally, lived on a diet which might be called mixed French and English. I asked him about this, in the light of what he'd already told me on the subject of food.

BR   The guys who didn't take to French food, it was mainly that they were put off by all sorts of fancy stuff in tins – goose livers, rillettes (tripes), andouillette (sausage made of chitterlings). We weren't recommended to eat charcuterie.

GF   Because it was fatty?

BR   More because it was manufactured, so you couldn't tell where it came from. As a culture, the French tended to eat fresh food, anyway, so we did. We ate horsemeat, for sure, and when I got boils that time, I was told to eat horse because it's a cleaner meat than beef, or so the French say. It was the same with cows – you weren't to eat the fillet, the tournedos, because it's not a part of the meat that works, it just lies there and does nothing, according to the French. You'd only to eat working muscle, there were fewer toxins in it. Especially in the north of France, not so much towards the south, there were separate horse and beef butchers, in the same establishment, maybe, but boucherie chevaline one side and boeuf on the other.

GF   Did you have any French friends outside cycling?

BR   No. It takes a long time to get to know the French, and certainly to be invited into their home. Darrigade has never been to Poulidor's place, for instance. Even still.

Elliott was not selected for the regional Ile-de-France team, as he had been in 1956, and, for the '58 Tour, joined an Internations conglomerate, alongside Robinson and two other Englishmen: Stan Brittain (third in the recent Peace Race and overall winner of the Tour of Sweden) and Ron Coe, one of Britain's top professionals, current road-race champion.

The obvious leader of this motley crew of riders of whose individual talent there was no doubt but whose experience in the Tour de France had been either tried well or not tried at all, was the Austrian, Adolf Christian, third overall the year before. However, when Robinson approached him to discuss the deal with him – if we (ie the three Brits and one Irish) rode for him would he split the takings – Christian wasn't interested. Robinson had no truck with that and Christian's refusal effectively split the team from the outset. The four cross-Channel men rode together, ate together and followed the tactics discussed by Robinson and Elliot who shared a room. The Tour record marks all four with an asterisk to indicate 'first-time rider'.

The press beefed up Gaul's potential for the win, 'especially if it's cold' – the Luxemburger hated the heat – and the pages of the Equipe were dotted with inset publicity boxes. It was noted that the French riders were wearing jerseys made of wool blended with rhovyl, a proprietary name for a mixture of synthetic materials which made the wool more absorbent and soft. A big splash told readers that the Citroën camionettes accompanying the race as team service vehicles (replacing the heavy lorries hitherto supplied by the organisation) were 'robust, speedy, practical, with their two doors, front and side...' Mornay were advertising their *Rock 'n Roll* perfume as 'the most dynamic in the world'. The race radio was inaugurated and, for the first time, the gentlemen of the press were provided with a press room and a *permanence*, a large hall commandeered in the stage finish towns – school, town hall, community centre – in which were installed telephones and radios both for the influx of information and the means of diffusing it. The race doctor could now dispose of a fully equipped medical back-up team, capable of dealing with most emergencies. The publicity caravan had been regimented and streamlined – cars selling papers, commercial vehicles, music blasted out by loudspeakers at ear-splitting volume – and set off an hour and a half ahead of the peloton.

The modern era had arrived.

The riders reported and were processed through the various stages of registration and checks: any rider whose bike was adjudged to be faulty or substandard was issued with a Tour bike, yellow frame (as had every rider ridden a yellow-painted organisation bike between 1930 and 1948). Violet Mercier bikes, the green Helyetts, Bobet's own tint of yellow...They drew the regular mound of equipment, from riding caps to rain capes and visited Dr Dumas for a medical examination.

Stage 1 Brussels – Ghent 184km

One of the Internations' Danes, Fritz Ravn, punctured and had a 99km chase on his own to the finish and, although Elliott performed brilliantly to contain the speed of the main bunch, Ravn missed the time limit and was out. It was the first incontrovertible evidence, if any were needed, that the Internations were a team in name only. The *Equipe* columnist Bilan du Jour (Digest) said that what the *directeur*, Max Bulla, lacked was a valid leader. 'I'm talking about Brian Robinson, who rode with Gaul, Brankaert as well as Adriaenssens. All the other members of the team finished with the peloton, some minutes down.'

Stage 6 Caen – Saint-Brieuc 223km

Elliott was normally a placid individual. On this day he gave vent to a real torrent of Celtic fury. On the run-in to the Breton market town, the Irishman was well-placed against two Belgian riders, Van Geneugden and Desmet, but they switched him, first into the outside bend then, as he tried to get past down the barrier, they pushed across to stop him. So enraged was Elliott that he put these allegations direct to a journalist and said: 'You can write that, I'll sign it.' He added that someone had pulled his jersey on the sprint into Dunkerque on Stage 2. 'But I'm a decent feller, if I was a no-good, I'd have swept the track the same way the Belgians did to me today and Van Geneugden would be in hospital.'

His fury was intensified by the insouciance of his nominal leader Christian, for whom he had worked hard all day to keep him up with the leaders in a strong break. Not that he wanted thanks or even pay-back – what he'd done was 'normal'. He did, however, expect some kind of response, a certain sympathy in the man's reaction. Instead? Austere indifference or else gloomy silence. Elliott had been coaching the Austrian along, telling him the time gaps, urging him to get stuck in – 'We need to roll, here, we've got a fifteen minutes' advance' – to which the po-faced Teuton replied: 'Five minutes or fifteen, what's the difference?'

The press picked up on the fact that the Internations riders did not only not speak the same language *per se*, but neither did they share any fluency in the common language of bike-racing. The Danes, especially, were, it was clear, riding to a separate personal agenda. When Elliott and Christian attacked – and Elliott, like Robinson, was looking for stage wins – the first to react was one of their own team, the Dane Andresen, who understood neither French nor English. Robinson immediately rode him down and shook a fist in his face. 'It was the only way I could get the idea across'...such as *Don't attack, you moron, they're in our team.*

Meanwhile, at the back of the race, the more experienced Barbosa refused to wait for his fellow Portugese in the team, the new boy, Batista, because 'it's not my role'.

Elliott, relayed by Robinson earlier in the race, had moved from 47th to 23rd overall: it was a debt he soon repaid in full.

L'Equipe 3 July, lead story:
'Pour la première fois, un anglais a gagné une étape du Tour mais...Brian Robinson a failli d'être victime de son "fair play".' For the first time an Englishman has won a Tour stage but...Brian Robinson was nearly a victim of his fair play, which, because the French think it out of place in professional sport, as peculiar as other English eccentricities – tea-time, the weekend, gentleman – they always leave in its English spelling.

The 170km from Saint-Brieuc to Brest followed narrow, twisting roads over the sharply undulating Breton countryside, constantly buffeted by wind and exposed to fine drizzle. The individual time-trial loomed and, even though the big hitters of the peloton were hoping for a more tranquil day, the conditions militated against it and they were all, once more, strung out, battling with the elements and the terrain if not each other. A number of breaks went early, but when the sporadic agitation died down and the bunch regrouped after 50km, Robinson attacked to be joined by the French regional, Dotto, a short while later, and then by the Italian, Padovan.

Robinson's account was written up in detail. They'd ridden through teeming rain towards the finish in Brest 'soaked to the bone':

> Early in our escape, Dotto was going really hard – it hurt my legs to follow him, but he was undoubtedly pushing too big a gear. Bit by bit he slowed down and then he didn't give me any trouble. I really took over the break. I attacked 30km from home. I wanted to see what shape my companions were in. Perhaps I should have pushed on. But, I truly believed that I was going to win the sprint, particularly because there was a hill to come and I knew the Italian weakened every time the road went up. Even though he hadn't done much work in the break, he looked tired. [Italian riders had a well deserved reputation as wheel-suckers.] Had I been completely new to Brittany and relied on the profile in the Tour magazine, where it seemed that the finish had a long drop into the town, I should have thought my chances of beating Padovan considerably smaller. But from last year's Tour de l'Ouest, I knew this drop was followed

by a considerable rise for the final run-in and that would be to my advantage.

After snaking round the hairpin, I switched from 52x14 to the 16 sprocket. Padovan came past me about 400m out. I took his wheel immediately. The pace he was going at made him a sitting duck – a team-mate couldn't have led me out better. He went over to the left side of the road, hard against the spectators. This was a good move on his part because the wind was coming three-quarters from the right, so I'd be forced into the wind when I came back at him. When I saw 200m to go, I dropped my head and came alongside him. Just as I was about to go past, he lunged across into me and squeezed me onto the right side of the road. I let him get clear and launched another attack on the left. He zigzagged across and baulked me again. So, then, across the line, what was I supposed to do? I certainly didn't shake hands with him. Max Bulla said I should make an official protest but I wasn't thinking about that. I only made the protest on his insistence, plus that of a number of journalist friends. Padovan's Italian team manager, Alfredo Binda, defended him, of course, which was a bit droll – the night before, Binda had been clamouring about tightening up on infringements in sprints.

Even though Padovan had been named the winner, on the line there was a mass of people congratulating Robinson and it seemed that, because of his reluctance to protest, he was, indeed, going to be a victim of his very British sense of fair play. Even so, wrote the journalist, 'decency has its limits, in the Tour de France as elsewhere'.

When Robinson went up to room number 302 in the Hotel Vauban, which he was sharing with the Irishman, to get his massage, there was champagne on ice, ordered by Elliott – he'd met Bulla, heard the news and come back, his face beaming. Enter Bulla: 'It's done, the jury of commissaires has decided to relegate Padovan.' The French reporter, naturally, played up Robinson's long-suffering, immobile, very *British* temperament.

His casual remark, at a press conference – 'I ought not to have needed the jury to beat Padovan' – masked a very profound delight and, to steal a pun, the eyes had it – gleaming with pleasure. He also said, in characteristic understatement: 'I shall ride tomorrow.' That meant he intended to put some effort into the 46km time-trial on the Chateaulin circuit to limit his losses on overall standing. This left open the possibility of launching another attack before Dax and the first Pyrenean stages. He also said that he was 'proud of being the first rider from across the Channel to win a stage of the Tour but I really should have been the second. The journalists all tell me that Shay Elliott was fouled just as badly yesterday to finish second in Saint-Brieuc, but the judges wouldn't listen to his protest.' The boos of the crowd when

Graczyk (in green), Voorting (in yellow) and Padovan with his bouquet as stage winner had made their lap of honour was patent enough sign that it didn't take a jury or Robinson to tell the real story.

As for Padovan, he was furious, lamenting his ill fortune – second to Hassenforder in Perpignan the year before, second in Bordeaux and then in Paris, to Darrigade, and now second again. 'It's too much,' he cried, imploring all the gods in creation to come to his deserved aid. Then he moaned that he went too soon. 'Think of it, three hundred metres. I was sure I was stronger than Robinson. Especially at that moment. The Giro was good for me and I have better form now than I had in Italy.' In which case, rejoined the journalist who listened to him, *why didn't you show it?*

Invited to give their opinion, Jean Bobet (now a journalist) suggested that the Italian sprinter had made a mistake in going too early, that Robinson read the attack perfectly but had been badly switched and was the rightful victor; Valentin Huot (French regional) agreed – the road had been wide enough for a fair sprint and Robinson ought to have held up his hand in protest the moment that Padovan blocked him; Albert Bouvet (French regional), said 'you'd have to be blind not to have seen the misconduct...the better man won.'

Robinson assessed the significance. 'My first reaction was that I needed that win. The stage was worth about £230, but I got the contracts afterwards – 20 at £40 each...I'm set for another year, I thought.' His aim was always to finish each season with the price of a saloon car, around £1,000, in the bank.

Wadley remarked on the chaotic state of the room Robinson and Elliott shared. After the evening meal it was still heaped with clothes, gloves, towels, shoes, bidons, spare tyres, pumps, musettes, in a general mishmash which some French riders referred to as *une assiette anglaise*...an English plateful, alluding to the English habit of heaping vegetables on a plate with the meat, where the French tend to serve them separately. However, before bed, both riders had packed the aluminium Tour suitcase marked with their name and race number and their kit for the morning was neatly laid out on and under a chair. French style, everything in order.

The win occasioned more general reflexions on Robinson as a man and a rider, especially his astonishing ability to adapt. The perception, misguided and incorrigibly insular, held by a large proportion of racing cyclists in Britain, was that their top men – what the French called 'over-Channel riders' – were the equal of top riders on the continent and that victory in the Tour of Britain qualified a man to mix it with them. From this shaky tenet, they concluded that it wouldn't be long before the home race was as big an event as the Tour de France, as if the gulf between the two were no more than a line between two squares on a hopscotch grid. This may seem laughable now but, in some quarters, a very British sense of superiority had, somehow, survived and endured through a long and self-imposed exile from the realities of road-racing, the staple of the continental scene. The intrinsic toughness of the Tour de France, since its beginnings, largely rooted in its arcane and draconian regulations, the country's multifarious terrain, the intense pressure of public interest, the fact that the Tour generally drew the very best riders from across Europe (where both the Giro and, especially the Vuelta, remained more identifiably national tours dominated by home riders) made any comparison with the fledgling Tour of Britain absurd. Together with the additional problems faced by men without affiliation of either national or regional teams, the transition from Pennines to Pyrenees became rather more arduous than simply drumming up the fare for the cross-Channel ferry, as the blazers of the British cycling authority saw it.

Living in France, speaking the language competently enough not to be duped by sharp-nosed agents or promoters, and to know what terms were being offered in a contract as well as the more routine business of not only feeling at home in the peloton but able to assert your position in it, all this took considerable flexibility. Even the diet can deter. From the land of lard to olive oil and green salad, vinaigrette [in my childhood home, lettuce was served with a dressing of Sarsons malt vinegar mixed with granulated sugar], queer bread you couldn't make toast of, a bewildering array of stinky, sloppy or hard cheeses, undercooked meat, poached fish without batter, no decent brew of tea, coffee made with chicory, raw vegetables (choucroute), hard bits of fatty meat called sausage, which isn't a proper sausage by any stretch of the imagination, not so that you could fry it, no eggs and bacon and baked beans, in fact no eggs at all, nothing close to a hearty roast with gravy*, not to mention what they did with most of an animal's inedible inside bits and a good few of the inedible outside bits and expected you to eat them. A pint of good ale? Forget it. And the chocolate tasted like syrup...

None of this culinary difference bothered Robinson, although whenever he and Shirley arrived back in Yorkshire at the end of the season, they did stop at a chippie for that familiar taste of home. Many a Brit has languished on the 'continong', desperately homesick, everything forrin, hankering for home food, fish 'n chips, bangers and mash, liver and bacon, good old Yorkshire pud, none of your fancy French muck. Such vexatious resentments, for that's what they are, breed retrusive, dog-in-the-manger attitudes, a down-in-the-mouth comportment to add to the proverbial stiff upper lip which makes the French laugh. In their view, the result of constipation and an inefficient liver.

---

* To the French, gravy was sauce and the Italian admiral Francesco Caraccioli once said 'The English have sixty religious sects and only one sauce' although this is not thought to have influenced Horatio Nelson in his decision to have him hanged at the yardarm after the uprising in Naples, 1799.

It's not enough, either, merely to speak the language, you must learn to do the language, as well, to take it on, to feel it. This requires a certain charm, a liking for the host nation which does not allow for insincerity or, that most odious of traits to the French, hypocrisy. Granted, the French can seem, and be, very proprietorial about what they consider to be exclusively their own: cheese... wine ... being right...That does not preclude them from evincing a certain self-deprecation – in a style perhaps not immediately obvious as funny to the sarcastic Brit – and valuing *politesse* as an essential to social intercourse.

'Robinson is a sage' said *L'Equipe*. The word 'sage' covers a range of meanings, wise, prudent, sober-minded, discreet in behaviour, sensible. 'Brian, who has become the most Parisian of all the British and deploys the language of our suburbs, is riding his fourth Tour de France. In learning French he has also learnt to race in the French manner. And the best of it is that his great friend, Elliott, thinks in exactly the same way.' (Throughout the Tour, in the hotel as well as on the road, the two men spoke French together because, as one of them said, it was too much bother to think of the English. By contrast, Brittain and Coe could muster no more than a dozen words of French.) The inference we draw is that the more experienced men had adapted as bike racers, they wished to be seen as men on a par with their companions in the peloton, from whatever country. They were racing in France and wished to blend in, not to be marked out as that distinct oddity, coureurs anglais, a species of humankind undiscovered before Robinson and Hoar rode into Paris in 1955.

It has been claimed that the men who went to France from Britain had to cope with a more debilitating fear of failure than novice French professionals because they faced a longer journey back to base, whereas the locals could easily slink home. This is to miss the point. Not cutting it as a professional strikes to a rider's heart whether he is a bus ride away from where he started or a long-haul flight. All those men who did establish themselves and make a career on the continent did so through intrinsic ability, mental resilience and a willingness to adapt to what must have seemed, at the outset, the very contrary conditions of racing and living. Robinson was never dogged by fear of failure because he worked on a simple logic: the men he was racing against in France might have a different background, upbringing and nurture, but they were only men, like him, bike riders. What they had done to get to the peloton mattered not. What mattered is what they had to learn to do once they were in the peloton, just as he had. End of story.

For his riding in the break which led to his victory, Robinson received the prize sponsored by the manufacturer of a fizzy drink called Pschitt, mimicking the sound of the effervescent pop as the cap flipped off the neck of the bottle. (This may have been prompted by the Schweppes advertising slogan 'Schhhh...you know who.' If so, it was a disastrous miscalculation to any English ear.) Thus Robinson was declared 'The most Pschitt rider of the stage'. For this he won 100,000 francs to add to the 200,000 francs he took for the stage victory.

That same morning, the other members of the Internations team (who, so far, hadn't won a cent) suggested that Robinson and Elliott should share their winnings with the rest of the men. Given that Robinson had almost had to punch one of them to stop him from attacking Elliott, this was a bit rich. Robinson, Elliott and Brittain agreed to work together from there on. (Sadly, Ron Coe had just retired.)

The effort seems not to have cost him dear: he delivered the best time of the Internations in the time-trial won, unexpectedly, by the low-gear twiddler Gaul, who beat the discipline's ace, Anquetil, who rode big gears with metronomic fluency, by seven seconds.

Stage 14 Pau –Bagnères-de-Luchon 129km

In an article headed L'Anglais sans peine, (English without tears), an *Equipe* journalist wrote: 'I will always remember, as one of the most defining moments of the 1958 Tour, of human achievement, this white jersey circled with two bands of black rising up behind Gaul on the summit of the Peyresourde: Brian Robinson. We knew the English were good at climbing – they conquered Everest – but we've never seen an Englishman riding at the side of a climber with wings, the most famous of them all, on a first category col, in the Tour de France.'

No matter that the two men who conquered Everest in 1953 came, one from New Zealand, the other from Nepal, Robinson had, this day, scrapped with two of the sport's best ever climbers, Bahamontes and Gaul, up to and over the final climb of the day, the Peyresourde. He showed the raw energy (the journo wrote) of an island race which does not buckle, an admirable quality, and 'if Brian slipped back for a while it was to come back more strongly'. (As Napoleon Bonaparte said, ruefully: 'The English don't know when they're beaten.')

The report went on to compare him to Robinson Crusoe, stranded on an unknown shore, fending for himself, and, with that self-reliance bred of natural stolidity and inner belief, digging deep into his own natural resource.* Perhaps, the writer speculates, just as Crusoe educated Man Friday, Brian Robinson would teach the British about road-racing 'which, at the moment, some see as a strip-tease show. He may teach them the familiar aspects of our progressive civilisation: the mechanics of the chainwheel, the art of repairing

---

* The town of Plessis-Robinson, six kilometres outside Paris to the south, takes its name from Defoe's book. A restaurateur of what was then Plessis-Piquet, inspired by the tale of Crusoe, opened a *guingette* (café-bar with dancing) called *Au Grand Robinson* and, in 1909, the town was renamed because of its popularity.

a puncture, the hunt for bottles of beer…Consider the British alpinists who first climbed the mountains. These new Britons have exchanged the ice pick for a pump and crampons for forty-five teeth.'

Very French: slightly affected humour, play on words, starchy allusions, bags of affection and, beneath the apparent light mockery, a most genuine esteem for a man who was cleaving to them and their way of life and doing things. And, in the context of what, at the time, was not an entirely cordial entente, the British application to join the European Economic Community, precursor to the EU, in 1961, was vetoed by the French President Charles de Gaulle, who thought that the UK was too tied to the USA to be of any benefit to Europe. It must be said that the application was not backed either by a unified Whitehall or Westminster – only the Liberals were unanimous on the subject – nor by a majority of the trade union membership or the public.

An *Equipe* reporter based in London, Maurice Simon, commenting on the notion being touted that Robinson has proved to the English that they can play a role in international cycling, notes that people ask him, 'Who is this Brian Robinson?' his name having appeared, miraculously, on the sports pages of a press which rarely looked beyond football, cricket, rugby, swimming and horse-racing. (The *Daily Herald* had devoted a quarter of a page to Robinson's exploits.) 'Where is he placed? Can he win the Tour de France?' To these questions, Simon replied: 'This he is the ex-maker of coffins from Yorkshire.' The director of the Union of Bike Manufacturers, a Mr Palin, boasted that Robinson's performances had produced 'an enormous interest in cycling'.

Before the start of the stage, the celebrated boulevardier Charles Trenet (his most famous song probably *La Mer*) turned up to flash his smile, take Gaul's bike for a quick spin and then climb into a black Citroën DS to follow the race.

Bahamontes was in cracking form. The Spanish fans were out in huge numbers to see the Eagle of Toledo ride the Pyrenean cols and he repaid their loyalty with a crushing display of power: he led the way over three days' of mountains, Aubisque…Aspin and Peyresourde… Ares and Portet d'Aspet. Gaul, hampered by a bout of mild sickness earlier in the race, stayed with a small bunch of elite riders, including Anquetil, Bobet, Geminiani and, remarkably, Robinson. He stayed with them over every Pyrenean pass and, when Gaul accelerated on the Aspin (Stage 15) only Robinson and Geminiani could go with him. As they approached the col, Robinson prudently dropped back to rejoin Bobet and company, knowing that he could make up any deficit on the descent into the valley. From the foot of the Aspin to the Peyresourde and on over the final climb, still in the small bunch of big men, Robinson launched onto what is one of the fastest downhills in the Pyrenees. After the first four kilometres or so of hairpins, the road straightens much of the way into Bagnères-de-Luchon and the ride is a whistle-in-the-ears breeze. The lead followers all came in together.

The race then swept north out of the mountains into Toulouse where both Elliott and Robinson spent most of the night on the loo, severe stomach upset occasioned by over-exposure to sun, extreme physical stress, perhaps a slight chill from the descents – the Aubisque was thick with mist – and, maybe, some tainted food or water. It was (is) the sort of minor ailment which bike riders suffer intermittently. Battered by the extreme demands of stage-racing, their immune system becomes fragile and vulnerable to any hint of infection. However, the ministrations of Dr Dumas and their *soigneur* Richardot restored them both on the eve of a beast of a ride.

Stage 18 Mont Ventoux, time-trial 21.5km

Robinson never extended himself at full stretch in time-trials in the early or middle part of a stage race. A gain of two minutes against the clock could expend so much energy that it might cost much greater losses the following day. On Ventoux, however, he lost even more time than a sensibly contained ride ought to have done because, for reasons unexplained, his mechanic fitted a freewheel block with no cog between the 14 and 23 sprockets. He finished in 1h 9m 51s, over seven minutes' down on the winner, Gaul. Brittain clocked 1h 15m 36s, Elliott 1h 20m 45s.

Stage 19 Carpentras – Gap 178km

Across the lavender fields and olive groves of the Drôme, in scorching heat, over a succession of cols: the Perty, 1302m, to the north of Ventoux, out of the valley of the Ouvèze, the Foreyssasse, 1040m, both cols high and long enough to be stinkers in this approach to the High Alps, capped with a final torment over the Sentinelle, 980m, before the drop into Gap.

As the men with whom he had crossed the Pyrenees went off up the road in a series of attacks ignited by Geminiani (now in yellow) and the French national team to put time into Gaul, Robinson stayed put. 'I was not taken by surprise,' he said. 'I had half a dozen chances to go but I just couldn't do anything about it.' The fact is, he was severely weakened and dehydrated by diarrhoea and running out of power. He punctured three kilometres out of Gap and Brittain remained with him while he changed the tyre. 'I hadn't enough strength even to give him a turn at the front and he took me all the way to the finish. Stan's been a great help all day.' His ambition to finish in the top ten was over. He had suffered what the French press called *un knock-down*. Down but not out.

It was on the next stage, towards Briançon, that his Tour ended. The stomach upset had deteriorated into a violent dysentery. Stomach pains, diarrhoea, extreme dehydration, exhaustion. Le plus Schitt de l'Etape took on a bitter irony. He spent a wretched night and consulted Dr Dumas in the morning. It was quite plain that he couldn't continue but the will to go on, as ever, usurped the protests of both mind and body. Abandoning was so utterly miserable and demoralising, so utterly conclusive an act, and Robinson, as noted by Maitland among others, had that rare capacity in the best athletes to drive himself, physically, into a state of complete, if temporary, paralysis, unable either to move or speak. He got on the bike at the start line, struggled up the long valley of the Ubaye into Barcelonnette, but, on the slopes of the col de Vars, some fifteen kilometres on, he faltered at last, and stopped. Next morning, in the town which echoed his name, he watched his two companions Brittain and Elliott head off in a downpour. The rain persisted all day, towards Aix-les-Bains over a cruel obstacle course of big summits, Lautaret, Luitel-Chamrousse, Porte, Cucheron and Granier.

Robinson returned to the caravan in Bry-sur-Marne. He was in no condition to ride for another two weeks, at least, once more a season pivoting on the big race had stuttered to a disappointing halt. By the working agreements of the day, there was, of course, no recompense for illness or injury.

Gaul, at last, took the Tour. Geminiani lost yellow, Anquetil cracked on the stage into Aix-les-Bains and Elliott came in 'cold, muddy, with torn jersey and shorts, grazed arms and legs' in Wadley's words. Two punctures, a crash in mist on the Luitel, a broken free wheel but he made it. Brittain, at 54 minutes on Gaul, was outside the time limit but, in view of the awful weather, he was allowed to start next day. Both outsiders made it to Paris. Not so Anquetil, who abandoned on the eve of the individual time-trial with a lung infection. Of that awful day on the Col de Porte in the Alps he described his own private misery, a description which carries a more general application to what those riders went through:

> From the first hairpins, I thought I'd lost my mind. I was at less than 60%. I wish I knew why. It was as if my lungs were stuffed with cotton wool. I was suffocating. When I stood on the pedals I must have looked like a fish chucked on the grass of a riverbank. [He was a passionate angler.] The final jolts before…before what? What was happening? I felt cold to the bone. My muscles were inert. They were as stiff as the branches of the pines shaking in the wind. I kept tugging at the levers to change the gears. Bigger or smaller, the same result: no power. When Gem went past, I was incapable of taking his wheel. It was finished, I'd lost the Tour, certain. Louison Bobet came up alongside: 'Jacques, I'll wait for you.' I told him, 'No Louis, there's no point.'

The twelve men of the Internations team shared a meagre final pot of 965,000 francs, (£772), secured for them by the two lone finishers.

A little more than a week after the Tour arrived in Paris, Pierre Chany wrote what must be for a contemporary audience, fifty years later, a striking piece in *L'Equipe* entitled LE DOPING GAGNE DU TERRAIN...Doping gains ground. Chany, born in 1922, was arrested and imprisoned by the Vichy authorities in 1940. He escaped – on his birthday – from a train deporting him to forced labour in Germany. He joined first a branch of the Resistance, the Franc-Tireurs et Partisans (a partisan group of sharpshooters and snipers) then an Algerian regiment. He was wounded three times and awarded the *Croix de Guerre*. In 1953, the same year that the motorcycle squadron of the *Garde Républicaine* (charged, amongst other official duties, with escorting the President) took over the marshalling of the Tour de France, Chany became chief writer on cycling at *L'Equipe*. He covered forty-nine Tours and Anquetil said, in estimating his journalism: 'Don't ask me to tell you what happened during the race. There's someone more competent than I am to do that... Even I will wait until tomorrow's article by Pierre Chany in *L'Equipe* to find what I did, why and how I did it. What gives him authority is that he is competent, that he knows me and understands me. His version will be better than mine and it will become mine.'

On 29 July, Chany wrote, of the seventy-eight men who finished what many described as the hardest post-war Tour yet, that after only a few days' rest, they embarked on the classic (read 'punishing') round of criteriums. The pressure during the Tour itself, with so many prizes in contention – overall, mountains, points, combativity, team, stage – at ever-increasing speeds, three individual time-trials and no rest days [sic], compensated by late starts. Add to that, the intense heat of the Dog Days, the wretched wet and cold of the Alps, and it was no mystery that they arrived in a state of exhaustion. However, this was not the fault of the Tour alone, but an accumulation from a long season too overloaded with racing. In fact, most riders were on the road, in competition, from the beginning of February until October. (Robinson actually finished his season towards the middle of September. Paris-Tours, in which he did not always ride, marked the end for him. By that stage he was mentally empty, even if he was still in good enough shape physically.) 'Thus,' wrote Chany 'doping becomes the order of the day. "We load up and off we go." But, those who use drugs risk ruining their health irremediably.' Chany then cites René Vietto* who says he'd known young riders who'd died through excessive drug abuse. 'They are,' he said, mad to

---

* Vietto finished second in 1939, fifth in 1934 and 1947 and eighth in 1935. He wore the yellow jersey for fifteen stages during the 1938 Tour and for fourteen stages during the '47 race and was, thus, race leader for more days than anyone who never won the Tour de France overall.

swallow this stuff. There was,' wrote Chany, 'a battle to win.' He called on Dr Dumas, the *soigneurs*, the race controllers, all those of competence who had a conscience, to contribute to the struggle against doping, at the same time acknowledging that they lacked the means to apply more direct action. 'This requires a psychological war, backed by the federations, cycle clubs, *directeurs sportifs*, in fact by all those who do not want to shut their eyes and feign ignorance.' And, in an eerie pre-echo of what is being said today, Chany put aside the moral aspect and declared, firmly, 'this is a practical issue'.

In an extended interview for *Cycling* magazine in November 1958, Robinson said that whereas in the first Tour de France he rode, there were quite a few promenade stages, the last two years 'there had been anything but:'

> Every stage is like a classic one-day. That's why it's impossible to do well in the classics *and* the Tour. It's also why the Tour is tougher now than in, say, Coppi's time when one powerful team, led by a man of his quality, could control the race most of the way. Now the system is simply for everyone to keep battering until something gives way, so the tempo of the battle never ceases. This is why, to the public's surprise, the big boys appear to slip up in missing a break, they can't really help it. Some breaks in a race of this tempo must go without them. They try to let go the ones that don't appear to be dangerous. Sometimes their judgement is wrong. It's a gamble. If I've missed a break, I've missed it. The worst thing is still to get a puncture in the middle of a real battle. Positioning, of course, has a big effect on where you finish. The first year in the Tour, I was hanging on the back for three weeks. Now I know you've just got to be in the first thirty, otherwise little gaps keep opening up and you have to keep closing them. When the elastic eventually breaks, you're all used up through defensive riding. It's essential to place yourself very carefully, to pick the men to be watched and stay near them at all costs. For example, when Anquetil and Bobet were a minute up, it was obvious that Gaul and Brankart had to chase, so the one thing to do was quickly glue oneself to them. For me, this year, it was almost too easy. I was going so well...despite the fact that it was my toughest Tour yet, it was my most comfortable. I was at my absolute peak, as ripe as possible, unfortunately, for the effects of the daily changes from extreme cold to boiling heat. Once the germ arrived, I was too rich a territory for it to let go.'

After the Isle of Man meeting in 1959, at Elliott's instigation, Robinson, together with Anquetil, Coppi and Darrigade, crossed over to Ireland to ride as invited stars at the inauguration of a track in Dublin. The party stayed at the farm run by Elliott's parents – clay pigeon shooting in the afternoon and a long siesta. 'Which means that I've slept in the same room as Coppi,' Robinson told me.

GF   What was he like?

BR   He was a lovely guy, very nice manner, a gentle soul. He was completely the opposite of what he must have been like on the bike. I couldn't imagine him so aggressive and ruthless when he was racing and then so calm and cool and relaxed off the bike. Mind you, he was at the end of his career.

On the eve of the races, a grenade exploded on the velodrome, presumed to be the work of Irish National Cycling Association.*

---

* The long-established NCA refused to acknowledge the partition of Ireland, and was thus not recognised by the Union Cycliste International. It was known to have links with the Irish Republican Army (IRA).

1949: National Hill Climb Championships: Brian Robinson(left),Geoff Clarke, Trevor Smith, Brian Haskell, Tom Oldfield, Granville Hayley, Des Robinson (leaning on the family firm's cart – 'Joinery & Funeral Director' on the tailboard). (i)

National Hill Climb Championship 1950 (ii)

Peter Proctor, Bernard Pussey, Brian Robinson, Les Willmott (iii)

*First Tour de France,
with Hercules, 1955* (iv)

Tour de France, 1955, just before the start of Stage 4, at Namur, Belgium.
Brian Robinson is immediately behind the Commissaire's car. (v)

with Fred Krebs at the end of a stage (vi)

Tour de France, 1956, stage one – Reims–Liège, alongside André Darrigade, who won the stage. Robinson was third. (vii)

Parc des Princes at the finish of the 1956 Tour. Robinson finished 14th overall. (viii)

Leading the break, Milan–San Remo, 1957 (ix)

Ghent–Wevelghem, 1957, with Shay Elliott (x)

Tour de France, 1958, first stage win: stage 7, Saint-Brieuc–Brest. The Italian, Arrigo Padovan was relegated by the race jury for irregular riding in the final sprint. (xi)

In good company – the first ramp of the Col de Soulor, Tour de France, 1958, with all the favourites at the front: (l to r) Plankaert, Anquetil, Bauvin, Adriaenssens, Robinson, David (Geminiani behind), Nencini, Gaul, Anglade, Mahé. (xii)

"Come on, keep going, stick to it, we'll make it." For hours Elliott kept Robinson going during stage 14 of the 1959 Tour: Aurillac–Clermont-Ferrand. Elliott was eliminated for finishing outside the time limit; Robinson remained in the race through an ancient Tour regulation that stated that men currently in the top ten overall could not be eliminated for a late stage finish. (xiii)

Six days later, a rejuvenated Robinson won the 20th stage, from Annecy to Chalon-sur-Saône, with a margin of 20 minutes. (xiv)

CHALON : 20' D'AVANCE POUR L'ANGLAIS BRIAN ROBINSON

CETTE vingtième étape Annecy-Chalon-sur-Saône se court sur le mode mineur. Elle est la synthèse de ce que fut ce 46° Tour de France : ambiance d'indifférence, absence totale de combativité de la part de ceux dont on attendait des humeurs de bataille, victoire d'un coureur « sans-grade » favorisée par la passivité quasi générale d'un peloton engourdi. Dès le départ, on se rend compte que ce ne sera pas une journée d'actions éclatantes. Le peloton aborde groupé le col d'Echallon, dernier col comptant pour le Trophée St-Raphaël Quinquina (Grand Prix de la Montagne). Une tentative de Saint — rival direct de Gaul pour le Trophée — est « contrée » par ce dernier et c'est Dotto, ripostant à une attaque de Robinson, qui passe en tête, précédant l'Anglais de 10'' et le peloton de 35''. Dans la descente du col, Brian Robinson s'enfuit et lâche Dotto, qui sera absorbé par le peloton. Dès lors, on assiste à l'aimable spectacle d'un coureur prenant minute sur minute au peloton qui se chauffe au soleil, tel un lézard paresseux. A l'arrivée, Brian Robinson compte 20' 6'' d'avance sur le peloton qui se présente groupé à Chalon. Seul Robic — qui compte vingt minutes de retard et qui sera éliminé — et le Polonais Wierucki (qui, malade, a abandonné) sont absents. Bahamontes garde évidemment son maillot jaune.

LES ARRIVEES A CHALON-SUR-SAONE

1. Brian ROBINSON (Inter), du groupe Rapha-Geminiani, les 202 km. en 5 h. 52' 21'' (avec bonification) ; 5 h. 51' 21''), moyenne horaire : 34 km. 397 ; 2. Fadevan, à 20' 6'' (avec bonification : 6 h. 11' 57'') ; 3. Darrigade ; 4. Cazala ; 5. Van Geneugden ; 6. Le Buhotel ; 7. Van Aerde ; 8. Anquetil ; 9. Buysse ; 10. Damen ; 11. Gismondi ; 12. Sabbadini ; 13. Baffi ; 14. De Bruyne ; 15. Picot ; 16. Saint ; 17. Traxel ; 18. Huot ; 19. Groussard ; 20. Foleschi ; 21. Bruni ; 22. Graczyk ; 23. Contori ; 24. Hoorelbeke ; 25. Thomin ; 26. Vermeulin ; 27. Fabbri ; 28. Anglade ; 29. Janssens ; 30. Bleneau ; 31. Rivière ; 32. Mahé ; 33. Friedrich ; 34. Kersten ; 35. Planckaert ; 36. Sutton ; 37. Brankart ; 38. Dalberghe ; 39. Bergaud ; 40. Bono ; 41. Forestier ; 42. Bisilliat ; 43. Rohrbach ; 44. Pauwels ; 45. Bolzan ; etc.

LE CLASSEMENT GENERAL

1. BAHAMONTES (E), 112 h. 4' 58'' ; 2. Anglade, à 5' 40'' ; 3. Mahé, à 8' 56'' ; 4. Anquetil, à 10' 14'' ; 5. Baldini, à 11' 16'' ; 6. Hoevenaers, à 11' 28'' ; 7. Adriaenssens, à 11' 44'' ; 8. Rivière, à 12' 34'' ; 9. Pauwels, à 20' 2'' ; 10. Saint, à 20' 19'' ; 11. Gaul, à 21' 26'' ; 12. Brankart, à 22' 58'' ; 13. Bergaud, à 34' 33'' ; 14. Mananneque, à 55' 28'' ; 15. Dotto, à 59' 20'' ; 16. Darrigade, à 59' 40'' ; 17. Robinson, à 1 h. 2' 57'' ; 18. Friedrich, à 1 h. 3' 47'' ; 19. Planckaert, à 1 h. 5' 11'' ; 20. Vermeulin, à 1 h. 10' 7'' ; 21. Foleschi, à 1 h. 14' 40'' ; 22. Van Aerde, à 1 h. 16' 48'' ; 23. Desmet, à 1 h. 19' 17'' ; 24. Graf, à 1 h. 19' 30'' ; 25. Thomin, à 3 h. 26' 59'' ; 26. Quaheille, à 1 h. 34' 16'' ; 27. Janssens, à 1 h. 34' 52'' ; 28. Gismondi, à 1 h. 39' 5'' ; 29. Damen, à 1 h. 10'' ; 30. Hoorelbeke, à 1 h. 39' 28'' ; etc.

TOUR DE FRANCE 1959 ETAPE ANNECY CHALON-S-SAONE

ROBINSON ET SUTTON, LES DEUX ANGLAIS, SE PREPARENT A LA DOUCHE

QUELQUE PART ENTRE ANNECY ET CHALON, ROBINSON, SOLITAIRE, FONCE VERS SA VICTOIRE

55

How the French press saw it (xv)

Riding in the Herne Hill 'Coppi meeting', 1958. Nino Defillipis in the background (xvi)

Leading Dotto and Anquetil on the Col de l'Iseran, 1959 (xvii)

World Championship road race, 1960   (xviii)

A final Tour – with Shay Elliott and Ken Laidlaw   (xix)

Robinson (with André Foucher) takes a drink on the Col du Granier (xx)

*'In memory of our youth' – a card
from Nicolas Barone with whom
Robinson rode for two years in the
Saint Raphaël-Geminiani team* (xxi)

at home, in what passes for retirement… (xxii)

… and with Graeme Fife, overlooking the Yorkshire moors (xxiii)

9: GOING FOR BROKE

'The slow, loud throbbing of an engine...all along the route, spectators look up rhythmically, a wave of raised heads towards the noisy insect looking down at them from 100 metres. It's the ambulance helicopter, sponsored by Aspro.'

Aspro had funded the medical service of the Tour for some time ('Phew...thanks Aspro' their advertising slogan). Their helicopter was part of an increasingly modernised back-up for the Tour organisation. A second helicopter carried a film camera to record the passage of the race, the film developed each evening in the laboratory camionettes of the RTF (*Radiodiffusion Télévision Française*) and despatched, express, to Paris. A daily roundup was augmented by direct transmission from five stages – the flat second stage into Namur, over the Puy de Dôme, Tourmalet and Iseran, and the finale at the Parc des Princes. Prize money had been increased, a Prime de la Malchance (prize for the unluckiest rider) was sponsored, aptly, by the National Lottery, and Bobet admitted that he had made a 'gross personal error in riding the '58 Tour'. The French team, already split by the counterclaims of several established star riders – Anquetil, Bobet, Geminiani, Anglade – now had to accommodate a new arrival, the brilliant Roger Rivière, 23 years old, protégé of Geminiani. World record holder for the hour, twice world pursuit champion (he'd taken the national pursuit title at the age of 19 from Anquetil), winner of the Tour de l'Europe for amateurs, Rivière had oodles of class. He joined the rickety unity of the French national team on which Anglade turned his back to ride for the regional Centre-Midi and, for a second time, the Internations team was riding.

Robinson and Elliott missed the team meeting called for Tuesday before the Thursday start, but were in sanguine mood. They joined Christian, with another Austrian rider, two more Danes (none of the prickly foursome of '58 was there), a Pole, two Portugese and three Englishmen, John Andrews, Tony Hewson and Victor Sutton.* This latter trio had been riding as independents in France. Hewson spoke in glowing terms of Robinson when I talked to him. 'He was a brilliant rider, tremendously gutsy and very focussed, and I was very much in awe of him, his experience, and we were aiming to copy what he had achieved. As far as we were concerned, he had a godlike aura about him and it's a shame he never got the adulation that Simpson got. But, he is immensely taciturn. He never pushed himself forward in the same way.'

---

* For more detail on them, see Tony Hewson's entertaining *In Pursuit of Stardom*, Mousehold Press.

As a member of the Rapha-Geminiani team, Robinson's bike was fitted with Campagnolo gears, Stronglight cranks and pedals, Duban freewheel, Brampton chain, Mafac brakes, PIVO bars and rims, Geminiani toe-clips, Dunlop-Reynolds tyres (which he swapped for his favoured Italian make.) He appeared in a photograph, alongside Rivière, used for publicity, puffing the efficacy of the banana, packful of vitamins, a handy way to reconstitute muscle power. 'Riders pick up their musettes,' says the caption, 'and go through the contents. Some goes straight into the pockets but many riders eat the bananas straightaway. Here see Rivière (winner of the sixth stage time-trial the day before) and, behind him, Robinson, eating their banana, knowing that it is an energising food, the preferred fruit of champions.'

On the other side of the page, an advertisement for Toblerone, 'ever inimitable' – milk, almonds, honey, Swiss quality with French chocolate.

Stage 5 Rouen – Rennes 286km

Robinson had left Richardot's massage table and was relaxing in the hotel room he shared with Elliott. A knock on the door. It was Raymond Louviot. 'Brian, I need you to translate, could you come down, please?'

Robinson went down to find his manager sitting with a twenty-one year old Englishman from Nottingham. He'd been racing as an independent, based in the Breton market town of Saint-Brieuc since Easter and Louviot wanted to sign him for a new incarnation of the Rapha-Saint-Raphaël team, which, in the following season, would be co-sponsored by the bike manufacturer, Gitane, as Rapha-Gitane. The young son of a Harworth (in Nottinghamshire) miner, Tom Simpson, had begun as a track rider – bronze in the Rome Olympics team pursuit, 1956, reigning British pursuit champion – and had already shown remarkable talent on the road in Britanny and the Route de France. Louviot was offering him 800 francs per month, far more than Robinson, in his fifth year as a professional, was earning. 'That was a bit of a sickener for me but, as events proved, he was well worth it.' He translated the terms, Simpson agreed and signed. A month later, he won the fourth and fifth stages of the Tour de l'Ouest and, in the autumn, came an astonishing fourth in the Worlds' road race.

Stage 8 La Rochelle – Bordeaux, 201km

The Hôtel des Quatre Soeurs, centre of Bordeaux, in the room shared by Robinson and Elliott. The Irishman is as red as the lobsters which are the speciality of La Rochelle – he made a solo break of 160km in the full blaze of the Charente and Gironde sun, took the Combativity prize (now sponsored by Manor, vin doux naturel, l'âme du Roussillon) but was caught and, on the Bordeaux track, lost (as he feared he would) to the French regional Michel Dejouhannet. Robinson, relaxing on his bed in a vest, felicitates him on being scrapper of the day. Shay, already disappointed not to have won in

Namur – he attacked on the last hill up into the citadel, but weakened and was overtaken by the Italian ace Vito Favero – says, 'better a stage win than combativity'. However, the total prize money for that day's ride exceeded all that the Internations team had won in toto since the start in Mulhouse. For comparison: at the end of the next day's (ninth) stage, the Internations team was bottom of the prize take, with 352,603 francs; the French national team had already scooped 4.5 million.

During that ninth stage, (Bordeaux–Bayonne), the blistering heat continued. Riders stopped at fountains in town squares to douse themselves with water, darted into *bistrots* and rummaged, shamelessly, through bar refrigerators for cold drinks, grabbed water bottles held out by spectators. Darrigade was spotted dumping his bike and sprinting a hundred metres to grab a bottle of lemonade. Leading the charge for refreshment, the Spaniards, 'men of the hot lands' whose resistance to the sun might have been stiffer.

To combat thirst, Dr Dumas advised consumption of carbonic water, such as Vichy, vitamin C, sipping at hot drinks like tea or salty soup, this last a quite unpleasant taste but most salubrious in extreme heat against dehydration. As for the doctor, he was travelling with bottles of chilled beer. 'Above all, don't copy me,' he admonished.

The French rider, Privat, ignored this advice the following day, (Bayonne – Bagnères-de-Bigorre), over the Tourmalet. On the approach to the mountain, through the small town of Pierrefitte-Nestalas, he got the bonk, a creeping seizure of lost power which begins in the stomach, paralyses the legs and then hisses like an untuned radio in the head. He began to wobble. Neither the *directeur* Bidot's Peugeot 203 nor the mechanic's Renault Dauphine is on hand to help. A journalist driving alongside him advises him to stop at the table of the feed-station and grab a musette – he'll lose no more than a hundred metres. Privat ignores him. Instead, he dumps his bike at the side of the road, goes into a *bistrot*, swigs two bottles of beer and retrieves the bike, having lost nearly four hundred metres on the lead group. He sets off, his face clenched in a grimace of suffering as the other riders dig into their musettes. Once on the climb, they have trouble trying to digest and, one by one, slip back. Privat, however, breathing more easily, his system responding nicely to the temporary boost of the alcohol and the ping of the cold fizz, pedals strongly over the col and comes second at the finish.

Sutton performed magnificently, this day, riding the great mountain in the company of Anquetil, Bobet, Baldini, Robinson and others as they forced the pace through Saint-Sauveur. He was, according to Wadley's report, pushing too big a gear and, had his goggles not misted up on the descent, he would have finished in this elite group. Robinson said that, as they rode up the Tourmalet, his fellow Yorkshireman 'even started talking about the race, the heat and other riders on the mountain. I told him to shut up'. At the foot of the climb, Elliott's chain broke and he lost nearly half an hour.

Although Sutton showed great class as a rider, he had not that adaptability which made life in France so manageable. He craved home cooking – 'Christ, I could do with some of me mother's Yorkshire pudding and gravy', to which Robinson retorted, 'France is famous for food, you're spoiled for choice, man'.

The start of Stage 11, to Saint-Gaudens, over the Aspin and the Peyresourde, was brought forward by seven minutes, in order to accommodate the television schedule for live transmission of the crossing of the Aspin. Plus ça change, as the man said, plus c'est la même chose. Robinson came in with the lead group.

Stage 13 Albi – Aurillac 219km
The eve of the stage, Robinson and his manager Ducazeaux had spent an hour scanning the map of the stage route, which crossed the départements of the Tarn and the Aveyron. The profile looked innocuous, a few climbs of no great height, but neither was there much by way of flat ground, rather a constant succession of rise and fall, which exaggerates the venom of the apparently insignificant Côte de Polissal 516m, followed by the Côte de Montsalvy 780m. Journalists, evoking the steep climbs of the Flemish towns, called this a 'wall'. And there remained the sawtooth climb to the finish in Aurillac, at 631m. Jean Bobet, now a journalist, stressed that it was a terribly tough day, calling for 45 x 24, a gearing more usually associated with mountains.

The field rolled out at 10.30am into close heat under a cloudless sky, pulsating with the sort of oppressive temperature that the returning champion, Gaul, hated. The undulations began almost at once and the pace was high. Robinson was among the first agitators, determined to make sure of a final top ten placing. At the first feeding station in Rodez, he and a number of outstanding rouleurs, Darrigade, Mahé, Dotto, Privat, Adriaenssens, Busto were 2m 30s up on a group of seven riders which included, notably, Anquetil, Anglade and Bahamontes, themselves ahead of a straggling main field, broken into several bits, in one of them, the yellow jersey Vermeulin, Bobet, Gaul, Rivière and a knot of Belgians. The Anquetil group accelerated and caught Robinson *et al.* hurtling down into the valley, 26km on at Villecomtal, the start of the Polissal, above the deep cleft of the Gorge du Lot and the rocky landscape of the Corrèze.

Dotto raised the tempo, a couple of riders fell away, Robinson pushed hard, trailed by Anquetil, crouched over the handlebars, his face clenched in effort, Bahamontes a little way further back, out of the saddle, staring into the hollow of the steep distance. The yellow jersey group was now at three minutes and, on the descent of the col, Bobet broke clear down the twisting road into Entraygues-sur-Truyère. Here, at a junction of the Lot with a lesser gorge, begins the climb of the Montsalvy. Ahead of Bobet, wrecked by the sudden jolt of another savage gradient on the 8km climb, Privat and Darrigade had been dropped, blown out. When Bobet caught them, he too was in trouble. A hundred metres back came Gaul, Rivière, Vermeulin. Bidot drove up and told Rivière to ride as hard as he could. Rivière objected: if he did, the Belgians would take his wheel and coast to the finish. Bidot brushed this aside. This was his chance to get rid of Gaul. Rivière responded and dropped Gaul, never happy going downhill, on the descent into Junhac. He raced on through the village, Gaul, overheated and stressed, pulled off at the fountain and dipped his head in and out of the water whilst his team mate, Goldschmidt, filled the bidons. Bobet and Privat went by.

Ahead of them Robinson and the others were still at high speed on the lumpy approach along narrow lanes to the finish, none of the climbs classified as such, each one hard enough to cost dear at the close of the stage, a final 80km of relentless up and down. All down the road, riders peeled off, spent, to recover. The Internations' team car overheated and the mechanics and Ducazeaux, dodging the gouts of steam, plied the sick vehicle with bidons of water. Robinson had no support.

At 2km from the large track in Aurillac, the leading group was together. One kilometre on, Bahamontes led, Robinson bridging the gap. They regrouped at the entrance to the cement track, Robinson on the Spaniard's wheel. One lap done, along the first straight and Robinson attacked into the banking, going strongly, the rest close behind, too close. On the final straight, he wilted, they shot past and Anglade won. On a smaller track the early burst might have succeeded, but...but there are, and can be, no *buts*. Two track stars, Forlini and Varnajo, who came up to congratulate Robinson at the finish, said as much, that if he'd left his effort for another fifty metres, he'd have won. He missed a win but gained much besides. The day, a masterly ride, took Robinson from eighteenth overall to ninth. (Gaul came in twenty minutes down, Elliott and Sutton in the main peloton which finished a further twelve minutes back.)

Stage 14 Aurillac – Clermont-Ferrand 231km
Overnight, Robinson suffered badly, once again his recalcitrant stomach. To the misery of pain and bodily discomfort, the added nightmare spectre of another abandon.

An advertisement showed a smiling Darrigade attributing the secret of his superb form to relaxing nights on a Simmons mattress. As for Rivière, he wore the pyjamas of champions, made by Doncho, soft, warm, of health-giving wool. If only...

I asked Robinson about this recurring gastric complaint.

GF   Was it ever diagnosed as anything more radical?

BR   No. All I can think of is that when we got into Aurillac, we were absolutely famished and the guy gave us some *pain d'épices*, which we wolfed down. It may have been stale or something, I don't know. And, of course, our body temperature was that hot, I suppose drinking a lot of chilled water may have had something to do with it. You were discouraged from drinking too much during the race – that was the thinking in those days – so you always had a mouth like…like a French bog, if you like.

Anquetil said that he rode ninety kilometres of this stage without eating or drinking. He admitted that all the bottles of liquid he saw were tempting but that this day he wanted to suffer and 'to hit the bull's eye'.

Diarrhoea is more often caused by dehydration and excess of sun than by tainted food so it may, simply, have been that Robinson's system, overstretched, dessicated and boiled, succumbed to the stress of the day rather than any immediate biophysical disorder. However, he had been forced to quit the Vuelta that year because of problems with his stomach and had been prescribed medication. After the stage finish in Bayonne, facing the Pyrenean stages, he stopped taking the tablets because he felt they were affecting his form. The strength of his ride into Aurillac suggested that he had made the right decision. Although it is impossible to say for sure whether pills could have prevented the recurrence of the stomach upset, it seems more likely that they would not. The swiftness of his recovery bears that out.

The evening after the finish in Aurillac, Jean Bobet, a graduate in English, went to see Robinson and Elliot in their hotel room. He fumbled for a pleasantry. Robinson reassured him, there was no need – 'We speak French here'. Bobet said that they had each, for some time, become continentals. Not much of an accolade in many English eyes, perhaps, but a sure sign of their professionalism as riders in the continental peloton competing in the Tour de France. But, their last Tour? They said so, quite freely. As Bobet put it, they'd shed that altogether British starchiness which prevented the queen's subjects from speaking candidly, of voicing their feelings, their malcontent, their disappointments. Sang-froid is one thing, grace under pressure, put up and shut up…a stiff upper lip rather less biddable to the Latin temperament.

Of their disaffection with the Tour, specifically the fact that they were riding for such a motley crew, Robinson gave the reasons: 'If the formula doesn't change, we'd rather stay at home. No team means no money. Sutton? He's a good guy but he's not in the race. We constantly have to go and look for him at the back.'

Elliott: 'Because we're linked to the national teams, we don't qualify for the money given by Simmons [for best daily and final overall performance] to the regional teams. How can we compete with the French and the Belgians? They've got twelve riders, they're much stronger than us.'

The Internations also had twelve riders, but without a united purpose or common cause.

There was, too, the lack of support from the cycling authorities in the United Kingdom who regarded the whole business of riding on the continent of Europe as a vulgar caper, an aberration not worthy of notice or encouragement. Riders who had competed for Great Britain in the Worlds' at Reims in 1958 were still waiting for their money.

Elliott, moreover, had an even more pressing reason to feel like an outcast. In 1953, he'd been beaten up, presumably by members of the IRA, while out on a training ride.

Elliott's decision to live in France and to take out residency was rooted in a more pressing need than bike racing. Indeed, he regarded Le Perreux as his home, ahead of Dublin, the city of his birth. Robinson was talking of a move to anglophone Jersey, in close enough proximity to France and where Shirley would feel less at a disadvantage. Bobet was, above all, impressed by the commitmen of the two men to their career as professionals. 'They practise their trade with the same fervour that their compatriots reserve exclusively for cricket. Alas for them.' Bobet's reference to cricket may well be a cliché; the evident respect for the fervour of these two lone giants of the road was heartfelt.

Robinson came to the start feeling awful, sick, enfeebled. Elliott, singled out by a commissaire for some irregularity in his turnout, was fined 500fr for being ill-dressed. The field set off for Clermont-Ferrand on another day of torrid heat. Robinson managed to stay with the bunch until the first attack went at Puy Mary, 67km out, and from then on, the ride was torture.

For six hours, Elliott nursed, cajoled, pushed, encouraged, talked to, relayed and helped his ailing friend. He poured water over his head, splashed his face gently, when the commissaires weren't looking planted his hand in the Englishman's back – of course, the commissaires did eventually see him and the fine ensued, to both riders, 2,500 francs and 30 seconds penalty, Elliott for giving the aid, Robinson for accepting it. There were times, said Robinson, when he probably wished Elliott would just shut up, that the constant babble of his voice, *come on, keep going, stick to it, we'll make it, come on Brian, come on,* would stop, go away, leave him in peace. But, if the words underscored the torment of sitting on the bike near incapable of effort, they also served as a continuous reminder that his friend was there, at his side, sheltering him from buffets of wind, leaning across to cool him down with a refreshing douse from the water bottle, riding with him, nursing him along *comme une mère poule*, said the journalist, the same term, remember, used for the Derny men who shielded the riders in the Bordeaux-Paris. Dr Dumas supplied glucose tablets – a necessary supplement for a rider who had voided so much solid food and could ingest none, but its accumulated effect was to cause gripe in the guts and to leave a foul taste in the mouth.

Grinding along behind these two riders, like the Grim Reaper, came the broom wagon, the besom attached to it reinforcing its role as the sweeper-up of discarded and broken bits of the race. And, Elliott's stream of words, the exhortation, jarring as it sounded much of the time, a barrage in his ears, was also an echo of his own unshaken will, to keep going until he dropped, never to give up, to ride until he could ride no longer. Mountaineers looking after others suffering from hypothermia in extreme cold do the same, they talk and talk and talk to keep them awake, for if they go to sleep, death follows close behind.

At the feed station in Riom, Elliott took both musettes and loaded up with all the extra bidons he could carry. He pressed his friend to eat, to supply some of the energy he was dredging up from somewhere just to keep going.

Robinson en perdition...they said, the French (translatable as 'distress') having something of the force of the earlier English sense of utter destruction, complete ruin, from the Latin *perdere*, to destroy.

As he observed this melancholy affair from the pillion of a motorbike, Jean Bobet thought how the forefathers of these two men had fought: the one to annexe and subjugate Ireland, the other to make it free. 'I was moved to see them so closely bound by distress. The solid strength of the one aiding the weakness of the other. They were not unaware of the futility of their persistence because they calculated the permissible time gaps all the way along their slow journey.' He concluded his account with an appeal to the fans who complain when the peloton goes too slowly. 'I have not told you everything but I am sure I have told you enough so that, from now on, you do not take potshots at cyclists.'

The riders called the *grupetto* at the back of the race in the mountains 'Darrigade's autobus', Darrigade the experienced pro who kept the slower moving bunch of non-climbers together at a speed which would just miss the time guillotine. 'If you stayed with them,' Robinson told me, 'you knew you were safe, it was an insurance policy.' No such indemnity for him or Elliott this day. They knew they were doomed. They came in forty-seven minutes down.

BR To be honest, I don't know how I got to the end. As to that rule that kept me in, I was as surprised as anyone.

The rule, invoked by Ducazeaux, gave a waiver to any man who had started the day in the top ten overall. Robinson was thus reinstated, Elliott, for all the selfless devotion he had shown, the sacrifice of his own race, was not. Robinson was mortified, even if Elliott insisted that he had come to the

Tour to help Robinson and that he had done. There were alpine stages to come and he, unlike his friend, was no climber. Robinson had a chance to come back and do something. It was typically throwaway and unassuming in the genial Irishman, whatever grievous disappointment it glossed over. Although Elliott was definitely out, the discussion about Robinson continued for some time and, when the blackboard of names for the individual time-trial was marked up next morning, beginning with the official *lanterne rouge*, the German Matthias Löder, Robinson was not, at first, included. Robinson, the actual *lanterne rouge*, nonetheless crept back up the overall classification. Setting off first, up the twelve kilometres of the Puy-de-Dôme's conical volcanic outcrop, he acquitted himself well, finishing in the middle order. Hassenforder, over eight minutes down on the winner, Bahamontes, was excluded on time. Bahamontes recorded 36m 15s, his nearest challengers three Frenchmen, the only men to beat forty minutes: Anglade, at 3m, Rivière at 3m 37s, Anquetil at 3m 42s.

During the Rest Day in Saint-Etienne, after the time-trial, Robinson had begun to recover his strength, thanks to the kindly attentions of Dr Dumas and ample quantities of yoghurt. Now, boring into his mind, a determination to do something to repay Elliott's courageous help.

Stage 17 Saint-Etienne – Grenoble 197km
Another day of fierce heat and café raids. Bahamontes, sensing that this was his Tour, attacked hard on the Col de Romeyère 1069m, some 20.4km of climbing and, apart from a brief flat halfway, at around a steady 8 and 8.5%. He led Gaul over and then, unusually for him, descended at risk, Gaul close behind. The two men relayed each other all the way to the finish on the Grenoble track where Gaul took the sprint and Bahamontes the yellow jersey, with an advantage of 4m 2s over Hoevenaers. Robinson and Sutton came in with the following bunch of thirty-six riders.

Stage 18 Grenoble – Aosta 243km ...Bastille Day
The route crossed three monster cols: the Galibier 2556m, the Iseran 2770m, highest pass in Europe, the Petit Saint-Bernard 2188m and down into Italy.

After the taxing ascent of the Giant of the Alps, the sinuous descent and the short hop over the Télégraphe, in biting cold, followed by the long drag up the valley in driving rain, the peloton was strewn along the lower slopes of the Iseran. At the very back of the field, Louison Bobet, who had been growing weaker, day by day, was now ill and despondent. He knew his race was over but there was one thing left to accomplish: to ride to the roof of the Tour. He had never ridden the Iseran and, before he quit, he said, 'I wanted to plant the last banner on its summit'. At the col, he stopped, climbed off, put on a raincoat given to him by a *soigneur* as the Italian champion Gino Bartali (Tour winner in 1938 and '48) stood holding his bike. Bobet emptied his pockets, boarded the ambulance and bid farewell to the *Grande Boucle*.

For the rest of the riders, the descent of the Iseran was, in that most evocative term of French journalistic hyperbole, *infernale*, hellish. The road awash with melting snow and pelting rain, the corners became even more perilous to negotiate, a terrible strain on nerves, muscles, bike-handling. The ascent of the Petit Saint-Bernard took the riders into an alleyway of ice-bank sidewalls and another frightful descent – a slurry of mud across the tarmac and fog added to the inherent difficulties. In extreme cold, the riders' fingers froze and could hardly work the brake levers, the tyres were constantly at risk of sliding, and always the clock ticked menace in their heads…to beat time, to beat time. Sutton, to whom this kind of descending was new, had a wretched day of it and came in six minutes down. Ducazeaux was scathing. 'Sutton descends worse than Dotto, and that's saying something. If he had stayed with Robinson the team would have won the 200,000fr day's prize.'

Robinson himself survived a puncture and was beginning to show something like his previous form. He was with the lead group on the fast descent towards the finish, a mere two kilometres' out of Aosta when his back tyre rolled off. He lost contact, of course, and arrived with seven other riders forty-seven seconds down. He led the sprint in and placed seventh on the stage. He unleashed his wrath on the mechanics…their stupid error had cost him an even better placing. Nevertheless, he moved up from the back of the field to 42nd overall.

Stage 19 Aosta – Annecy 251km
Robinson finished the day, the last of the alpine stages, thirty-six minutes adrift, looking fresh and in fizzy good spirits. That evening, the mechanics fitted a pair of very light Italian-made wheels to his pale blue Geminiani frame, carrying lightweight time-trial tyres. Robinson spent the time before supper scrutinising, once more, the profile of the next day's stage: 202km to Chalon-sur-Saône – a drop to the foot of the third category Forêt d'Echallon 963m, a lumpy middle section and a steady descent into the old town, once residence of the kings of Burgundy.

Le tout pour le tout…going for broke.

Several factors persuaded him that this was a stage for a solo break: most of the riders were physically and mentally tired after the alps, their thoughts were on the time-trial, the last stage into Paris and the scramble for points in the team competition; the hilly terrain of the Jura and the Saône-et-Loire suited him, 'his kind of country' and, foremost, he badly needed and wanted to have a go, to give Elliott's sacrifice meaning. He also needed to put on a show. Before the Tour started, in Mulhouse, Daniel Dousset, the criterium agent, had told him and Elliott that if they did not thrust themselves out of the anonymity of the Internations team, there would be no contracts. Robbed of the opportunity of a win in Aosta when his tyre rolled off, this stage it had to be. (After the birth of their second child, Robinson and his wife had decided to leave the site at Bry and Shirley and the two children, Michelle and Martin-Louis, took to the road, going where the racing took them. It greatly lessened the emotional strain of separation, a curious vagabondage, the family as one, pa earning the money on the move. In the amalgam of all that they were putting into success on the road as financial investment, there was much hanging on a stage win.)

The lightweight wheels and tyres made no great material difference, a few seconds advantage, maybe, but their effect on morale was potent. The tyres would be more prone to puncture and, if it rained, their silk walls would take in water and swell the tube. However, feeling good about riding a lighter machine had considerable psychological value and this was a day for focus, concentrated will and pointed ambition.

'One man alone had the courage to shake off his chains and set off on an adventure, the Englishman, Robinson, the reprieved man of Clermont,' wrote the *Equipe* reporter.

On the approach to Bellegarde, Robinson moved to the front of the bunch. He knew the town from having ridden a criterium there: a sharp bend in the road led onto the steep climb up through a stony gorge towards the Forêt d'Echallon. It was an ideal point to cut loose and disappear. This he did, followed at once by the climber, Jean Dotto, a former team-mate, riding for the French Centre-Midi regional team. 'Although we were riding in national teams I had been asked by my trade team-mate, Gérard Saint, (of the French regional Ouest-Sud-Ouest team) if I would help him. It was the last day to count towards the mountains classification. He asked me to take him over the top of the next col after he'd led up the first, but he couldn't hang on. [Saint and his immediate rival in that competition, his team mate Valentin Huot, had a violent argument after Huot pulled Saint's jersey near the top of a climb. Huot eventually came fourth overall in the competition, Saint third, but he also won the overall Combativity prize.] Robinson said: 'Jean Dotto was there too, screaming for me to wait for him as we climbed the Echallon. I decided to drop him as the French team would be chasing and he wasn't much of a descender. They caught him, but didn't bother about me. That descent was a bit hairy, mind you – I was on 8oz tyres and there was a lot of gravel about, so I was afraid of puncturing.'

Dotto reached the summit ten seconds ahead of Robinson but was not very quick downhill. On the descent through the trees into Oyonnax, riding at hectic pace, clipping corners, cutting a line as close to straight as he could, Robinson dropped Dotto. He pushed on alone, another 140km ahead of him – once the distance of the Grand Prix des Nations' individual time-trial – tracked by Ducazeaux in the team Peugeot. When he reached a minute advance, he knew the gauntlet was down. Forty kilometres on, he had a lead of five minutes and eased off a little, to ride within himself. Even so and despite an intermittent headwind, he continued to gain time. 'After a while, you get into a sort of breathing rhythm which ties in well with things going through your head, such as *I'm going to win, I'm going to win...this is the day for Shay.* My mind was sharp, my legs were good and my morale was formidable, fully psyched up. With one hour to go, I knew the win was in the bag but I had to put that out of my head and just get on with the job. Even so, it was a real comfort to know that and I didn't let up till I crossed the line.'

Some way out from the finish, the motorbike with the slate drove up to show him the time advantage: *Pel 19' Reste 36km.*

Afterwards, in the euphoria of the win, he said, 'I still had a little left in hand'.

He rode down the long straight to the line in Chalon-sur-Saône, cheered all the way by a big crowd, the wooden fencing draped with a Martini banner, the Tour director Jean Goddet, in his trademark khaki bush shirt, shorts and knee-length socks, a motorcyclist and officer of the Garde Républicaine escort waiting to applaud the lone winner as he raised his arms and rolled in to victory, *Robinson le puncheur*...Robinson the hard-hitter.

He says: 'It's difficult to describe the feelings of satisfaction, stimulation, pleasure, excitement, all these things and, of course, the public appreciation is so overwhelming it brings tears of joy, also the fact that the family back at home, friends and all share in that pleasure. Even today, when someone reminds me of those super moments, it stirs the blood.'

A nice touch – second on the stage: Padovan, who beat Darrigade in the bunch sprint.

Bellegarde played a significant role in another rider's fortunes that day. Robic was dropped and had to ride the remainder of the stage alone. The difference was that he was in the decline of his career and already weak, with little hope of beating the time limit. The more Robinson drew away from the peloton, the graver Robic's plight became. At the side of the road in towns and villages, eager children born after the days of his pomp – he won the Tour in 1947 – cheered him as he slogged past, hunched over the handlebars, hailing him *Biquet*... Kid, don't give up.*

Antoine Blondin, anxious to save Robic's day, had driven up alongside Robinson *en route* and reports the conversation thus:

'Hello, Brian, *want you to stop.* [in English]. Won't you stop? You're eliminating Robic. What's it to you if you win with only a slight advance? Let him catch up on the time gaps – it's you who're making them.'

---

* Robic had been paying 2500 francs fines for slitting the sides of his jersey so that he could more easily slip newspapers underneath them at the cols. The Tour organisers reacted harshly to damage to their property.

'And if I get caught…?'

'Okay, listen: ride to the finish and stop short of the line, then cross it when you judge it the right moment to take your victory and to save the beaten innocent who's paying the price of it.'

Blondin seemed happy with the logic of this. It had no effect on Robinson, however. He merely pushed harder on the pedals, indifferent to the appeals and, as Blondin records, 'answered them in cruel terms evincing that other aspect of *fair play*: may the strongest on the day be wholly the strongest'. Robic came in forty-one minutes down on Robinson and, despite an impassioned plea laced with an acrimonious tirade to which Goddet remained impervious, he was eliminated.

For Robinson, honour, prizes – stage, team, combativity – contracts*, a telling punch, indeed.

There remained the 69km time-trial into Dijon, won by Rivière, and the last stage, a mammoth 331km, to Paris. Bahamontes held a lead of four minutes over Anglade, a little over five on Anquetil and Rivière. The French nationals might surely have gone onto the offensive and worn Bahamontes down in the long haul from Dijon? The Tour was still theirs to take. The Spaniard was mercurial, he had never ridden the Tour with anything like consistency and fixed purpose – magnificent one day, hardly even there the next. Coppi, who had signed him to his trade team, Tricofilina, said that he could have won both the Giro and the Tour that year, 'but this man is a job to handle. He's as stubborn as a mule'. (He refused to ride the Italian tour.) This year, though, the mule found a calm and steady handler in the Spanish team *directeur*, the ex-racer, Dalmacio Langarica. 'All you have to do with Federico is to calm him down nine days out of ten,' he said. 'If you didn't, he would kill himself fighting just when he felt like it, no matter how unimportant the rider was.' In short, Bahamontes learnt to use his head. It helped that his main Spanish rival, Jesús Loroño, wasn't riding – they did not get on. Finally, the French team, as ever at odds, had one united contrary aim: to prevent Anglade from winning. He came second.

A photograph taken at the final stage start in Dijon shows Bahamontes, in yellow, leaning against the back wing of a Citroën DS, talking to René Latour, to his right, crouching, his friend Robinson, to his left, standing, the new man Sutton, the former carpenter from Doncaster, who had shown so well in the mountains, now 331km away from completing his first *Grande Boucle*.

---

* Again for comparison, Bahamontes landed sixty post-Tour contracts at 200,000 francs a time.

On 12 September, on a contract organised by Dousset, Robinson crossed the Atlantic from Le Havre in the FLANDRE, a liner of the French Compagnie Générale Transatlantique, to New York (a fare of $229) to ride the first of the season's whirligig of Six-Day races. The weather was appalling, the ocean lashing the ship with thirty foot high waves and most of the eight hundred passengers kept to their cabins. Robinson and seven of the other riders he was travelling with, were not afflicted with sea sickness and lived the life of Riley in the saloon, personal service by the stewards who always took to sportsmen.

BR   Which Riley was that, then?

GF   History doesn't record. Could be any of a number.

BR   Shay was Irish, of course.

GF   There you are, then.

Robinson had learnt the craft of riding wooden tracks at omnium meetings in Basle, Zürich, Copenhagen and on one rickety outdoor wooden vélodrôme in Brittany, used for stage finishes.

The old Madison Square Gardens, built in 1879, had been designed to accommodate a cycle track. It put on various cycling events and then hosted the first Six-Days race in December 1891. (The strict Sabbath observance laws did not permit any form of sporting contest on a Sunday, in accordance with the fourth of the Ten Commandments: 'Remember the Sabbath day, to keep it holy.') Individual riders, 144 hours on the track, round and round and round incessantly like squirrels (the French slang for them), tormented by sleep deprivation, paranoid hallucinations, delusions, crying fits, terminal exhaustion, riding in an unventilated fug of tobacco fumes, heat vapour from the arc lights, the bodily exhalations of the spectators in what was billed as the 'dizzy ride to nowhere'. When the black sprinter, Major Taylor, 'The Fastest Bike rider in the World', was forced to get some sleep, his handlers woke him after only fifteen minutes and told him he'd overslept. They gave him a capsule containing white powder which, they said, cost $65 an ounce and would keep him awake for the rest of the race, then they plonked him back on his bike. It was bicarbonate of soda but Taylor rode on for another eighteen hours without pause. Another track ace, Charles W. Miller, was off the track for a total of only fifteen and a half hours – nine and a half hours of sleep, five and a half for shaving and washing and, on the final Saturday afternoon, clad in a special pink and white cycling shirt and shorts, half an hour to marry his fiancée in the Garden.

Six-Day bike racers came out of this purgatorial insanity asphyxiated, broken, eyes skeletally sunken, having driven themselves loopy for a baying public inside the hall until the public outside the hall called for a halt to the bestiality. (Voyeuristic sane members of the public used to pay to view the tormented cavortings of the insane, lunatics, in bedlam.)

The Six Days evoked the same scenario. Entertainment? Sadistic callousness, rather.

The Six-Day was, wrote a *New York Times* reporter, in 1897:

An athletic contest in which participants 'go queer' in their heads and strain their powers until their faces become hideous with the tortures that rack them is not sport. It is brutality. Days and weeks of recuperation will be needed to put the Madison Garden racers in condition, and it is likely that some of them will never recover from the strain.

New York State put a stop to the spectacle in 1898. The legislature passed the Collins Law which forbade the participants in a Six-Day race to ride for more than twelve hours in any twenty-four hour period. In response, someone came up with the idea of two-man teams and, in 1899, the new format was launched at the indoor sports arena first built in downtown Manhattan in 1879. Hence the term Madison for the two-up track race. From 1899 to 1901, if a man's partner dropped out, he could continue to ride alone, twelve hours out of the twenty-four, for the individual distance prize. From 1902 onwards, remnants of teams could form new teams, thus ensuring more complete fields and better racing throughout the whole week.

Just as in Paris at the Vél d'Hiv, Madison Square Gardens was a favourite haunt of show business names, who came to have supper and see the racing from the centre of the arena after the theatres closed. Enrico Caruso, John Barrymore, Al Jolson, Eddie Cantor, Jimmy 'Schnozz' Durante, Bob Hope were all 'Six-Day nuts'. So, too, the famous theatrical duo, Alfred Lunt and his wife Lynne Fontaine, famous for putting on a dizzying round of repertoire. Once, when they were on stage together, they dried and looked at each other in puzzlement. The prompter whispered, no response, he whispered again, at which Alfred turned to the wings and said: 'We know the line. Which one of us says it?'

Tin Pan Alley song pluggers hovered by the public address microphones hoping to wow the spectators with a new number and the upper tiers were haunted by bums and loafers who, for just over a dollar a day, could have a warm berth and intermittent amusement. Fans crowded in laden with food hampers, wine jugs and Prohibition booze. That great chronicler of life on Broadway, Damon Runyon, wrote : 'If you got to get drunk, there's no place better to get drunk than the Six-Day Bike Race.'

The arena was cleared of people on the fifth day and it cost another admission for the final twenty-four hours.

Hustlers and pickpockets flocked to the old Garden to lift wallets, clothes stowed under seats, shoes…'If you saw some guy walking down the street in his bare feet, you knew he had just come from the bike race.' Floating (i.e.peripatetic) crap games, set up to evade the law against gambling, moved into the Garden, and if Nathan Detroit, a character in *Guys and Dolls* based on Runyon's writings, didn't exist in name he sure as hell was true to life:

> Why, it's good old reliable Nathan, Nathan, Nathan, Nathan Detroit,
>
> If you're looking for action, he'll turn it to spot,
>
> Even when the heat is on, it's never too hot.
>
> But for the good old reliable Nathan, oh it's only just a short walk,
>
> To the oldest established permanent floating crap game in New Yawk.
>
> Frank Loesser, music and lyrics Guys and Dolls

The wooden tracks were, for the most part, portable and when Robinson and his partner, the American Erwin Pesek, arrived at the Garden track for the start of the racing, the carpenters were still building it. They finished ten minutes before the gun.

The programme describes Pesek as 'a fine jammer [who] has figured in more spills than any other present day rider'. *Jam* was slang for the eyeballs out action when teams are trying to gain a lap advantage on the rest of the field. The editorial of the *New York Times* on 9 September 1961 records that, when a jam was taking place 'the racket was prodigious...twenty-four athletes in a bedlam of pedaling spread out entirely round the track. These were the bad-tempered, frenzied moments when some team had decided to steal a lap.' [Interesting that the writer alludes to a bedlam, ie madhouse.] As to Pesek's propensity for spillage, not encouraging. Among the other riders: Robinson's friend Varnajo, his Internations team-mate Barbosa and the crack Italian pairing of Leandro Faggin and Ferdinando Terruzzi. Robinson was very strong after a season on the road but lacking in pace – long stages blunt the speed – so he had to take off for the primes from nine or ten laps out (it was quite a small track) and hang on – or not – when the quickies mounted their surge for the line. He was having a wonderful good time. 'You needed very quick reflexes, more so than on the road. The nights were a bit boring, just trundling round on your own in the empty place, but the jamming sessions were great. And the food produced by the Italian restaurant in the basement was excellent.'

Budget for the kitchen, feeding riders, working reporters and race personnel: $10,000. The menu included chicken, lamb chops, boiled and baked ham, steaks, bacon, mounds of assorted fruit and vegetables, rice, spaghetti, oatmeal and cereals, salad, prune juice, fig juice, grape and grapefruit juice and a case of clam juice to settle nervous stomachs. The old Madison Garden had housed Barnum and Bailey's circus and the subterranean area of the arena was known for the pervading stink of the elephant dung and, though the whole place had an old smell about it, Robinson was, as he said, 'having a laugh', and no bad weather to ride in, either. True to form, Pesek fell off on every session, whether from mischance or a muddled need to live up to his reputation. However, he and Robinson were going well. Until, on the fifth day, in the rush of a jamming session, as he grabbed hold of Pesek to sling him into the action, the man came on but his bike simply disappeared. A wheel collapsed? The frame split? The forks falling to bits? Whatever, Robinson let Pesek drop, too – 'What else was I to do?' – and they were out, Pesek with a broken collarbone. 'It was sad, really, I was going great, the crowd, not that it was a very big crowd, was enjoying it and I had twelve hours to get another partner. We were lying third on points, too.' Ted Smith, an American paired with the Canadian Pat Murphy, was suffering from a saddle boil and Robinson approached him: since it was likely he was going to have to quit, why not let his man ride with Robinson? Smith refused, soldiered on and then quit half an hour after the twelve-hour cut-off, which meant Robinson was out. 'I was a bit sick about that,' he said.

Terruzzi, who won the event with Faggin, and with whom Robinson had trained on the wooden track, was full of praise for the Yorkshireman and had Robinson, towards the end of his career, been still keen on bike-riding, he might have pushed for more track contracts. There would be the problem of finding a compatible partner, naturally, as well as the prevailing difficulty of money: to make a profit from the track, a rider would have to ride the entire gruelling, winter-long round of Six-Day races – in north and south America and across Europe – and Robinson was, by this time, sick of travelling. Nor was he much interested in simply flogging himself to make ends meet. He had a talent for the discipline, undoubtedly, but one element of the Six-Day didn't sit wholly comfortably with him. The excitement of the racing had to be augmented with conscious showmanship, what Ernest Hemingway described, in *A Moveable Feast*, as 'the slow circling and the final plunge into the driving purity of speed'. Riders were expected to play up to the audience expectation of thrills and spills – crashes just avoided, madcap interventions, crazy last-minute swoops off the top of the banking…all that required considerable adroitness and any rider who had spent a season in the continental peloton was bound to be adroit. But, as Robinson put it, 'you have to be a bit savvy…the public aren't all *that* daft', that is, they can see through mere trickery, it has to look authentic and such histrionic antics were not his style. He never rode at the famous Paris arena, the big Vél d'Hiv, where teams of three could jack up the speeds even faster. Although he says that he found the Six-Day fairly easy, less stressful than road-racing, the track was a tough way of earning bread. The high G-forces which clamp down on a rider's head and shoulders on the tight curves and steep banking – Basle was particularly sharp, 'like a Wall of Death', he said – add to the physical toll. But, he never came off, he was fly and a beautifully balanced bike rider.

The receipts from the Madison Gardens event were disappointing and a projected ride in Chicago was cancelled. The infamous gangster Al Capone had once funded a Six-Day race in Chicago but, perversely, decided that the riders should gyrate round the track in a clockwise direction, instead of the convention, established in ancient Greece, of circling an oval stadium counterclockwise. (There is a reason for this: the heart being located on the left side of the chest, the widdershins rotation puts less strain on it. In fact, a rider at Capone's eccentric meeting suffered a heart attack as a direct result of this change of direction.) The atmosphere in the indoor arenas of the wooden tracks was always thick with tobacco fumes. 'It taught me to smoke,' says Robinson, the proxy inhaler. However, he took home $800, (about £200), a nice bonus. They also had three days free for sightseeing in the city before the ship sailed home to Southhampton. The menu for 4 October: Canteloupe melon with sherry, consommé, fillet of sole Deauvillaise (creamy white wine sauce with a hint of mustard), asparagus sauce gribiche (vinaigrette with chopped hard-boiled egg, cornichons, capers and *fines herbes*), poularde du Mans en casserole (a fattened pullet), salade chiffonade, pear Belle-Hélène, wafers, fresh fruit.

10: GREAT BRITAIN RIDES AGAIN

In England everything stops for tea. In France, everything stops for Le Tour…If an enemy of France were planning to invade the country, this would be an appropriate time to start it. The people have no time for other news during Tour de France month. The newspapers are full of it; television and radio give it priority coverage; it is the main topic of conversation in cafés and bars; anyone will supply details of the race more readily than the more political news.

Robinson, in an article for *World Sports* 1959.

Five years on from their first appearance in the Tour de France, Great Britain fielded another team, including Robinson, naturally, and the young man whose contract he had helped negotiate with Louviot the year before: Tom Simpson. Simpson, a rider of outstanding ability, always acknowledged his debt to Robinson, both on and off the road. In particular, just as his older friend and team-mate had taken his own first lesson in the crucial skill of descending on the wheel of a master, Kubler, that day on the Ventoux, so he initiated Simpson. Descending long alpine roads at extreme speed takes an exaggerated level of nerve, refined skill, poise and balance, mercurial reflexes and what develops as an intuitive capacity to read a road. The thinking mind must put aside any weighing of potential risk, the possibility of mechanical failure – a blow-out, broken forks - the sudden jolt of coming on an unlooked for hazard. As well as the primary task of getting to the bottom as quickly as he can, the faster and more intelligent the line of descent a rider takes, the less he has to apply the brakes and increase friction on the rims. In extreme temperatures, the rims are liable to overheat, anyway. This happened to Robinson's cost the year before: the adhesive on one tyre liquefied and caused the tubular to roll off.

GF   When that does happen, how do you put it out of your mind?

BR   Straight away, you don't dwell on it. You can't afford to.

Simpson was not at all sure of himself, to begin with – a familiar situation for all neo-pros – but he was absolutely sure that he needed to learn and that Robinson could teach him. Robinson obliged. *Take my wheel*…the best way of learning how to so something is to do it, to feel it, to absorb the advice into the immediacy of personal experience, to merge the rationale of the brain with the rhythm of the body. Don't think about it, just do it. Easy enough to say, but overriding the natural impulse to caution is a hard lesson. There was, too, that most powerful of imperatives at play: descending was part of the job and without the skill a man would always be at a disadvantage, especially if he was no climber – and not all climbers are good descenders. For any rider who couldn't get up the climbs fast, it was essential that they be able to get down them fast, to recoup lost time.

Robinson thought very highly of the ambitious new man. On the eve of the Mont Faron time-trial, in the hotel room they shared, they discussed whether or not to ride lighter but also less robust 28-spoke wheels. They agreed to chance it. They went to sleep. At about 3am, Robinson woke. Simpson was sitting up in bed shouting, '28 spokes...28 spokes...' Next morning, Simpson had no recollection of this. He won the event but both men finished on wheels severely out of true.

GF   I've driven up there, it's a savage ascent. What was it like on the day?

BR   The top five kilometres of the climb were unsurfaced, not poor but no tarmac. The whole route, though, was lined with people, all down to the bottom. What with car horns and all, they made a hell of a noise – that was something you had to get used to.

GF   What about the fumes from the cars and motorbikes?

BR   The cars didn't tend to bother you and the motorbikes only came up close when the photographer wanted a picture, otherwise they kept their distance, they knew that petrol fumes would be a problem. On the big climbs, cars were banned, they just took up too much room, so the mechanics had to ride pillion on motorbikes, with two spare wheels. Like the Mavic service bike nowadays.

Robinson reflected on time-trialling. Professional roadmen had a similar distaste for them to his, because they forced a rider to extend himself to the limit. A specialist like Anquetil depended on his superiority against the clock both to gain time and, as important, to reinforce his psychological, predatory dominance. When he lost time to Poulidor on the famous duel up the Puy-de-Dôme on the 1964 Tour, he went into the final time-trial with a bare thirteen second advantage on his great rival. 'Twelve more than I need,' he said, as much a message to cow Poulidor as a statement of bald truth. He, though, was an exception. To finish several minutes down on the winner damaged reputation and many pros were inclined to pull out rather than post a slow time. English clubmen would surely not understand this attitude, but most of them rode for the pleasure of the game. French amateur and Italian *dilettante* mean just that, love and delight. For Robinson it was a job, 'and once I put my leg over a bike, then work begins. If I don't work hard enough then there isn't any money and that's the only goal in mind. The best time-trial I ever did was the Grand Prix Martini à Genève round Lake Geneva in 1956. Jacques [Anquetil] won it, as he did a number of times, and I got within three minutes of him which, over 50 miles, wasn't bad. I was steaming.' An evident note of pride. He came fifth. Otherwise, the race against the clock was never to his liking, he merely got on with it when required to.

Professional freelancers, in whatever sphere, have that same insistence on doing a job. No overlay of romantic fancy or sentiment, no call on artistic flair or competitive brilliance, no call upon imagination or athletic prowess alters that.

Noël Coward, exasperated with the witterings of an actor who said he couldn't properly address a line until he knew what underlay the words, what was his motive, snapped in those acerbic clipped tones: 'Your motivation is the cheque at the end of the week, now, get on with the job.' And a noted Broadway songwriter, when asked what came first, the words or the music, replied, deadpan: 'The phone call.'

At the beginning of the year, Robinson had driven south from Yorkshire, collected Simpson from Sutton near Doncaster, the home of his wife Helen's parents, and on across the Channel down to the training camp, this time based in Palavas-Plage, near Narbonne in south-west France. They lived in a house owned by Gilbert Bauvin (second to Walkowiak in the 1956 Tour). Bauvin had a friend, a butcher, who was keen to promote the place.* They trained for a month in the warm sunshine, discussed the year's objectives with Louviot, and then embarked on the early season's racing on the Côte d'Azur, the warm-up shorter events, the Paris-Nice – which, Robinson said, always put him on form – and the annual helter-skelter of one-day and stage races before July.

I asked Robinson about Simpson.

> There was never a dull moment when Tom was around. There'd be a fun game of boules, a trick bike ride, whatever, jokes and pranks. I was always pleased to be in his company. I never saw him in a bad mood, even when he fell off the bike he seemed to be able to shrug off any feeling sorry for himself. We used to room together and it was a pleasant time in my time as a pro, with Tom in the same team.

Shirley had stayed behind in England. Robinson, Elliott and Simpson shared a sparsely furnished apartment in north-east Paris belonging to a friend of Varnajo, that they took for a year. Thirty pounds per month, a cooker and beds. Every Monday they happened to be in Paris, which wasn't often, they went to a bike shop on the Place de la République where Louviot had rented some cellar space as a depot for his team men. Robinson says they

---

* Whether the fact that Brigitte Bardot got married there helped or not, the small town, on the Languedoc coast, eventually grew into a major resort.

were probably a bit of a nuisance, cluttering up the place, asking for this, clamouring for that. The Paris pied-à-terre didn't get used much but it was, at least, a base.

Some time in May 1960, the two Englishmen had five weekdays off between races. Robinson lit off back to Yorkshire for a break and Simpson stayed on. He wanted to buy a car. Robinson advised him to get something reasonable, like a Peugeot 203, and gave him the address of one of the team car drivers. He came back to the flat to see 'a bloody great Aston Martin convertible parked outside. I clumped up the three flights to the flat and said: "What's that pram you've got downstairs, Tom?" "Oh, don't you like it?" "It's a super car but it's no good for bike riders, plus it'll drink a hell of a lot of juice." He just shrugged and smiled. That was him, impulsive. I never saw the car after that – I think he got it back to England, somehow.'

And so began what the French call the *train-train*, the daily grind, of races, Robinson inducting Simpson into the tricks of the trade. During one stage of the Tour du Sud-Est, Simpson, still acclimatising to the serpentine bends of the steep descents, was all over the place. One particular descent, says Robinson, wasn't that tricky, the corners weren't unusually tight, but the new man was in trouble. He came off. Robinson didn't mince words. 'Get on my wheel, for Christ's sake', which Simpson did. Even so, he came off another three times, and three times Robinson, urging him 'Come on, come on, stick on' rode him back to the bunch. However, Simpson won the race overall and, if the lessons he got from the more experienced hand were bruising, they were timely.

The two Rapha-Gitane men arrived in Lille just before the start of the 1960 Tour de France to join six other compatriots as only the third Great Britain team ever to ride the race. The warring BLRC and NCU had agreed to unite and form the British Cycling Federation [see Appendix I]. In principle, this suggested that any BCF team invited by the Tour organisers would represent the cream of British cycling. It was, perhaps, a bit more than a pious hope, although there was no compelling evidence of much enthusiasm from across the water. Andrews, Brittain and Sutton were back, John Kennedy, Harry Reynolds and Norman Sheil (twice pursuit World champion) had been racing as independents in France. Elliott and Hewson had withdrawn and, as late as a week before the Tour, an eighth man had still not been named. Robinson had some while earlier contacted the BCF and pressed for the inclusion of Owen Blower, fifth in that year's Tour of Britain. His advice was ignored. First on the BCF's list of possible riders was Bedwell, who didn't want to ride. Given his bad experience in the '55 Tour, and the reasons for it, he, surely, wasn't a sound choice, in any case. Brian Haskell didn't want to ride either. Three days before the Tour's *Grand Départ*, they contacted their final hope, John Kennedy, resident in Belgium, where he had been racing regularly. That he was conveniently placed for the start in Lille may have swayed their decision. Selected earlier in the year, Kennedy had renounced, because of painful saddles sores. He'd recovered, answered the summons and pitched up in Lille.

The fact that they were racing as Great Britain was of little import to Robinson, the nominal team leader. He had ridden for so long as a freelance that the only loyalty that had any claim on him was to his work. Do well, amass contracts, job done. Victory is sweet, the bouquet, the lap of honour, the applause are a pleasure, but the moment doesn't last, only the gain on the win. For, as the lady said: 'A kiss on the hand / May be quite continental / But diamonds are a girl's best friend. / A kiss may be grand / But it won't pay the rental...' Of course, Robinson would not have been a bike racer in the first place had his competitive drive not been out of the ordinary. He was a top-flight athlete and of the breed made to win races. Calculating odds, however, is central to bike racing and, for riders who lacked full team support, the fruits of labour had to be scrapped for. His hard-headed approach may not have endeared him to the fresher-faced men but that was of no concern to him. He applied practicalities, as ever, to the second half of the Tour's opening stage, a 27.8km individual time-trial, finishing on the cycle track in Brussels. Simpson rode out of his skin to come fifth (he lost time when he fell in the tunnel leading onto the Heysel track). Robinson, more savvy, rode in with his hands on the tops, his time respectable. He told Wadley that he could have clipped it by at least a minute but why expend effort for a small gain which might cost him a much heavier deficit later?

One thing that might have reassured him, this year, was the recent claim made by the Tour's chief mechanic that the glueing on of tyres had much improved. (Wooden rims, he said, were a thing of the past.) Tyres, ever lighter and stronger, now continued to stick even when the rims overheated on descents. He claimed.

The *Equipe* writers named Simpson as leader of the Great Britain team, largely, one imagines, because he had a more ostentatious nature than Robinson. He played up to the journalists, aped the French archetype of the British milord, always joking and clowning, on the surface taking nothing seriously. Happily for journalists, ever pressed for colour to primp their prose, Simpson delivered good copy. They voted him the friendliest rider in the Tour. (Riders of tart humour who did not cooperate were assessed for their *prix citron*, the lemon prize.) He was also the most maladroit – he fell a dozen times during the race, often through taking unnecessary risks. This is by no means to diminish his innate outstanding ability as a bike rider, only, in these early days, his bike-handling. Asked about the neophyte, Adriaenssens called him 'a fine rider' and, when asked about his climbing ability, said that he had so much class that he would adapt.

The GB team's *directeur sportif*, Ducazeaux, knew that his team hadn't the strength to mount anything much in the way of all-out attack. The lack of experience apart, they, like the other smaller teams, had only eight men; the national teams, Belgium, France, Italy, Spain, had fourteen. The Belgians and Italians had been agitating for two teams apiece. Had not the French their own national team *and* four, lately five, regional teams? Like his senior man Robinson, who'd begun his career fighting the unequal odds of big combines, Ducazeaux said they must wait, ever on the lookout for an opportune moment to strike. To this end, he said, he'd invented a new sort of rider: the vigilant. This wasn't Simpson's style, at all. Of him, the *directeur* said: 'He is all fire, all flame. To damp him down a bit, one has to be persuasive, one has to amuse him.' This impetuosity was dangerous, however, and Bidot, Georges Ronsse and Alfredo Binda, *directeurs* of the French, Belgian and Italian teams, had detailed certain of their men to watch out for and sit on Simpson if he got too uppity. They were right to watch him. He initiated and urged on a good break on the second stage, came third and missed taking the yellow jersey by twenty-two seconds.

Ducazeaux's opportunist strategy had ample scope for operation to begin with. The Tour began exceptionally fast. After eight stages, the average speed was 41.224kph. Anquetil had lately become the first Frenchman to win the Giro d'Italia and was not riding, nor was Gaul. After two days of the race, Bahamontes, moody, unpredictable and obstinate, withdrew. A photograph shows him sitting on his suitcase, alone, like a downcast orphan, on the station platform at Dunkerque, before wheeling his bike towards the train at the start of the long journey back to Spain.

On the fourth stage, Sheil's forks broke, he lost five minutes waiting for a spare bike and was given the wrong machine (suited to Robinson who was much shorter in height). He had a wearisome chase, mostly on his own, after a peloton travelling at 43.5kph, for eighty kilometres into Caen. He missed the time limit by fifty-five seconds but the commissaires took pity because of his bad luck and reinstated him. Brittain, weakened with food poisoning, had to pull out on the stage into Bordeaux. The rest of the team headed on for the Pyrenees.

Stage 10 Mont-de-Marsan – Pau 228km
Robinson and Simpson crossed the Aubisque in company with an elite group in pursuit of the Italian Graziano Battistini. His compatriot, Gastone Nencini, a known reckless descender, hurtled off down the mountain, closely followed by the two Britons. Simpson took a bad fall, Robinson stopped, gave him a wheel so he could press on and then waited for the team car to get himself back on the road. He chased after Simpson and they joined Adriaenssens, in yellow, and Baldini, in a frantic race after Rivière, Nencini, Battistini, Rostollan and Manzaneque. This group of five took the stage by two minutes. Robinson and Simpson would surely have been with them had it not been for the crash. Simpson said that the tyre had rolled off and blamed

the mechanics. Robinson and Ducazeaux examined the buckled wheel: no, not the mechanics' fault. Simpson did not brake well – part of keeping the line is the ability to brake at the right point, not to yank at the levers to make sudden decelerations. Simpson bowed to their experience. Sutton limped in ten minutes' down, in some disarray. Behind him, Andrews, Kennedy, Reynolds and Sheil, who had each taken a hammering.

Stage 11 Pau – Bagnères-de-Luchon 161km
A hard stage, indeed, over the Tourmalet, Aspin and Peyresourde.

They climbed through banks of mist into bright sunshine and back into cloud, the lead group together, none wishing to stir any action, ahead of them the young Swiss rider, Kurt Gimmi (who stayed away to the finish). Three kilometres from the top of the Peyresourde, Nencini attacked. The headstrong Simpson immediately took his wheel. Two kilometres on, he had blown completely. 'He changed up – *up* – and sprinted away,' said Simpson. 'I could do nothing – not even breathe or see straight. I have never been in such a state.'

The following group came past, Robinson and Sutton with them. Way back down the field, Andrews was struggling and out of touch. Sheil made the finish four minutes after the time cut and was eliminated.

Stage 12 Luchon – Toulouse 176km
Out of Luchon, the route went over the minor Col des Ares but Kennedy had nothing left. He fell off the back and was in for a hard ride. On the fast descent of the Portet d'Aspet, Reynolds fell, broke his collarbone and was being flown to Toulouse even as the race radio announced the abandonment of Andrews at the back of the race.

Some eighty kilometres from the finish, the riders had to negotiate a dark tunnel, five hundred metres long, worn out of the living rock by the waters of the river Arize near the famous palaeolithic cave of the Mas d'Azil. The lead group plunged in, their shadows cast in moving fresco on the rock walls by the pale lights. Despite warnings that the road was slippery, from water dripping out of the limestone, there was a big pile-up and one of the favourites, Anglade, took a bad fall. Robinson, delayed by a puncture, Simpson and Sutton by broken toe clips, were in the following group. They, too, sole survivors, now, of the GB team, got caught up in a prang in front of them and plodded on to arrive in Toulouse some fifteen minutes down.

Stage 13 Toulouse – Millau 224km
The race route crossed the lumpy region of the Cévennes, a broken limestone plateau – the *Lévézou* – riven with cuts and ravines, another of those undulating stages which suited Robinson's attacking temperament. Ten

minutes out of the ville rose, ('pink town'), named for the blush of its roof tiles, he set off alone, got thirty-five seconds in ten kilometres, decided that the bunch was not going to let him get more and sat up. He was keen for the three remnants of the GB team to contest the £500 prize awarded to the best three finishers of the eight-man teams but, when they came in on the cinder track at Millau, some distance down on the winner, their chances of doing so looked slim. The Rest Day followed.

11 July, Lozère

Noon had sounded, the mass was said, the sun grilled the Causses, [from Latin *calx* chalk], the horizon was lost in the haze. There was no sign of life either on the bare ridges or in the gorges which were etched with a menacing checkerwork of shadows. Only a thin line of men marked the road like stitching, having emerged from caves somewhere and stuck in place to provide small, hot oases of humanity. We had just crossed the Col de Perjuret and were plunging headlong into tight twisty turns, each for himself and God for all. Except for one man...

We saw Rostollan on a corner, running back up the road, gesticulating, shouting: 'Roger's crashed. Roger's crashed.' It was impossible to halt the toboggan ride we'd launched on. No one had seen Rivière disappear, not one of his companions, none of the spectators. For five minutes, we thought he'd vapourised, pure and simple removed from the map of the world, of which the immense, chaotic terrain surrounding us indicated the scale. Yet, he lay, twenty metres away, below the road, hidden by a fold in the ground, stricken with some paralysis which prevented him from making the smallest movement, the faintest call for help. His head lay on a pillow of stones, his eyes open. And all this work of nature surrounding him formed a rocky shroud. (Antoine Blondin, report in *L'Equipe*.)

Rivière's back was broken. He never rode again and died at the age of forty. After the accident, doctors found evidence that he had taken painkillers. Rivière himself blamed his mechanics, then his brakes (they were in perfect order) and finally admitted having taken Palfium, an amphetamine. This almost certainly so fuddled his senses that either he could not work the brakes properly or simply did not apply them at all.

Stage 15 Aignon – Gap 187km

On the descent of the Col de Perty, Simpson broke away with four other riders (two Belgian, two French) and they worked hard to ride clear for the remaining eighty kilometres. Simpson's overextended effort had spent him. The cannier Belgians took first and second. He finished third but took the day's combativity prize. It was a brave ride but further testimony to his inexperience, careless of tactics in the rush to do well.

Stage 16 Gap – Briançon 172km
Robinson was up with the leaders over the Vars and then the Izoard, but had a blowout and crashed on the descent and lost contact. Simpson fell at the start of the Izoard and badly hurt a leg muscle. He rode the rest of the race in some pain. Cooked by the sun and effort on the ascent of the Izoard, in the freezing draught of wind on the descent, Sutton caught a severe chill and had to withdraw. Perhaps he'd failed to stuff a newspaper under his jersey to insulate the front of his body. (Keeping the stomach warm, at all costs… Robinson himself habitually used brown paper or a piece of nylon.)

In the final 83km time-trial, Robinson (28th) and Simpson (29th) were separated by eleven seconds, only, and they reached the Parc des Princes 26th and 29th overall. Interviewed at the finish, Robinson said he was not sure whether, as he had indicated earlier, this would be his last Tour, after all.

Nencini, whose second place in that year's Giro had owed not a little to the ardent helping hands of the *tifosi*, pushing him up mountains – standard Italian practice for their men against the hated interlopers…they spat at Anquetil – had no such help in the Tour and won it from his compatriot Battistini.

Back in England, Robinson rode, and won, the first British professional-independent hill climb championship. 'I rode off form and only after some persuasion,' he said in an interview in *Coureur* the following March. Off form is shorthand for physically drained and mentally exhausted after the season's racing on the continent. 'Tom Simpson had a couple of entry forms and didn't want to ride because he thought he might be beaten. I decided to have a bash and the result you know. Incidentally, 1, 2, 3 for the Huddersfield Road Club.'

That closing remark hints at his pride in the club to which he still belonged and marks the deep vein of innate loyalty in him, a loyalty which the hodgepodge national team could not tap. Like many other riders who were dissatisfied with the inequality and imbalance of the Tour's selection procedure, he wanted a return to trade teams, where the loyalty which operated in all other racing throughout the year was at a premium. That loyalty had to be shelved during the Tour de France where the nominal unity of national and regional teams was largely artificial, the glue that held them together a shared interest in prize money. This anomaly was complicated by the fact that men from the same trade teams, who rode together in every race apart from the Tour, suddenly found themselves dumped in opposition. It was not all roses for men picked in the national teams, either, particularly the French, whose proclivity to squabbling and internecine discord made life very difficult for men like Anglade, Graczyk, Mahé and Saint. They expressed a desire to ride in regional teams in which they could express themselves better.

One evening in the autumn of 1960, a hopeful young English club rider who was working in Paris, saw Robinson and Simpson at the Gare du Nord. He recognised them, the star racers, mooching about in a railway station. He approached them. They, perhaps flattered by the attention, the obvious admiration, or simply from the courtesy that no-nonsense men of the two wheels incline to, said hello. They were waiting for Elliott to arrive. The young man rode with a local club, saw the two famous men a couple of times more on the road near Paris and still treasures the Geminiani track suit which he bought from Simpson.

That winter, as ever, Robinson returned to Mirfield. The money he might earn on the indoor tracks, riding show races or Six-Days – he was no star and could not command anything more than the bare minimum – would only just cover the hotel bills, which meant he'd in effect be working for nothing. He was, moreover, keen to be at home with Shirley and the children, enjoying not having to ride the bike. In fact, after the Hill Climb he put the bike in the garage and it stayed there until the following year…15 January, when all professional bike riders gave up skiing, walking and hunting to get down to fitness training. He either walked to work or took the car. It was the first time that he had had so complete a break from the two wheels. He even eschewed the Huddersfield club runs. Racing throughout the winter might bring him to the start of the season fitter but it would also leave him tired and jaded. A long layoff would only sharpen his desire to race in the spring. As he put it, 'I'll be enjoying all the events from criteriums under the street lights in Belgium to tearaway races in Brittany, the roadman's paradise.'

Pressed on the extent of this moratorium on riding, he said he just didn't feel like getting on the bike and reckoned that's probably how most of his team-mates felt, too. 'They'll be lying around getting fat, like I am.' (Over the winter, he had put on 2lbs.) 'As you can imagine, they're all in a pretty rough state.'

He then recalled that spring when brother Des attended the Simplex camp. They arrived fully fit and gave the rest of the party 'some real whackings', but once the racing started, they took a hammering. 'This is the secret of continental roadmen, to be able to pull everything out of the bag when not on peak form, even though these early season events aren't taken that seriously.' Racing instinct kicks in, plus experience, cunning and that intrinsic ability to economise with scrupulous care on work-rate…never to do more than is absolutely necessary until you have to. He cites the example of riding the long cols of the Pyrenees and Alps where it was essential to gauge effort so that, reaching the top, there was enough reserve left for recovery on the descent. 'This needs a fair amount of self-knowledge which can only be learned in training.'

For the spring training, he'd 'set up near some of the other riders, tag along with them, do the distances and, day by day, knock back the miles.'

His new companion in the peloton, Simpson, was doing just that, too, and in April he became the first British rider ever to win a Classic one-day race: the Ronde van Vlaanderen, beating the Belgian flahutes, hard men, on their home ground.

11: LIBERATED AT LAST…SORT OF

Grand Prix du Midi-Libre, four days in May…Critérium du Dauphiné-Libéré, seven days in June.

The *Midi-Libre*, 'Free Midi', newspaper, based in Montpellier, began publication in 1944, its title sounding a defiant blast against the Nazi occupation of France. The Midi, literally 'south', refers to the whole south of France, from the Italian border to the bay of Biscay, and was formerly ruled by princely families, quite independent of any authority in Paris. Part of it, to the east, was, for a long time, under the aegis of the Italian House of Savoy. To the peoples of the south, therefore, the concept of *liberty* has a dual force: liberty in principle, of course, but liberty, also, from any interference of royal government in the north.

The paper inaugurated the short stage-race which bore its name in 1949. Initially around 250km long, it was extended and, in 1961, the route, from Carcassonne in the Languedoc to Nîmes in Provence, ran 834km. Last run under the original name in 2002, the race foundered for lack of finance, was resurrected as Le Tour du Languedoc-Rousillon in 2004, but has now disappeared. In 1960, Robinson won one stage, came second in another and was placed seventh overall.

The *Dauphiné-Libéré* is another newspaper which clarions the message of freedom. The Dauphiné, formerly a province in the alpine region of south-eastern France, was ruled as an independent county by the Counts of Albon for three centuries until 1349, when it became part of the kingdom. However, it maintained its autonomy until 1457. The atavistic sense of that separateness persisted long. Perhaps taking his cue from the fact that the king of France was referred to as the 'father of his people', one of the Albon counts, in the 12th century, adopted a dolphin (French *dauphin*) as his badge to emphasise his own care of his people, just as dolphins are traditionally reputed to be the helpers of humankind. (In Greek myth, Arion, a poet and musician, is cast into the sea by mariners who envied his wealth, but a school of dolphins hears his last song and one of them bears him safely to land.) The count was thenceforth known as Dauphin and, by transference, his territory as the Dauphiné. When the lordship was sold to the king of France, to pay off debts, the treaty of agreement required that not only should the province be exempt from a number of taxes, but that the king's heir should, thereafter, be known as the Dauphin. That title died with the last king, but the area continues to be known by its adopted sobriquet and cleaves to a lingering pride in its former independence, its essential and unique freedoms. 'La Marseillaise' is not sung throughout France with equal enthusiasm.

The Dauphiné saw some of the worst of the final, bitter throes of the German army's desperate, bloody and doomed resistance to the uprising of the Forces Françaises de l'Intérieur, the FFI. The Critérium du Dauphiné-Libéré, generally seen as a warm-up race for the Tour de France, was first contested in 1947, again as a statement of release from the oppression of Nazi occupation.

Robinson had had a late start this year. He worked all winter in England – he and his father had to attend to an exceptional number of funerals because of a serious 'flu epidemic. He was kept busy making coffins and hadn't had much time off. Besides, there'd been so much fog through the winter that there was little chance of getting out on the bike anyway. As a result, he didn't start training until March and revised his programme to concentrate on stage races. The Four Days of Dunkerque and a stage win in the three-day Circuit des Monts d'Auvergne in May gave hint that the unaccustomed layoff had not greatly inhibited him. As Louviot said: 'Brian is a very reliable boy [thirty years old] who has given me much satisfaction. It does not matter a lot if he starts training later than the others. He will build up to his best form just as others are beginning to weaken.'

He then rode the Midi-Libre, not as team leader but as a team man, which was, he said, no bad thing. He was there to help his team-mates and then, when he got into form, they would help him. In a very strong field, including Louison Bobet, Joseph Groussard, Raymond Poulidor, a new man who had won that year's Milan-San Remo, and all the big French teams, Robinson came eighth overall. With but one day's rest, he set off for the Dauphiné-Libéré.

This was, said *L'Equipe* on 28 May, the eve of the departure, a very different Dauphiné-Libéré, the course was more human, more open to new blood. The field showed a number of younger riders, largely untried, as well as older, more experienced men. Many leaders of the peloton had been drawn, instead, to the Giro d'Italia, although the presence of the reigning Tour de France champion, Nencini, its Points' winner, Darrigade, and another prominent French rouleur, Graczyk, made this race 'very original'. Nencini, however, had spent two months in hospital after a bad crash in the Menton-Rome that spring, was overweight and lacked fitness. Present, too, were what one might call typical Dauphiné-Libéré winners – Lauredi, for example, and Dotto, with five wins between them, also Fachleitner, Lucien Lazaridès, Louison Bobet, all showing one thing in common: they were top rank climbers. In 1955 Walkowiak had come second to Bobet in the race and, next year…he won the Tour. The flatter Midi-Libre, which had just ended, favoured a *routier-sprinter*, such as that year's winner Joseph Groussard…and so the pre-race analysis went on, this rider's chances, that rider's strengths, an increasingly diffuse catch-all. Robinson gets a passing mention some way down the page.

The Rapha-Gitane team, managed by Louviot, with Geminiani as assistant – he'd retired from racing in 1960 – was very strong. As Robinson told me: 'We always took the biggest pile of money on offer because we were all hungry. When Geminiani had been riding with us, or Rivière, it made no difference, we didn't kowtow to them. We got on with the business, which was earning a crust and the crust was better in France. I don't remember that Geminiani took much of a part in the Dauphiné. He was an apprentice, learning the business, if you like, shaping down after his riding, and he couldn't have had a better tutor than Louviot.'

29 May 1961, Avignon

In 1309, Pope Clement V, a Frenchman entirely subservient to the French crown, moved the whole Papal court from Rome to Avignon. The Italian poet Petrarch, living there at the time, called the town 'a sink of vice'. Given that he had seen and fallen in love with the woman who inspired his poetic outpourings but never even spoke to her, one detects a trace of puritanical pique in his critique. The Pope set up in what had been the archbishop's palace and this Palais des Papes, within the cincture of the ancient ramparts, is the focal point of the city. Clement's successor, John XXII, was something of a wine buff and, as well as being drawn to the celebrated vintages of Burgundy, his taste extended to the as yet undistinguished wines of the Vaucluse, of which Avignon is the main city. These were soon known collectively as Vin du Pape, later Châteauneuf-du-Pape. The Papal imprimatur was worth a lot to any vintner. Gregory XI, last of the seven Popes who resided in Avignon during what was called the Babylonian Captivity (with reference to the exile of the children of Israel in Babylon), returned the papal court to Rome in 1377. Whether Petrarch considered this residency to have been a good thing or not is unknown. He'd moved into the countryside near Ventoux – and famously walked up it – and died three years before John and the rest packed their bags.

Stage 1 Avignon – Vals-les-Bains 213km

The fifteenth edition of the Dauphiné-Libéré rolled out from the huge courtyard in front of the Palais des Papes straight into the mistral. There are, the saying has it, three scourges of Provence: the parlement (because it interferes in everything), the Durance river (because its floods inundate everything) and the mistral (because it blows everything flat and scorches the life out of plants). The mistral (from Provençal *mistrau*, 'masterly') is a cold wind from the north or north-east which accelerates down the funnel of the Rhône valley and can reach a velocity of 90kph. In the 1969 Tour de France, the mistral hit the peloton at 70kph as it crossed the Camargue. The race directors took pity and allowed the riders to shelter behind the team cars for 50km. No such reprieve for the men of the Dauphiné this year:

they rode 75km into its teeth. The roads were, mercifully, flat to begin with and, despite the scarifying wind, the sun shone on low slopes cloaked with chestnut trees. Chestnuts were long a staple crop in the Midi, source of flour and animal food. The local bees swarm to the blossom, too, and their honey is pungent with the flavour of the nut. The peloton crowded together against the gale and crossed the Rhône at a relative dawdle. Into the lower Ardèche the ground became more hilly and two riders launched a suicidal attack – undulations and a high wind? Ideal conditions for an escape. Possibly. They were soon hauled back, but their impetus spurred other ambitions, and the speed gathered as the peloton began to fragment. A group of thirty riders, among them Robinson, eventually established a strong break and finished 7m 46s up on the following bunch containing Graczyk. Nencini, way off form, struggled in some eighteen minutes down. Later, Robinson praised the Italian's courage, merely to finish. Darrigade took the stage, shooting past two men who must have thought they had it sewn up fifteen metres from the line. Robinson finished thirteenth in the same time. Darrigade, now wearing the leader's gold jersey, made it clear that his intention was to imitate the routier-sprinter Groussard and win the Dauphiné.

Stage 2 a. (race on line) Vals-les-Bains – Valence 161km
Darrigade's plan sank. A bad knee hampered him severely, his team did not rally to his aid and he lost nearly eight minutes to the winner, Graczyk, obviously annoyed with his lapse the day before and keen to make redress. Robinson's young team-mate, Rolf Wolfshohl, reigning World cyclo-cross champion, came third, he himself finished with Darrigade in the main group.

Stage 2 b. (team time-trial) Valence – Romans, 37.2km
The Rapha-Gitane team won the stage, Robinson recorded the third best time and Wolfshohl and Gérard Thiélin were now first and second on general classification, Mastrotto ninth, at 7m 19s, Robinson tenth, at 7m 24s. Their *sous-directeur* Geminiani was cock-a-hoop. 'With Wolfshohl and Mastrotto we're going to play on velvet', like aristocrats, he meant. Mastrotto (a thick-set, powerful Frenchman from the Pyrenees), had come sixth in the previous year's Tour and was a noted climber – nicknamed the Bull of Béarn*. The German Wolfshohl, 23 years old, was strong but inexperienced on the road. However, Darrigade had predicted that he would become an outstanding rouleur and his strength would serve him well in the mountains. 'Rolf takes his role as leader very seriously,' said Geminiani. 'When he dismounted, he asked me for a comb. Great riders always think of how to present themselves handsomely on the podium. Think of Koblet.' (The French prized elegance,

---

* A former province, now the département of Pyrénées-Atlantiques.

chic in their riders, and still do.) He expanded on his theme. 'Everything's going well. It will be hard to take a lot of minutes out of the German and you'll see how hard he works over the cols. On the flat it's hard to contain the race, but in the mountains, just watch him go. And, if Wolfshohl does wobble, Mastrotto is there to take his place.' There was another private agenda in place. Mastrotto was intent on reselection for the French national team in that year's Tour. He wanted to impress Bidot when the manager came to see the racing – an attack in the mountains, for sure. He said that he'd have won the time-trial easily had it been an individual rather than team event.

When Wolfshohl complained that the course ahead was hard, Geminiani told him, 'All the better, the tougher it is, the better for you because you're on form'. He also spoke warmly of the ginger-haired Thiélin – who admitted that he'd never ridden so hard – and Pierre Everaert, who'd been dead in the saddle at the start but worked devotedly for the team. Robinson's later comment on these vapourings was laconic. 'So long as he had one of the team in the lead, he didn't care who it was.' At the time, he was preparing his own agenda.

Stage 3 Romans – Villefranche-sur-Saône 233km
The start in Romans was given some thirty metres away from a junior school and, behind its high walls, the kids were at play. They could hear the race but not see it. Zut. They escaped. Suddenly the whole gaggle of them was teeming out onto the road and the CRS had to round them up, assuredly the mildest, if not least elusive, of the targets that the Compagnie Républicaine de Sécurité, the redoubtable flying squad of the French military police, had ever encountered.

Forty kilometres from the start, along the valley of the Rhône, the French rider Claude Valdois attacked. Robinson and three others followed out of the bunch, Robinson to police the chase on Valdois. Fifty kilometres on, they caught him and drove on the escape. During the pursuit, Louviot came up alongside Robinson and told him, 'You can work, you know' and he needed no further encouragement. He knew this was his day and, naturally, having been allowed to join the escape he was obliged, by team loyalty, to win. Some eight kilometres from the finish, a sudden sharp hill offered Robinson an early chance to go for the win: it was just the sort of ground he favoured and a fierce attack on the steep slope would surely have catapulted him out of contact. However, he held fire and waited as the rest fell away leaving only him and Lach. He made his run for the line from a long way out, took the time bonus of ten seconds and, far more important, over ten minutes on the peloton. He was now race leader with 2m 50s on Wolfshohl, (2nd), 6m 22s on Thiélin (3rd) and a hefty ten minutes on Mastrotto, way down in the order. The team, too, was fully in charge of the order, well clear in that competition.

Geminiani, overflowing with pleasure, ever flamboyant and ready to lollygag, settling nicely into his new, self-elected role as puppet-master, strolled up to the journalists, a race cap pulled down over his aquiline nose, a cigarette drooping from his lips, hands in pockets. 'Things are going well, so well that soon my riders won't need me at all. Tomorrow I'm going to stop for lunch in a good restaurant. If you happen to know of one...?' The journalists clustered round whenever he held forth because he was raffish, showy and plied a smooth line in banter.

Robinson attended the press conference as new leader of the race. The press once again praised his command of correct French, answering even the subtlest of questions with aplomb. *Correct* embraces accuracy, precision and an indefinable quality of politeness. This is a people, after all, who have an academy of literary sages overseeing, maintaining and passing stern judgement on the purity of their language and blocking seditious attempts to contaminate it with nasty neologisms and foreign interlopers. As for Robinson and Wolfshohl, they formed a picturesque tandem, talking to each other in French, because the language of diplomacy had become the language of the peloton. One of their exchanges led directly to Robinson's stage win and the foundation of his overall victory. When Valdois attacked, Robinson, who thought the young German the strongest of their team, rode up next to him and asked what he thought. Wolfshohl said Robinson should go, try his luck, maybe it would work. Indeed, when I asked what relations were like within the team Robinson stressed that there was no ill feeling or variance. Everyone knew their job and got on with it. That was partly Louviot's great skill as *directeur*: firm but even-handed. Team tactics were his affair, and that brooked no argument. Robinson added that it was always a mistake to get caught by the manager at the tail of the field. If he thought they were slacking, Louviot would come up behind and blow his klaxon, lean out of the window and tell them to get back up to the front or, if a rider had punctured, he'd pick the nearest member of the team and tell him to wait to relay the man back up the road. 'Always better to be up at the front with the first twenty riders, that way you could see what was going on and stay out of trouble. And not to have to do any extra work.'

GF   Was there a lot of chatter, banter?

BR   On a long stage, around 250km, the first 100km or so would be what you might call leisurely, unless someone was stirring things up, otherwise you'd natter away. It passes the time and that's bike riders anywhere, enjoying a friendly conversation, like. When the hammer went down you'd all get down to business. It sometimes blew to bits right from the off, of course. Hassenforder was a devil. He'd often go to the front right at the start and announce: 'I win today', and like as not he would. If he'd taken the dope, that is. [Laughs]

GF   I can't remember where I read it, but apparently he experimented with Palfium, Maxiton, Tonedron, amphetamines, fed the stuff to one of his goldfish and then watched them all go round the bowl, to see if it had any marked effect over the others.

BR   He was half-mad, I'm sure. He's still alive, still goes out hunting every day. He was always crazy on rifles. It was a standing joke, you know, at the start of a stage, someone would call out: 'Who's fired up today?'

Robinson told the reporters: 'I'm happy to win this stage because it's my son Martin-Louis's birthday tomorrow [1 June]. I didn't want to miss that. I want to be a good husband *and* a good racer so it's important to build up my palmarès. I don't know if I can win the race overall but I'm sure our team will take it. I didn't intend to attack, because Wolfshohl held the jersey. It was the shape of the race which decided it and our position is now even stronger.' Asked whether this was his first leader's jersey, he replied that he'd worn the white jersey in the Tour du Sud-Est in 1955, his first stage race in France. Because of inexperience he lost it in the mountains the following day. 'I don't fear the mountains, now, but I'm still not in great form.'

One of the journalists at the press conference pointed out that this is not what Valdois and Lach (3rd and 4th on the stage) had said. Robinson smiled. 'I don't know. I'm behind where I was in previous years, not close to the usual output of training. My nervous system is not as strong.' (Meaning that he didn't feel as sharp as he would normally feel at this point.)

Had he made a decision about the Tour de France?

'Nothing formal, but my calendar isn't particularly full and my form's a bit late in coming, although I have been improving over the last month. So I hope to do my best performance yet in the Tour. I need to have a strong team round me for that and I'd choose to have my friends Elliott and Simpson riding with me. There's no question any more of my riding practically in isolation – I'd rather not ride the race at all. So, we'll see. Now for Grenoble and I'm going to defend my jersey.'

After the press conference, he went off to join Shirley and the children in the caravan for tea, a happy pause – she got the winner's bouquet – and, next morning, they were there at the start to see the race pull out, at 9 o'clock.

The starts tended to be at 9am, sometimes at 10am. Reveille at 6am, wash, get dressed, down for breakfast, beefsteak and pasta, back to the room to rest. They didn't always get a massage before the race, but if rain threatened, they'd apply olive oil to their legs and arms. 'Olive oil mixed with a bit of cheap eau de cologne.'

GF   So you wouldn't go off smelling like a Spanish short-order cook?

BR   More like a eunuch.

GF   Did you do that French thing of rubbing down with eau de cologne?

BR   At the end of a one-day race, if there wasn't anywhere to wash, you'd certainly rub down with eau de cologne – cheap, bought from the supermarket, or even just plain alcohol.

GF   What did you do after the stage finish?

BR   Back to the hotel for tea and biscottes, around 4pm, usually, because it was a long time till supper, then a shower and lie down to wait for your massage.

GF   You didn't read?

BR   No. Just rest, really, settle your body down into a normal quiet state. Sometimes you felt red hot – from the heat and the exertion – and you had to cool down. I always told the guys at training camp, it was my maxim, I suppose: if you can sit down, sit, if you can lie down, lie down. You might get half an hour or so free time before the evening meal, when you'd maybe have a gentle stroll into town or sit in the hotel garden if there was one, to have a chat with the other guys. That was when Jock Wadley would pitch up to take notes for his Diary, or other journalists, of course. They wouldn't come in when we were eating – whether or not because the restaurant steered them away, on the manager's orders, perhaps, I don't know.

GF   But access to the riders was pretty open?

BR   Oh, yes, not just to journalists, either. Members of the public would come up, any time, when you were out and about, at the stage start, rarely at the finish because you got off back to the hotel as quick as you could. There was none of what goes on today – the team buses and such which have made all the difference, no bodyguards, not even Jacques [Anquetil]. If you didn't want to be pestered, you fended them off yourself.

Stage 4 Châtillon-sur-Chalaronne – Thonon-les-Bains 223km

The route crossed the path of his famous solo victory in the '59 Tour, on to the ring of mountains round Geneva and down to the shores of Lac Léman. An attack went off from the front, sixty kilometres from the finish on Mont Salève, through plantations of strawberries, above Annemasse. Rapha-Gitane had no need to respond and the attack fizzled out: the three leaders were held up by a level crossing barrier for one and a half minutes as an interminably long freight train rumbled past. The peloton was in somnolent mood, too, either apprehensive of the high mountains of the next stage or else reining in impatience. Various riders attempted to break out but the race was gripped implacably by Robinson, Wolfshohl and Thiélin (1st, 2nd and 3rd on GC), who snuffed out the attacks, backed up by Mastrotto, Bernard Ignolin and Everaert. Another rider accidentally slipped on gravel, collided with Thiélin and pitched him over, and Mastrotto slid off on a bend, but the Rapha men swept them up at once. The crash left Mastrotto with a ripped jersey, the paint on his frame scratched and his left hip and side badly enough grazed to warrant medical attention. This was a blow. Bidot was due next day to see how this Pyrenean mountain man went in the cols.

That evening. Hotel room, shared by Robinson and Everaert*, Thonon-les-Bains.

Through a large window, a view out across a line of trees in a park, Lac Léman and the Jura mountains in the far distance. Lying on one bed, Louis Bergaud waits for his turn on the massage table. On the adjacent bed, Wolfshohl sits over a cup of tea, a slice of bread, a pat of butter and an enormous pot of jam. Robinson, naked, perches over the bidet in which he is soaking his feet. He's just given his legs a go over with the electric razor – some riders used to wet shave their legs. Geminiani holds court to the journalist in attendance.

'A *directeur sportif*'s job is the most relaxing in the world, if there weren't all these flights of stairs to climb.' He taps Wolfshohl on the shoulder. 'Your appetite okay? This Wolf thinks only of eating and making breaks.' Wolfshohl, his mouth full of food, does not speak but nods politely. Bergaud chips in. 'I don't mind him eating, I just wish he'd cut us some slack. You need to tell him, Raphaël. He goes after everyone. He's going to eliminate us all, him, too.' Geminiani chuckles. 'It's hard tomorrow, boys, mountains, but we're in the top three and we've got the best climbers. Not too tired, Brian?'

'No, I hardly turned a pedal, same with Wolfshohl and Mastrotto.'

'Ah, my friend, Mastrotto did well today. I know him, the big man. When he digs in and starts going at it with his ears back, watch out. After he crashed, I put a lightweight tyre on his back wheel. You should have seen the way he got back on. At the finish, he was bitching about having had enough of this flat country.'

Robinson remarks: 'Flat, he calls it. He's got a nerve.'

'He'll get what he wants tomorrow. But beware the day after tomorrow – the Laffrey, it's a wall, eight kilometres of it. Hey, Wolf, if you open up too wide at the bottom, you may just finish up in the gorge.'

Wolfshohl takes this in and then asks: 'What time's dinner?'

Geminiani gives him a lesson in tradition. 'Henri Desgrange said that a stage-race rider collects his thoughts at dinner. You all need to agree on that. Okay, cheerio, boys, I'm off to see the others.' He leaves a fresh gold jersey for Robinson and, on the way out says, aside, to the journalist accompanying him: 'Wolfshohl has all the dynamism of a guy of twenty-three, he doesn't know his trade, yet, but he'll be a good climber. He can take back the jersey, which Robinson will defend, that's to be expected. We can't lose this race but

---

* Everaert and Robinson were good friends. The Frenchman lived in Dunkerque and Robinson and family often stopped to stay after they had crossed the Channel.

each rider takes his chance. I can't deliberately sacrifice Wolfshohl, Thiélin, Mastrotto, they ride their own race. I ask only that they don't go off with dangerous rivals, like Adriaensses,'

Stage 5 Thonon-les-Bains — Chambéry (Cols de Saxe, Colombière and Revard) 206km
Wind and rain. The Rapha-Gitane outfit is strong and in command but, on the Revard, Mastrotto attacks and takes Robinson by surprise. He's shaken. Thiélin and the hit-man Wolfshohl try to follow, but in vain. Wolfshohl held Mastrotto's wheel for about a kilometre and then faded. On the climb of the Colombière, a number of riders fell away, including Darrigade and Nencini.

In Chambéry, Mastrotto was beaten by Mahé but went to third overall, displacing Thiélin. Having called Mastrotto's actions 'a fair demolition job' L'Equipe went on: 'The Rapha-Gitane riders today gave us a spectacular exhibition of tight-rope walking without nets. The opposition to them was nowhere.'

Robinson came in with the bunch at ten seconds. Mastrotto took a five-second time bonus but was still over six minutes down on the leader.

At the finish, Mastrotto went off, his eyes lowered, avoiding the blatant fury of Thiélin. Wolfshohl shrugged and Mastrotto began to explain his tactics to the reporters. Geminiani intervened: 'Eloquence isn't his forte. He's sincere in what he does.' Read: he does as he likes and hasn't got the gift of the gab to explain why. Thiélin breaks in: 'What is he thinking of? All right, we've got the top three, we've got a guy out in front who can win the stage and he attacks, causes panic in the bunch, drops Robinson, assassinates Wolfshohl…if he'd won, okay, maybe, but no, he gets beaten in the sprint. Result: we've all got sore legs and we've lost money. That's what you call a really good day's work.'

Geminiani: 'Let's not exaggerate. Mastrotto did an excellent job.'

Thiélin: 'So did Mahé, and he's not someone we can ignore.'

Geminiani: 'The tactic was right. And there's the race overall to consider. Raymond isn't always so inspired. He's entitled to have his say.'

Thiélin: 'He needs to warn us, then. We don't see him all day and suddenly he disappears up the mountainside, without a word.'

Geminiani: 'Right. Enough. No more talk, boys. This is a bike race, not a travelling show. If Raymond rides off like a postman, it makes no odds. Think what you like. Frankly, I think there's no need to dramatise. There are two stages left and we're in a bloody good position, dammit.'

There was some background to this. Geminiani said that the idea of a team leader simply didn't exist at the time. It was Anquetil (whom he later managed) who changed that. At the end of the '50s, the beginning of the '60s, the main strategy was to create diversion. A team pretended to be relying on one man as leader then marked a rider from a rival team by sending him out on the attack. The effect was to protect their real leader. This is what Geminiani hints at but his opinion is distinctly partisan and based on his own dealings with Anquetil. In 1955 the entire French team signed a mutually binding contract with Bobet to help him win the Tour in return for his winnings. There was, too, the internal strife in the postwar Italian team about the cogent claims of both Bartali and Coppi to leadership.

When Robinson set off for his prize-winning ride along the Saône, Geminiani insisted, 'I didn't for one second think about final victory, even if I knew from riding with him that he could certainly accomplish something over eight days. So, I was very clear about that. Then, forty-eight hours later, I decided to give Mastrotto a free hand on Mont Revard. One might smile at that, but Bidot was visiting the Dauphiné before making his final selection for the Tour and I didn't want one of my best riders to miss out.'

There was, however, general astonishment at Mastrotto's behaviour, even if Bidot himself said that, in the perspective of the Tour de France, Mastrotto had done the right thing. (He picked him.) And in the perspective of the Dauphiné...?

Stage 6 Chambéry – Briançon 210km (Cols de Laffrey, Ornon, Lautaret)
On this second day of climbing, three Spaniards, of no threat to the overall placings, were allowed to break early on and left to it. Mastrotto, peeved at the early error which cost him a genuine chance to win the race and still anxious to prove to Bidot that he was in roaring form, made a reckless attack which Mahé, also eager to impress the French manager, damped down by sitting on his wheel. The peloton was jittery, Robinson kept his cool and Wolfshohl, succumbing to the pressure of his first major stage race, went under. He lost six minutes on the day.

The route went through Grenoble and over the Laffrey where, in March 1815, Napoleon's invading force of a little over a thousand men, which had marched up from Antibes after his escape from Elba, was confronted by the garrison sent out by the governor of Grenoble. Napoleon opened his coat to reveal the star of the Légion d'Honneur and walked up to the jittery line of infantry and said: 'Here is your Emperor, fire if you will.' Most of the troops facing him were veterans of his campaigns. They broke ranks and crowded round him and from Grenoble, the Imperial eagle, as Napoleon himself put it, flew triumphantly on to Paris.

From the Laffrey, over the Ornon, on through Bourg d'Oisans up to the Col du Lautaret and the long descent into Briançon. At the finish, Mastrotto was still bristling, anxious, if not desperate, to attract Bidot's attention and convince the French manager of his form. 'I could have done some damage had I attacked at the foot of the Lautaret because I was feeling exceptionally good. But, because of Robinson's position, I had to put the brakes on.' Mahé had punctured twice on the descent of the Ornon and, despite a wearing chase to get back on, raced up the final col with style, in the company of Privat. (Mahé, Mastrotto and Privat were all reselected in the French national team for the Tour.)

Robinson spent the day monitoring his rivals in the main group. His racing acumen was finely tuned, by now. Indeed, Simpson was wont to say: 'If only I had your head, Brian' to which Robinson's riposte was: 'If only I had your legs.'

Manzaneque broke clear of Gimenez-Quillez to cross the Lautaret in the lead and win the stage comfortably. Their third partner in the escape, Marigil, who crossed the Lautaret after Manzaneque, trailed in nine and a half minutes' down: on the 80kph descent, his steering went suddenly awry and the bike started to shudder. Marigil applied the back brake and came slowly to a halt. He lifted the machine and the front forks and wheels dropped out. That close to wipe out and serious injury. Manzaneque lived in a small town called Campo de Criptana in the centre of Spain, where Don Quixote famously tilted at windmills in Cervantes' eponymous novel.

Stage 7 Briançon – Grenoble (Col de la-Croix-Haute) 223km
The route of the final stage ran south across the Col de la Croix-Haute and then back to Grenoble. Although the race was more or less locked up, the Rapha-Gitane team took control.

GF   How does a team block attacks?

BR   Well, put it the other way round, how do you disrupt a team that is trying to control the race? You need to infiltrate them at the front and mess them about, break their rhythm. Of couse, they won't just let you into their line so that takes a bit of doing, you need to fight for a place, muscle your way in, and then you can slow them down, just by closing up the gaps on their men as they try to come through on the relay, so there's no space for them in the line. If there's a heavy side wind and you form an echelon, what you do is worm your way into the line and if, say, four of their front men go a bit quick and you can slip in behind them, you hold the line back and let a gap open, which means that their next guys have that gap to bridge, plus giving you a mouthful as they swing out and past. If the Belgians formed echelon, they'd put one of their big men at the back, to act like a doorman. Not easy to jump in there. They were big guys and ready to give you some argy-bargy with elbows and shoulders. That last stage of the Dauphiné, Wolfshohl went off on the attack. He was smarting at losing so much time, I guess. There was no chance of him taking the lead back from me, but my friends in the team said 'We're not having this,' and chased him down. That kept the speed up, too, so no one else attacked. The team was fantastic as far as I was concerned.

GF There really was no back-biting?

BR Oh, no. Mastrotto was doing what he had to do, it was his livelihood.

The Frenchman Novak did get clear, for a long while in company with Posti. Over the col, Novak, alone again, was eventually all but caught by a counter-attacking group stirred by the Belgian de Wolf. Novak held them at bay and raced onto the track in Grenoble with an advance of some fifty metres. To his enormous dismay, he lost it. De Wolf surged out of the chasing pack and sprinted past to snatch the victory. Darrigade mounted another specialist display of his track craft and took the bunch sprint ahead of Graczyk and a triumphant Robinson. He was, understandably, in jubilant mood. 'I wonder what Tom Simpson will say about this. I thought I was too old to keep racing.' (At that precise moment, Wim Van Est, now thirty-nine years old, was celebrating his third win in the Bordeaux-Paris.)

The sponsor of the race, the *Dauphiné-Libéré* newspaper headlined its page:

ROBINSON a gagné, c'est justice!

ROBINSON wins. Justice is done.

'This victory, altogether logical, is recompense for a conscientious *routier* [professional, mercenary] who has confirmed his quality in several Tours de France and was bound to know success, one day. Above all his daring, then his consistency, finally his courage, provided the opportunity, on this occasion, to take his first great international win. It's only just.' The reward, apart from popular recognition and fulsome plaudits in the press, was a rise in his wages and increased fees at criteriums.

He told Wadley that 'there was a time when having the yellow jersey in such a race would have worried me. Not this time. I slept at night and, during the race itself, everything went just right.' He also confided that he would, after all, ride the Tour de France. 'I feel in great shape and I hope Tom and I can work together. On paper, our Tour team is not strong, but you never know, there may be some pleasant surprises in store. I would like to bring off my third stage win and help Tom take one or two. Then I could think about retiring next year.'

12: A FINAL TOUR

I wanted to clarify and expatiate on Robinson's verdict that overuse of the brakes had caused Simpson's crash on the Aubisque in the 1960 Tour. I phoned one evening to arrange a time for us to talk.

GF   Would 10 o'clock tomorrow morning be all right?

BR   Yes, that's fine, I can delay going out.

GF   I don't want to interrupt.

BR   No, I only go off for some shopping on the bike, that's fine.

Next morning I rang. The voice answered: 'There's no one at home.'

GF   I was just about to ask if there was anyone in. (We discuss the weather – bright sun up there, pouring with rain down here – and the state of the vegetables in the garden up there, down here. Then to business.) I want to ask you about using brakes on downhill, especially those long mountain descents.

BR   You don't do it. (Laughs.) We used to have a competition on Holme Moss, last one to apply the brakes...result, scars and bruises. The main thing is to get your line right into and out of the bends. Of course you have to slow into a hairpin which means using the brakes, but otherwise you go as straight as you can, directly along the line where you're looking. You'll go where your eyes are looking. If you follow a guy down and you see his line isn't quite right you can correct it yourself, take as wide a sweep as possible. If there's a bit of gravel spilling onto the side of the road, for instance, you need more space – if you go too tight you may lose it.

GF   What if you *do* lose it – like that time on the Portet d'Aspet when you wound up down a farm track, I guess you took the safest course out of what could have been an up and over. Does the thought of it linger for long?

BR   Oh, no, it doesn't linger, you just get on with the next bit of the job. I suppose when it does linger, that's the time to quit. I remember coming into Aurillac that day, down the hairpins, I lost it and found myself hurtling across country, off road. I got two punctures, front and back and lost a few places, but at least I was still upright. Confidence is the thing. I learnt a lot from the Italian and Swiss riders who were pretty expert because they did so much of it, descending, I mean. It's important to put all your weight on the saddle and, generally, keep your hands on the tops because you have a better viewpoint that way. Unless you're chasing and need a more aerodynamic position, in which case you go on the drops. Really, you develop an intuition. You certainly don't think about what you're doing, you just let it go. It's the same as riding in a tight-packed bunch, you get so that you can hear the slightest click which warns you something's not right and you say 'Eh up' and you're alert. So long as you don't do anything daft or different from what everyone else is doing – you have to rely on other riders, of course, as they rely on you.

As a footnote to this, the Universal brake pads of the time were made of asbestos fibre and not very efficient. Aluminium rims were almost impossible to get a grip on when they were wet. Side pull brakes, which most riders used, were, compared to those available today, fairly crude (except for the Campagnolo version, which Robinson used) and the pressure they applied wasn't even. In sum, braking was not such a comfortable option anyway.

Tour de France, 25 June 1961, Grand Départ, Rouen
Elliott was riding and his hesitations of previous years were gone. It's a tribute to his quality as a man that, having been reluctant to commit himself to a race in which the pickings were so hard-won *and* in the light of his elimination in 1959, that he did ride. A man of his strength and brilliance might have made a better living in the smaller races riding for his trade team. The friendship with Robinson was an undoubted spur and the presence of Simpson (despite a knee injury) confirmed it. The team would, at least, have a solid core. Of the other members, Elliott was less hopeful. Having seen them racing in the Isle of Man a week before the Tour, the Irishman – riding for Great Britain - was convinced that most of them were below the standard required for the Tour. Robinson shared his scepticism. Ron Coe, Ian Moore, George O'Brien and Peter Ryalls were all based in Britain and had little real idea what lay in store. Brittain came back along with three other men who had been racing with him in Brive: Vin Denson, Ken Laidlaw (who'd been in France for only six weeks on a temporary pro licence) and Sean Ryan. Albert Hitchen, a sprinter, made up the dozen.

Robinson had told Wadley after the '55 Tour, that before the race there was always a certain amount of scraping around for riders to make up the numbers. Consequently, given the wide disparity between national, French regional, mongrel and scratch teams, there was a number of men riding who really were not best prepared. That they should fail to make the grade was not surprising, albeit a major blow to their morale.

Talking to another journalist at the *permanence* in Rouen, Wadley gave his opinion on the British team. The journalist, from Nantes, replied: 'But of course, Robinson, Elliott and Simpson aren't British, they're French.' So, too, but genetically, the GB *directeur*, André Mater.

Mater, dapper, wire-rimmed spectacles, hair cut en brosse, attentive and sympathetic, ardent cycling fan, gave his business as jeweller, trading as

Jacques Mater, located on the rue Sainte-Anne in the second arrondissement of Paris. In fact, he owned a *maison à gros numéro* (brothel), the Hôtel de l'Escale on the rue Blondel, some distance away in the same arrondissement, in the Saint-Denis red-light district. He had acted as *directeur sportif* for the Reims bicycle club, (with which Hassenforder began his career as an amateur) and looked after Hewson, Sutton and Andrews during their sojourn in France. A man with plenty of money, Mater was open-handed, debonair, gregarious. He'd never been a racing cyclist but he knew the business, even if he deferred to his *éminence grise* Robinson for advice on tactics.

Stage 1a. Rouen – Versailles 136km

The race began with a familiar split stage. Elliott was up at the front with a breakaway group of fifteen riders, among them his trade team-mate Anquetil and the ace rouleur, Darrigade, who took his fifth win on an opening stage in six Tours. Robinson and the rest of the GB men came in with the following bunch, save O'Brien, already struggling, half a minute down, last man in the field. Gaul missed out on the break – Anquetil had warned his rivals that he would lead from start to finish. Technically, he did so, by winning the afternoon 28.5km time-trial, in blistering heat. For the first time since Bobet was named leader of a French team, in 1955, the Norman was undisputed chief of the French national team. In a seigneurial manner, therefore, he needed to assert the principle of unity by declaring not only his target but his capacity to achieve it. He did both, putting more than two and a half minutes into Albert Bouvet, French champion and Worlds' silver in the pursuit. Simpson, chary of putting too much strain on his bad knee, posted what was a poor time for him and looked very unhappy and ill-at-ease.

Stage 2 Pontoise – Roubaix 230km

The French have a saying *avoir l'air de revenir de Pontoise* meaning to be out of touch. This may be explained by the fact that, one day in the deep midwinter of 1437, when snow lay all about, Pontoise castle was stormed by soldiers led by the famous English man of unmitigated and indiscriminate violence, John Talbot, first Earl of Shrewsbury, and taken without resistance. Because they were all clad in white tunics, the defenders of Pontoise did not see them coming. Durh. Otherwise, Pontoise is a fairly nondescript place, inexplicably twinned with Sevenoaks, where I live. You can't have everything.

Rain made the pavé of the Hell of the North doubly treacherous. Denson punctured and was relayed back by Hitchen, Moore and Ryan to a peloton scorching on at high speed. It was a stark initiation into the high tempo of the Tour de France. Minus Ryan, they came onto the famous Roubaix track in a trailing group, together with Simpson who was suffering cruelly with the pain in his knee. Once again, O'Brien came in last to beat the time limit by a whisker. Ryan, way down, in company with two French nationals, Mahé and Privat, was eliminated. Three Spaniards and one German rider were also eliminated, two Germans abandoned.

Stage 3 Roubaix – Charleroi 197.5km

Mater detailed Laidlaw to nurse Simpson, who was now in such pain that he could barely ride. It soon became apparent that if they stayed together, they were both going to be eliminated. Laidlaw faced that bitter dilemma: to desert or knuckle under to a suicidal duty. Simpson, in a last burst of derring-do, hauled the young Scot up the fearsome Mur de Grammont, a 25% cobbled climb he'd flown up in the spring, when he won the Ronde. The picture shows Simpson gasping with effort at the top, his front tyre almost flat, as was he. Over the top, they caught up with three Italian riders. Simpson told Laidlaw to hook on to them and then he climbed off. The Italo-Scottish quartet made the finish a measly twenty-two seconds outside the time limit but were reinstated. Mater pleaded for Laidlaw and Brittain, but could do nothing to help Ryalls, who had missed the cut, too. He was evicted. As well as Simpson, O'Brien and Moore both abandoned.

Stage 4 Charleroi – Metz, 237.5km

The GB team lost two more men: Brittain and Hitchen both abandoned. Brittain was forced out because he had fallen on some hotel stairs and had a badly wrenched ankle. He was, it seems, also vexed by the points system imposed by Mater to reward teamwork.

Stage 5 Metz – Strasbourg 221km

Coe abandoned, ill from sunstroke.

Stage 7 Belfort – Chalon-sur-Saône 214.5km

Whatever memories stirred for Robinson this day, as the race headed for the line where he had triumphed two years before, the harsher reality of riding in a team already reduced, after a mere five days of the race, to four men, was uppermost in his mind. Undecided at the start of his season about whether he'd ride the Tour this year or not, and prompted to do so largely because of the good showing in the Midi-Libre and the Dauphiné with his trade team, the feeling grew that the British national team would never be strong enough to have any chance of competing with the others or to give him the support he needed to make any sort of showing.

When one of Elliott's pedals broke, Laidlaw and Denson stopped to ride him back, bit-and-bit, to within two hundred metres of the peloton. Robinson waited to help them bridge the final gap. But it was clear, even then, that any aspirations he might have had for a high placing in the race were dashed. The thankless chasing they were required to do day after day had sapped and finished off the inexperienced men and left the rest with little reserve for anything but mere survival.

Mater took notes about the men in his charge:

Ryalls, O'Brien, Moore, Ryan: too young, not strong enough.

Hitchen: has possibilities but is inexperienced in continenal racing.

Brittain: a puzzle – obviously has the class but doesn't seem able to live up to his amateur reputation.

Coe: good, but insisted on wearing a crash hat in hot weather. Others have had accidents such as he had but have been able to dispense with crash hat.

Denson: very good but imprudent in drinking too much.

Simpson: a great rider who should not have started the race with so bad a knee.

To explain: it wasn't an excessive consumption of alcohol of which he was accusing Denson, but of water. As already noted, the received wisdom preached that water diluted food and that in-take of liquids during the race should be minimal.

As to Mater's strictures on crash hats and hyper-hydration…*autre temps, autres moeurs.*

Stage 9 Saint-Etienne – Grenoble 230km

The route went up through the forest outside Saint-Etienne over the Col du Grand Bois* 1161m (also known as the Col de la République) and then over a series of ever higher climbs towards the finish: Col de Couz 624m, Col du Granier 1134m, Col du Cucheron 1139m, Col de Porte 1326m in the Massif de la Chartreuse below which, to the south, sits Grenoble.

Denson's stomach was in turmoil and, some way into the first day of serious climbing, he abandoned and sat, forlorn, wrapped in a blanket in the back of the sag wagon. Wadley believed that his metabolism was upset as much by underdone steaks as by guzzling too much water. It was a sad end for a rider at the start of a solid career on the continent, much of it as a domestique for Anquetil.

On the Granier, Elliott was riding strongly, Laidlaw some way back and Robinson down the field. Elliott, generally not at home in the mountains, was a man of buoyant spirit, strong and willing and he'd said that this year he wanted to have a real go on the big climbs. On this first major ascent of the Tour, he had stuck with a group containing the yellow jersey, Anquetil, Gaul, Mastrotto, and others. Gaul crossed the col ahead of Anquetil, who had

---

* Roger Rivière, a year on from his terrible accident, was there at the side of the road, cheering Anquetil on over the col.

punctured. Wasn't this against etiquette, to attack when a rival punctured on a climb? Ah, but hadn't Anquetil attacked when Gaul punctured on the first part of the stage out of Rouen and taken five minutes out of the Luxemburger? Alas for Elliott, his forks broke and, once he'd remounted on a spare bike, he, too, punctured. Gaul crashed on the descent of the Cucheron but rode on, with a bruised shoulder.

Stage 14 Montpellier – Perpignan, 174km
In the course of many conversations with Robinson, what became manifestly clear was that although making a career as a continental roadman in one of the toughest eras of a tough sport posed enormous difficulties, he managed without complaint or exaggerated personal struggle. When I put this to him, he said: 'I suppose it was difficult but I didn't find it difficult.' The essential hardheaded pragmatism. Except that this is his core. His manner belies that. His disposition is mild, he's easy-going, friendly, open and good-humoured, unpretentious, of a deprecating wit and quick to laughter. He still gets impatient with himself – over this past winter of enforced inaction followed by the painful crawl back to fitness he showed bursts of frustration, the undamped spark of the competitive spirit, no doubt. But, there is never a flicker of outward show or flimflam. He is a man entirely without side.

I think his singular capacity always to reduce a problem to its rudiments in order to solve it and then to get on with the job is the single most influential part of his considerable legacy: that he went to France to race and proved that it could be done was remarkable enough in itself. But the way he did it, the acceptance that to race on the continent – in that epoch, anyway – demanded total immersion, was the crucial lesson that many riders who sought to follow him could not accommodate, to their cost. Laidlaw, in that Tour, nearly quit because he felt so isolated.

Having spent only six weeks in France before the race, he had little grasp of French. At the team table, the conversation was habitually in French – Mater spoke no English – which cut him out. On this stage to the foot of the Pyrenees, Wadley in the press car drove up beside the Scot who had dropped off the back of the main bunch and was riding along in the middle of the road, plainly waiting for his *directeur* to arrive.

'What's the matter Ken?' Wadley called out, noting the sullen look, aware, too, that the man had complained of a stomach ache.

'Cheesed off…nobody to talk to…'

Mater drove up. Since they shared no language, Laidlaw interleaved his tirade – he wanted to pack – with gesticulated emphasis about quitting, climbing off, abandoning this abomination of a bike race, with which the Scot was rare fashit, the noo. The queer exchange concluded, Laidlaw pedalled back to the bunch. Wadley came alongside again and said that if he walked away from the Tour he would regret it for the rest of his life.

Later that day, Laidlaw had found his spirits again and was off the front, on the attack, in such roaring haste to get to the finish that the French sent their man, Robert Cazala, up the road to sit on his wheel. The pair was caught, inevitably, and Laidlaw had to drop back again to get treatment for his stomach. He reached the finish only just inside the time limit, herded in by the broom wagon. Robinson had finished some way down. Next day, into Toulouse, Elliott, who had featured in most attacks, had been named most combative rider of the day. A publicity picture shows him in a wheelchair, holding his trophy, being towed along the Toulouse track by Anquetil on his bike.

On stage 16, Toulouse – Superbagnères 208km, Laidlaw mounted a full-blooded attack at the foot of the final climb, included for the first time in this Tour, to the ski station above Bagnères-de-Luchon. It was mad. His break reached thirty-five seconds ahead of the chase but, with fifteen kilometres still to ride, it began to shrink as quickly as it had opened up, he was caught and, eventually, struggled to the top into a storm – hail, rain, lightning. He won the day's combativity award.

Stage 17 Luchon – Pau 197km
It seemed quite possible that Robinson would net the diminished GB team their third combativity prize. On this queen of stages, over the Peyresourde, Aspin, Tourmalet and Aubisque, he went clear with the leaders of a small breakaway, Emmanuel Busto, a French Centre-Midi regional, and Marcel Queheille, Ouest-Sud-Ouest. He went over the col 1m 15s down on Busto but over a minute ahead of Gaul and others. He then caught, and dropped, Busto on the descent.

A cold damp mist had invested the Tourmalet and Robinson lost ground, trailing Anquetil, Gaul and others, including Busto, to the col some fifty metres back. At the top of the Aubisque, Busto had gone away again and crossed twenty-five seconds up on Gaul. Robinson was suffering, by now, but hung on and reached the finish in Pau only four and a half minutes down. Elliott and Laidlaw lost over twenty-five minutes.

Pau was once called Ville Anglaise. Used as a resting stop by English troops marching north after victory in the Peninsular War, Pau drew an increasing number of English visitors, thereafter. They indulged in fox-hunting and in 1856 built the oldest golf couirse in Europe outside Britain. By 1860, a third of the city's population was British.

The 1961 GB team brought the most men home in Paris to date – Elliott 46th, Robinson 53rd, Laidlaw 65th, of seventy-two finishers. It was, nevertheless, further testimony, if any were needed, to the inadequacy of the British team selection, preparation, induction and management. The untried members of the team did their best, but it was a long way short of even basic requirement. The unfledged men, for all their pluck, were unschooled, inexperienced, off the pace, and it takes a bit more than pluck to ride such a race. Surely Robinson's mood had darkened.

BR   I don't remember, really, but I suppose you're right. I was getting pretty sick of the travelling for sure, the money I was earning wasn't that good, and without trade teams in the Tour, I wasn't going to be faring any better. The Dauphiné win, of course, gave me a terrific boost, and it just went to show what could be done with a well organised team. In the Tour, we never had that and the lack of it came at a price. (The GB team won least of all the teams, £488. The French nationals, thanks to Anquetil's overall victory, Darrigade's green jersey and nine stage wins, scooped £13,031. Holland, second bottom, won £683 and then Spain, £1,096.)

GF   That Tour must have tipped the balance for you?

BR   I guess it did.

At the end of that season, after the criterium circuit had wound down, Robinson joined Anquetil (with his wife, Janine), Darrigade, Bahamontes and Geminiani, still ready to turn a pedal for money, in an exhibition criterium in Benidorm. Today's glitzy Costa Blanca resort of mega hotels and skyscraper apartment blocks – it's known as The Manhattan of Spain or Beniyork – provider of all-year-round touristica, destination of 'wide-bodied jets loaded with wide-bodied holidaymakers'. The birthplace of the package holiday, Benidorm was formerly a small fishing village in Valencia, on the east coast of Spain. The then mayor, with an eye to the commercial possibilities inherent in white-sand beaches, dependable sunshine and cheap living as an attraction to foreign visitors, mounted a publicity campaign which included Tour de France stars racing round the cobbled precincts of what was at the time a tiny harbour. The trip, organised by Dousset, lasted a week, the money was good, the racing more of a stunt ride than serious competition and it counted as a lighthearted perk at the conclusion of a hard year.

GF   Anquetil?

BR   A gentleman. The public didn't like him because of the way he rode, I imagine, he was that ruthless about winning, and he was rather shy in some ways, came across as a bit prickly. But not with other riders. He was always polite, friendly, outgoing and a man of his word: if he promised money, it would always be paid. For all his standing as a rider, he didn't put on airs. It was a job and he did it well, a complete professional and a good man to be with.

GF   Bahamontes?

BR   He was a great comic. I liked him a lot and, of course, he played up to the public in Benidorm, that time – they were his people.

On 3 October 1961, exactly a month before Robinson's thirty-first birthday, the morning edition of *France-Soir* made an announcement which, had it come four years earlier, might have changed the trajectory of his professional career: the Tour organisation had relented to pressure and declared that the1962 race would be contested by trade teams. They'd invited some twenty-two journalists, long-time critics of their dogged objection to trade teams, to attend an open-forum conference on 4 October. The paper talked it down as merely cosmetic: there'd be no discussion, the decision had, in fact, already been made.

Three years before, Jacques Goddet, the Tour director, had set his face against the introduction of trade teams, despite a persistent campaign in their favour. 'I want above all to make the Tour de France international. To do that, I must rely on the participation of national teams. Only they can help broaden our scope and attract foreign entries, in particular from the East [ie of Europe] – I hope to welcome their teams before long. I remain resolutely opposed to trade teams in the anarchic state which prevails amongst them at present. For the moment, unless there is some ruling imposed which guarantees absolutely the moral honesty and the collective sporting spirit of cycling, I will not change my mind.' He was afraid that powerful trade combinations would gather, and monopolise, star riders of different nationalities under their aegis. That, he emphasised, he would never tolerate. It behoved the trade teams to preserve a certain national integrity to match the Tour's international status.

As soon as the leak was made public, Jacques Goddet and Félix Lévitain phoned round and hastily summoned the journos to a meeting that afternoon at 5pm. Two hours into the session, after a certain amount of back-tracking and special pleading, smoothing of ruffled tempers and reassurance, Goddet and Lévitain made a formal pronouncement: trade teams it would be. (There had been sporadic talk of inviting national teams every four years only to coincide with the Olympic cycle, but without great enthusiasm.) This changed the situation across the board. Trade sponsors now looked to *directeur sportifs* to shape their selection round the year's most lucrative publicity splash, the Tour de France. Instantly, everything was focussed on the Tour: training, equipment, philosophy, the entire structure of the sport. Despite a majority in favour, a rump of opinion in France remained unconvinced, still attached to the national and regional teams, perhaps swayed by sentiment, even nostalgia. The hard truth was, however, that the amorphous conglomerates riding under national or regional colours certainly did dilute, if not jeopardise, the commercial interests of the sponsors, but without those sponsors the sport simply would not survive. Conflicting interests, therefore: purity of sport per se and sport as commercial milch cow. Demonstrably, the old system greatly disadvantaged some riders, Robinson for one, even if he was not the most prominent. That disadvantage was, in its consequences, preeminently, financial. This was manifestly unjust. The sport was professional and the interests of its practitioners should weigh more heavily on any vapouring by the administrators about what was and was not desirable in the greater scheme of things. A large number of riders selected for the biggest bike race in the world had been grossly underpaid. This was rank inequality and if a clamour for equality had driven *the* Revolution it should drive this one, too.

One journalist, Maurice Vidal, championing the anti-trade teams lobby, denounced what he saw as a grubby capitulation. His thesis was, nonetheless, puzzling. Recent Tours had been substandard, he said: Bahamontes had won in '59 because of the disarray of the opposition…the '60 race had begun like a whirlwind. but the tragic accident to Riviére had robbed it of its probable winner. This was hard on Nencini, whom Latour, for one, described as the best all-round rider in the Tour…in 1961, a total domination by Anquetil had roused bitter criticism. Anquetil was whistled and booed at the finish in the Parc des Princes and Goddet had referred to him as 'a yellow dwarf' because of what he called his cynical lack of audacity in the race. He had, so many critics contended, simply ridden on the basis of limiting his losses without any of that panache which ought to attach to victory. Vidal concluded his polemic: 'Faithful to what has always been our principle in regarding cycling as a sport not commerce, and in wishing to extend its competition to as many nations as possible, we cannot approve of the meretricious demands to which it has fallen prey. The proud achievement of the Tour de France was to construct a barrier against the encroachment of business interests. The last dyke has just given way. The consequences will be grave.'

Even after the decision had been made, the wrangling, complex, heated and acrimonious, went on.

Goddet, in an attempt to rationalise the decision, said that the problems arising from the participation of national teams were threefold. As the French selections in recent times had amply illustrated, it was hard to establish any unity of purpose or harmony of relations amongst riders who spent most of the year riding against each other for different trade marques. It led to internal quarrels, discord and dissent and, not infrequently, accusations of treachery made by a rider who thought the rest were either plotting against his interests or simply squeezing him out. This jarred with the heroic ethos of the Tour. Secondly, a rider like Gaul from tiny Luxemburg had nothing close to the strength of a big national team to support him. This created a shocking imbalance in the structure of the Tour. Thirdly, the French regional teams had no intrinsic cohesion and were patently there to make up the numbers, no more than a foil to the elite class. His opponents probably said that all these objections were entirely reasonable and that the solution was to replace the heterogeneous teams with teams of dependable loyalty. Therefore, trade teams it was, for six years. National and regional teams returned in 1967 and '68, resurfacing like ghosts at the banquet, before Vidal's dyke was breached a second time and remains so.

There had been more widespread rumblings about the Tour's distinct loss of personality. On 3 August 1961, *L'Equipe* published a distempered letter from a doctor who decried a century of mechanisation, during which human beings had been overtaken by technology in a universe where mathematics ruled supreme. 'People,' he wrote, 'yearn for simple and healthy contact. In cycling, the reverse has happened. It's become a complicated sport of multifarious classifications, varying types of machine, and subject to a mysterious organisation and curious tactics which are difficult to comprehend. Further: the *directeurs sportifs* are in control, moving their pawns (the riders) about with more or less virtuosity. [And this long before the advent of earpieces.] The doctor notes a profound change in the psychology of racing. Anquetil has become 'a sort of pedalling robot, taciturn, dour, not given to witticisms, not prone to passages of weakness, not able to deliver brilliant feats of riding. Cold, calculating, pitiless. In short, the very opposite of what the average Frenchman looks for in a French rider. Anquetil does not see that such mechanised rationality triumphs only on ground where the automaton is superior to the man because of its regularity. Despite the lyricism of the journalists, the Tour has become dehumanised and the public feels it. It no longer knows whether what a rider achieves is thanks to the *directeur sportif*, the team, the equipment, drugs or all four together.' He concludes: 'Once a legend for all time, the Tour is now defined by the graph of an impulse calculated by an electronic brain.'

The man was clearly overwrought and overfond of his hyperbolic verbal idiosyncrasy, as well as being hot against robots, but the jibe about Anquetil's manner of victory – the limiting losses approach – and the despotic nature of team tactics had become a hardy perennial for the disgruntled nostalgists. (His strictures about Anquetil's lack of brilliance are laughable.)

Nowadays, people bitch about the advent of the hermetically-sealed team buses, the louring presence of bodyguards (sorry intervention, that), the pampered inaccessibility of the riders, the remoteness of what had once been very much a popular event, ie for the people. All a pity, granted, but all part of a jumpy modern social climate. Certain riders in the recent past have, by their paranoia, changed the mood radically, tightened the encirclement of the ring fence, and that's to be regretted. But, there are still ways of getting to talk to riders, even if the security hedges round them are that bit thicker these days. I've hopped over the barriers without a pass more than once. As Hilaire Belloc advised, it is pointless to lament the changes for the worse in today's world, it would be better to search out its novel graces.

One consequence of the altered system was that the Tour lost something of its lode in the weighting of the season: where national and regional managers had delayed their team selection until quite late on, the riders were kept in suspense and had to race that much harder to draw attention to themselves. (As did Mastrotto in the '61 Dauphiné.) Since trade teams now dominated all season round, the spring races lost something of their brio and cachet to a rather functional approach. Lesser riders tended to be more chary of over-extending themselves too early at risk of missing out on selection later. But, in any system, there will always be an extenuation on hand for anyone who seeks an excuse for his own shortcomings.

The shape of the sport was also altered significantly by the arrival of big sponsors like Ford Motors. Dousset had much to do with prompting their involvement. The commercial possibilities of publicity through the Tour de France in particular were hugely attractive, but the arrival of the moguls had serious consequences. In the restructuring of teams, those who had ridden for the national selections and those who had competed in the regional outfits were shuffled into two packs, first and second string. The old teams were broken up, men who had ridden together, sometimes for years, suddenly found themselves out and had to find a place elsewhere. In the Helyett-Saint-Raphaël team of 1962, for example, the first flight included Anquetil, Rudi Altig, Stablinski, Graczyk, Everaert. Robinson was relegated to the second tier, with scant hope of a ride in the major races.

In any event, the shift of power came too late for him. He had spent around eight months of each of the past seven years competing on the road, whether in stage races or one-day events or the circus of post-Tour criteriums – one year he rode thirty-five of them. Life in a suitcase, away from family and home, long training rides on his own, a compelling sense that, at his age, he wasn't going to improve in performance...all factors which hastened on a decision that was already in the offing. Life as a pro cyclist was becoming a grind and, when the enjoyment goes, it's time to stop. An awful lot of gallivanting about Europe, putting up in some crummy flea-pit hotels, hounded by the constant drive to make money by placing well if not winning. Add to that the ungrateful isolation of the mongrel teams in which he had to ride the Tour. As he put it, he rode everything that came along because he had to. Like any freelance, he did not know the meaning of the word *no*. Yes was the ticket to a livelihood.

As ever, at the end of a season, tired out mentally and physically, glad to be shot of the bike for a few months, he went back to Yorkshire, stopped at the chip'ole out of Mirfield and was glad to be home. He knew, too, that in the welter of feelings which tugged him this way and that – Shirley and the children...the instinct of the born racer – he would have to choose.

Cycling hadn't lost its grip on him but it wasn't paying well and, given his age and the hammering his frame had taken, it would soon be paying even less. The first Tour, which had begun the adventure, was, he says, 'magic, painful magic but magic…it's what every bike rider aspires to, every roadie, anyway. And I did feel part of a big history when I rode it for the first time. But, gradually, you realise what the stakes are and it gets harder to match them to how you're doing. When I had to abandon after that crash and broke a small bone in my wrist – there was no way I could have ridden the cobblestones with that – the feeling was of being left out, all at sea, altogether out. I went home with the sense that nobody wanted me, the race was going on without me, that was me, done. I suppose that feeling always lurks and it got to the point when I felt I'd done my time and I needed to walk away, not be forced out. When I did make the decision, I had no pangs about it. The fact is, it's fine when you're in top shape but if you're not it's damned hard, a real struggle and you know you're badly up against it. The slog of travelling, too…it was a job for a single man, really.'

EPILOGUE

Late afternoon on 2 June 2010, the sky beyond my workroom windows blue and cloudless, the sun warm on the vegetables in the raised beds, the poppies bursting into flower, birds singing away in the silver birch beyond the garden gate. The phone rings. It's Robinson, apologising for tardy response – they've only just got back from the Wednesday ride.

'One of the guys had a broken chain. We found him by the side of the road thinking about calling a taxi. I always carry the tools and I had a spare link – which reminds me, I should get a replacement. But we did sixty miles, which is the furthest yet this year, so I'm pleased.'

We talk about this and that and getting off the bike to walk, which, in all conscience we do not do or even contemplate.

'I have got off this year, I'm ashamed to say, but there it is.'

Following such an injury, through such a winter, months of enforced inaction, a slow slow recuperation, fighting to get back to any kind of fitness, in his eightieth year, vexed about having to get off the bike…?

In the early spring of 1962, the Robinsons, Brian, Shirley and the two children, Martin and Michelle, packed their bags and headed off in the Riley, towing the caravan, down to Grenoble. Robinson did training rides of around 100km per day and waited, with no great confidence, for a telegram telling him to report to Nancy, for the beginning of the Tour de France. It never came. Robinson himself knew that this was to be the final sally. He'd started training late, and, as he put it, when they got to France 'I just buggered about, to be honest, it was a swansong, sort of thing. I knew I wouldn't be picked for the Tour and I wasn't riding well'. He rode the Tour du Sud-Est in late April and the Tour of Germany a month later. It rained nearly all week, he had no real interest in the race and, when his team-mate Altig packed, he climbed off, too. Was it on the last day? Altig gave him a lift…terrifying, a demonic German pro cyclist behind the wheel of a big motor, in a tearing hurry on the autobahn in driving rain….

Thirtieth in the Midi-Libre and an abandonment on the fifth stage of the Dauphiné followed by a busman's holiday in the sun, with the family, until the money ran out and they went home.

He did ride the Worlds that autumn but, when Simpson punctured and Robinson, without thinking, handed him a wheel, they were both disqualified. Only assistance from the neutral service car was allowed by way of making it a race of individuals. But Robinson had never done well in the race. He was always largely spent by then, the rest of the team generally had no acquaintance with continental racing, nor the miles in their legs for even survival over such distances – 296km that year, won by Stablinski, Elliott a fine second.

I'd asked him to say something about Simpson. It seemed right to post an envoi to him in a book about the man who had been his direct inspiration and mentor.

BR What happened to Tom was so very sad. It didn't need to have happened. He didn't need to boost his performance that way, he could do it mentally, he could drive himself over the top without any assistance from drugs. He was the one guy I knew who could excite himself without drugs. But, he'd thought it out and taken a conscious decision and it's always a personal choice. It's why he went from Paris, where we'd started when he first came over, to Belgium. I knew it was going on, of course. In Belgium it was obvious – the syringes came out during the races. It could have been vitamins, of course. But that's what put me off Belgium. I never liked riding with the Belgians, anyway. It was all rough and tumble, grunt and growl, there was nothing friendly about them. I'd see some Flandrian, twice my size, sticking some dope in him and think, 'How can I cope against that?' I must admit, too, that I was a bit scared of all that. And when you saw the scallywags who were doing it…that's why I rode stage races, because there was no question of using the stuff, then. I never pursued it because the general opinion was that if you were riding a day race it was all right, but on a stage race you have to think of the next day, what the after effects might be. Had someone come to me before that Milan-San Remo and said that if I took such and such I was pretty well sure to win, the decision might have been tough, but doping was never for me. A hit of coffee before a crit. and that was about all.

I did so well in the Milan-San Remo that one year because it came straight after the Paris-Nice and I was flying. There was another thing about Belgium, too: the roads were poor and the pavé, of course, they didn't suit a lightweight. And I never much took to flatlands, either. One of the reasons I only ever once rode the Four Days of Dunkerque, which is a big race – it's prestigious, but not hilly enough for me. The Ardennes were different – that was my sort of country. But Tom was pleased to go to Belgium. The thing is, though, you don't ride the Belgian classics on Evian water. Things were different in France. Of course it went on and Jacques was quite open about it – small trees don't grow in the jungle, he said – but he had such class and you can't turn a donkey into a race horse, whatever you squirt into its bloodstream. I think it's a bit like sex, in my day, at any rate, it was talked about a lot but more than it was done. Basically, I didn't want to know. And one of my lessons was seeing Malléjac by the side of the road on the Ventoux, on my first Tour. You're riding under such strain, on fire because the sun's so hot and you're so overheated with exertion, your head's banging away…all drugs do is take over the natural function so you can push yourself beyond what the body can strictly and safely tolerate. Denson said at the time that Simpson was struggling and he thought pills would get him over that.

Just before Christmas, in 1969, Robinson senior, sixty-five years old and just retired, collapsed, with angina. He never saw the New Year. Once a heavy smoker, he'd given up when he got appendicitis, aged sixty. The doctor said that everything was worn out. He'd continued to work 'on the tools', as they say in the trade, but, in the last few months of his life had grown progressively weaker.

Robinson took over the business more or less straight away and expanded it into a full-scale building firm. His father had bequeathed him a plot of land and on this the revamped Robinson company built four bungalows to sell, having first built a vicarage. The church was rapidly selling off the large properties in which vicars had been housed for a century or more and the grounds were usually so capacious that they could take a second dwelling, in addition. Thus the new enterprise thrived on the construction of vicarages and doctors' surgeries.

Robinson came back to normal life, as he called it, quite happily. It undoubtedly helped that his work entailed hard manual labour. It eased what is generally a quite painful transition from a protracted expenditure of extreme physical effort into a very much less intense regime. The metabolism, inured to a vast intake and burning of calories, has to adjust to milder demands. The body, tuned to high output of energy, is prone to close down. The hard toil of building work acted as a welcome alternative. (When Bernard Hinault retired, he started farming and didn't ride a bike at all for some twenty years.)

Surgery, that winter, cleared a problem he had with varicose veins. He did miss the life a bit, his friends, the whole routine of racing. 'But I'd done my time and I had no pangs about leaving it. It's fine when you're in top shape but if not, it's damned hard.' He then said a surprising thing. 'I'm not a great traveller, strange to say. I like familiar things. Rides with my mates on Wednesday and Saturday suit me well, even if it hurts to ride at the moment. I don't enjoy the bike as I did, which is sad, so I try to ignore it, But it'll get better, I hope.'

GF   Was there ever any thought of staying in cycling, somehow?

BR   I knew Benny Foster. He was a door-to-door salesman, heating oil, but involved in cycling administration. He'd got me a healthy contract to ride at the 1959 Isle of Man meeting in Elswick-Hopper colours. He went on to be the international team manager and he asked me if I'd consider coaching the Great Britain team. I said I'd do it for £3,000 a year and control of the riders. He said three grand was fine but that I'd never get control of the riders. This was a time when the officials were telling Reg Harris, who was World Champion, how he ought to train. Of course, they wouldn't wear it. It's an old problem in British cycling, the guys in charge sort of go on the basis that there are two ways of doing things – their way, the right way, anyone else's, the wrong way. I wasn't much bothered, though. It would have involved a lot of traipsing about and I'd had my fill of living out of a suitcase. I finished with a nice house and a good car and that was that. I needed to crack on and earn a living.

GF Did you go on riding?

BR No. There was no time. I did take up golf, joined the local club, which was a bit of social, too, but I only ever played on Wednesday nights, which was too infrequent so I never got any good at it. Apart from that it was all bed and work. Even Saturdays, there'd be a machine to see to. I get single-minded about things and I suppose that was a major contributor to our divorce, which came out of the blue, as far as I was concerned, a real shock, it knocked me really. I'd thought the life we had in France, by the Mediterranean and all, had been quite nice, but, you don't know. I realized later, of course, how tough it must have been for Shirely. I was so focussed on what I was doing. There's no other way of doing anything unless you do it all out, I think, not for me at any rate.

(He and Shirley separated in the late '70s and he remarried, Audrey, in 1980.)

GF When did you start riding again?

BR Let me think…'92. After I retired from the building work and had time.

Robinson, at my request, showed me the workshop in the old yard. He still works there, is in the process of laying new concrete floors and has just finished renovating the cottage opposite.

The shelves and surfaces are lined with the impedimenta of a joiner: moulding planes lined up like wooden books…a pigeonhole rack with small drawers where they kept the screws and fixings…blocks for various sized bits…the morticing machine, crosscut saw, planer… long abandoned spiders' webs draped with a winter coat of sawdust…racks for boards yet unshaped, some the remainder of the elm coffin boards from which he made the shelves I spoke of at the beginning of the book. The workshop tells of the continuum in the industry of his life. 'I never could be still, I had always to be doing.'

That he is conscious of being what this book heralds him to be, the great pioneer, is not apparent in anything of what he says about that time as a pro rider. Indeed, he would probably pooh-pooh the idea, even if he knows full well that the ascription is just. What does it matter, finally? He did what he did on a bike, did all he could on a bike, and, when it was time to quit that job, he quit without a backwards glance and got on with the next job. I asked him many questions, in the course of our putting this book together. Although, when the idea of a book was mooted, he professed a casual indifference to whether it were to exist or not, he gave me every assistance I asked for, trawling the depths of his memory as deep as he could go, not always with startling result, it must be said. But every detail, however apparently insignificant, adds to the texture and it is no easy thing to relocate and then recall the past. Redefining it is beyond most of us. You'd think that, having been there when it happened, we'd know. Alas, not so. Anyway, one day, answering to the curiosity which is the search engine for memory, I asked him about massage: had he been massaged before he became a professional rider?

'Oh yes. We used to go to Huddersfield rugby club on Mondays, which was our day off riding. There was a guy there who did half an hour for five shillings. Our kid Des was in the top echelon by then and he was more aware of stuff like that. He was much more up to the mark on things generally. I just followed on, really.'

I just followed on really.

2 July 2010

I walk, once more, across the gravel to the Robinson's house. The turbo has disappeared from the covered porch, a signal that recovery from the injury last winter is going well. The roof of the porch is latticed with sturdy tendrils of two types of vine, a German variety. Along one wall, a goodly stack of logs from the hewn sycamore which had been crowding one of the mature ash trees in the front garden. A new freezer in one corner, home of the stewed plums from the small orchard in the paddock adjoining the house's curtilage. Pears, apples, plums and a finely shaped walnut tree, the cutting brought back in the caravan from France some fifteen years ago.

At 8.55 next morning, Robinson and I set off to meet his friends in a pull-off at the bottom of the hill, me on bike borrowed from his son-in-law Martyn. The night before, Martyn had driven us, at my request, up Holme Moss so that I could check the exact distance of Robinson's record-breaking hill climb. From a shepherd's hut, dilapidated now as it had been when he did the ride on a warm late summer evening in 1951, with the wind behind him. The car's milometer reads 1.4 miles and, in the nacreous light of gathering dusk, we look from the windblown summit north across the ungainly sprawl of Huddersfield. There's a sign marking the offical end of the climb, now, a line across the road signalling a mile to go just above the start. Altitude on the summit 1719'/ 524m. I eventually dug out a Huddersfield RC official guide to the 1954 club hill climb, which gives the distance as 1 mile 500 yards on an average gradient of 1 in 7, won by Les Ingman (who rode in the Helsinki Olympics) in a time of 6m 46.2 s.

Our Saturday ride skirts the extended rise of Wessenden Head Moor on which the radio mast pinpointing the Moss stands. I'd had trouble setting the saddle height on the borrowed Airnimal. Robinson drops back and takes charge.

BR   Come through…come through, come on, don't mess about.

GF   What do you think?

BR   You're still riding like a dwarf.

I raise the saddle, he admonishes me, 'half an inch more…right' and we set off again.

Through New Mill over Hade Edge past Daisy Lee Moor, Snittlegate and over Crag Rats to Victoria. The moorland largely empty of sheep, to my surprise, the long drag of the hills entirely expected. 'Good for conditioning, these slopes,' I say, to no one in particular.

BR   What's that? Conditioner's what you put on your hair.

GF   There'd be no point putting any on yours.

The road straightens out and up past the wind farm on Spicer Hill to Millhouse and the Windmill café, built on the site of an old fulling mill – toasted tea cake or scones, tea or coffee. At an adjacent table to ours sits Brian Haskell, a stalwart of the Huddersfield RC, BLRC National Hill Climb champion several times in the 1950s, now cruelly afflicted with Parkinson's disease.

We pause at a viewpoint above Royd Moor, a panorama round all points of the compass, south over the Derbyshire Peak District and Kinder Scout 2088`… west towards the old packhorse route used for the carriage of salt from the Cheshire salt mines to Rotherham, Wakefield and south Yorkshire… The route home swings past the television mast by Hoylandswaine, down Cat Hill through open farm and moorland, sun shining, a light breeze, a nice tempo, back to Mirfield through Upper Hopton and along the old railway line, the Greenway cycle track which follows the Calder and Hebble canal all the way to Manchester.

Legend has it that Robin Hood is buried in the grounds of what was Kirklees Priory outside Mirfield. (The Three Nuns pub, just down the road from the Robinson house, alludes to this.) His cousin was the prioress and when he arrived, a wounded fugitive, the sisters either killed him or tended him to sufficient strength to allow for one final bowshot. Where the arrow fell, there he was laid to his final quietus. The spot is marked with a small iron palisade. As in so much folklore, there are indicators of some basis in historical fact. One Robert de Kyme, ward of the Earl of Huntingdon, as knight errant (mercenary) born in Nottingham in the early 13th century was related to the same prioress and twice outlawed.

Later that afternoon, we watched the televised coverage of the Prologue of the Tour de France, shots of Tony Martin waiting anxiously to see if his time would hold against Cancellara. It didn't and the pictures showed the young German in the close up and personal company of his girlfriend, cosily draped.

BR (wry smile) He'll not do well taking her around with him. He needs to keep his mind on the job.

GF Do you get a twinge when the Tour is on?

BR No. (pause) Sometimes, when they're going through the mountains, I think 'oh, we went over there...'

GF The state of the roads was so very different when you were riding. A friend told me the other day that they've laid new tarmac over the Tourmalet for this year's race and it's as smooth as a billiard table.

BR That's true. There was one long tunnel, I can't remember where...

GF Alps or Pyrenees?

BR Alps.

GF The Galibier?

BR Yes, I think so.

GF One of the first riders to go through it, in 1911, I think it was Georget, said that the people who'd dug the tunnel would have been better to dig it at the base of the mountain.

BR Ha. It was that long, dark and wet, from the seepage through the rock, you came out at the end blinking in the daylight. There was another tunnel, in the Pyrenees, where there was a mass crash, one time.

GF The Mas d'Azil?

BR Could be. In the dark, none of us could find our own bike so we just grabbed the nearest machine from the tangle and sorted it out later when we could see what we were at.

GF Was it your brother and father who first prompted you into racing?

BR Actually, I was dead set on getting a motorbike, but there was no money so I more or less drifted into bike-racing. I suppose the bug caught me. Odd, though, how your life might have turned out another way completely. I wanted to go to Australia when I was 21, coming out of my apprenticeship. They had good deals for tradesmen over there and I only didn't go because my mother was against it.

In the November 1958 issue of *Cycling*, Robinson ruminated on a future which might, therefore, have been quite different:

I believe no one is *born* to do anything. You must work at whatever you choose to do. You must get experience, you must take the general principles from others, even if you don't have detailed information. You must learn how to exploit your natural abilities – for instance, plan your racing, one year to sprint well, another to climb. Overall, you must be capable of self-criticism and self-analysis without lacking self-confidence and you must experiment a lot...The tempo of the road game on the continent has the effect of discharging the body very much the way a battery discharges. Two months, they say, is the absolute maximum a man can hold top form and that's the principle I work on.

He'd come a long way from the early flush of an amateurish willingness to 'have a bang' whenever the opportunity offered.

APPENDICES

The Bicycle Union, formed in 1878, organised and regulated bicycle racing in Britain, and was renamed the National Cyclists' Union in 1883. Public opposition to bicycle racing on the public highways was as vehement as the conspicuous detestation of cyclists – any cyclist of whatever stripe - in many contemporary motorists, notably and nastily White-Van-Man. Police even launched baton charges on racing cyclists. As the cycling historian Bernard Thompson writes in *Alpaca to Skinsuit*: 'Events organised by clubs in the 1880s, although taking place on quiet country roads, were constantly interrupted by the police. Often horse-mounted policemen charged at racers and threw sticks into their wheels.' Speaking as someone who has had a stick flung through a front wheel (in Egypt), I can vouch for the nastiness of that particular form of assault. At a time when a rider, mounted on what was widely perceived as a dangerous, unpredictable, outlandish new two-wheeled machine, could be prosecuted for 'pedalling furiously', ie at startling, therefore ungenteel, speed, the sight of unruly swarms of the varmints hurtling along the Queen's highways, not that respectably garbed, either, was not to be endured. In response to such marked antagonism, the NCU banned all cycle racing on public roads in 1890. Cyclists, a bolshie bunch even before the advent of the Bolsheviks, were not to be thwarted and set out to win back some, at least, of what they perceived to be their freedom of the road. The time-trial came into being. Participants gathered at secret locations to compete against each other, against the clock, setting off at one-minute intervals. In the view of purists, this delivered an absolute record time, the only true test, in their eyes, of distinction between one rider and another. The time-trial also had the advantage of being technically not a road race at all and, therefore, within the strict letter of the law, whether formulated by the NCU or the Palace of Westminster.

In 1876, an Englishman, Frank Dodds, had set what is registered as the first world record for the hour when he rode 26.508 km (16.471 miles) on an ordinary, that is a penny farthing machine. This exploit seems to have prompted the setting up of a national body to monitor competitive performance, hence the Bicycle Union in Britain, followed by other national federations, in quick order - France, the USA, Netherlands, Germany, Sweden. They were all soon at loggerheads, of course. The British Union denounced the laissez-faire attitude of the Union Vélocipédique de France for permitting so-called 'amateur' riders to compete for prizes of up to 2,000 Francs. Nevertheless, regulation was chancy, at best. When Henri Desgrange, future inaugurator of the Tour de France, beat the world hour record on the famous Buffalo Vélodrome in Paris, in May 1893, his manager bought him a sumptuous lunch and offered him a wad of bank notes which he could exchange for gold louis (a more dependable currency). Desgrange had to refuse, because of his amateur status. The timing of records, which meant that cyclists could compete against each other anywhere in the world, had begun sometime around 1880 and the fact that the British authorities cleaved to them more readily was at the root of a split – between road racing and time-trialling – which, from then on, divided the British racing scene from the continental, quite as effectively as the Channel separated Britain from Europe. So popular did racing against the clock become in Britain, partly fuelled by the amateur spirit of defiance, that it dominated the domestic scene for nearly a century. There was a certain mischievousness about the whole thing: start places and times were locked in a secret, complex code known only to competitors and not to be disclosed, even by the cycling press, to any interloper or officer of the law, a furtive practice which continued until quite recently.

The Road Racing (later time-trials) Council, set up in 1922, and the Road Records Association, which oversaw distance and place-to-place record attempts, jogged along uneasily with the NCU until 1942. A decree by the international ruling body, the Union Cycliste International (UCI) in 1933, had made all championship races, amateur and professional, massed-start events. Obedient to this diktat, when the Worlds came to Britain that year, the NCU located the road race on the motor-racing circuit at Brooklands near Weybridge in Surrey. The only other circuits available for massed-start racing on pre-war mainland Britain were at Crystal Palace, south London, Donington Park in Leicestershire; the Snaefell Mountain course on the Isle of Man was a special case. However, despite that bowing of the knee to UCI demands for a specific event, the NCU was not to be budged on the matter of massed-start racing on the road. They told clubs, instead, to organise races on closed circuits. Since there were few enough of these, the frustration of the road-riding lobby deepened. But the road-riding lobby was not to be silenced. In 1942, Percy Stallard organised a massed-start road race from Llangollen to Wolverhampton. He was instantly banned for life by the NCU and, in November of that year, he and a number of other malcontents formed the British League of Racing Cyclists, expressly to organise massed-start road races. Given that most cyclists consider one of the prime attractions of the beautiful machine to be the harmony, mental, physical and psychological, it engenders, there is at least curiosity value in the aspect of the various bodies set up to govern its deployment as a tool of competition being at each other's throats with the implacable savagery of feral cats. There is an unseemly tribalism at play in the internecine rivalry of bodies supposedly united in dedication to the furtherance of a sport they profess to love. Beneath that surface swirls a vehement and blinkered defence of the ground they have staked out as their own. Former sportsmen themselves, hankering for their own salad days in the saddle, they continue to act like the older clubmen browbeating the new sprogs in the club: their own lordship is long past, but some intransigent envy prevents them from standing aside for those whose day is now come. 'Put some time in' they say, time being the one thing old men have in ample supply. Men like H.H. England, editor of *Cycling*, was a very poisonous influence, says Robinson. His entrenched opposition to road racing helped to foment deep dissatisfaction among the racing fraternity.

A good bike rider has to reinvent himself in every race: a win on any one day never guarantees a win on another day. So, too, must every generation find itself and there are impediments enough, obstacles aplenty, without the intervention of the old farts who have done it once and think, accordingly, that they have done it for all time. Such pomposity is obstructive and unedifying. It smacks of the senior boys in a school bullying the juniors in belated revenge for the bullying they themselves had once suffered. Moreover, the disputes which centred on time-trial versus road racing in Britain had a pronounced moral tinge. Road-racing, said the against-the-clock timekeepers, was not and could not be a stringent test of class, because massed-start races might be won by a rider who could finagle his way to victory. They meant cheat. They meant skulduggery, low cunning. They meant brains over brawn. A marked contrast with the French attitude bred in the hard experience of elbow to elbow rivalry on the road. As Henri Desgrange put it: 'To win the Tour, it takes head and legs.'

Even so, France was not immune from such internal squabbling. During the government formed by various parties of the left, known as the Front Populaire (Popular Front) from 1936-1937, a federation to regulate sport was set up, the Fédération Sportive et Gymnastique du Travail (FSGT) – a sort of workers for sport and sport for workers body. As ever in France, politics is never far removed from any activity. Imperious and monopolistic, the FSGT would have no truck with any other sporting bodies, including the French cycling federation. The collaborating Vichy government dissolved the FSGT in 1940, although it was reborn later and continues to play a strictly non-authoritarian role in the stimulation of healthy and sporting activities in France.

After the war, when many of the vast number of concrete-strip aerodromes laid down in haste for fighter and bomber squadrons at the outset of fighting fell into desuetude, more closed circuits did offer for racing, but only in those areas where the RAF had been concentrated – mostly in eastern and southern England. The roads continued to beckon. Robinson's adaptation to continental-style racing, from so shuttered a background in Britain, is the more remarkable, a testimony not so much to his physique as his moral and mental resilience.

APPENDIX II

POUNDS, SHILLINGS and PENCE

Note on money symbols.

Pre-metric sterling money comprised pounds (symbol £), shillings (either s or the symbol /) and pence (d). Twelve pennies, or pence, made a shilling, twenty shillings made a pound. Thus £7 8s 4d stands for 'seven pounds, eight shillings and fourpence'. (Note the liaison in denonimation of pence.)

The currency also included a hexagonal threepenny bit (usually pronounced 'thrupenny') once silver, later alloy (copper, nickel and zinc), three bronze coins, penny, halfpenny and farthing (ie 'fourthing', embossed with a wren, the smallest English bird) worth a quarter of a penny. Three silver coins had laterally milled edges: the sixpenny bit, a two-shilling piece, known as a florin (from Latin flos, floris a flower, because the original coin had a lily stamped on it) and a two and sixpenny piece, 2s 6d, a half crown, (the obsolete silver crown, five shillings in value, was embossed with a crown), often referred to as 'half a dollar' at a time when four dollars US was equivalent to one sterling pound.

A single amount of shillings was designated thus: 8/-, pence, thus: 11d.

Slang called pennies 'coppers' (from the predominating ratio of copper in the alloy) – as in 'I've only got coppers' - and sixpence, shilling, florin and half crown 'silver'.

Money was sometimes abbreviated into colloquial 'l s d', standing for the original Roman coinage from which sterling values were, ultimately, derived: libra (a pound weight, originally of silver, and hence the abbreviation lb for the premetric 'pound'), solidus, of lesser value, and denarius, half a solidus. The metal of these coins varied in successive eras, but in sterling the paper pound replaced the gold sovereign coin after WWI, the shilling was silver and the penny, bronze. The conventional sign £ is no more than a florid, stylised L.

APPENDIX III

WARTIME RATIONING

In 1939, at the outbreak of war, Britain imported 70% of the foodstuffs it consumed each year, including more than 50% of its meat, 70% of its cheese and sugar, nearly 80% of fruits and about 90% of cereals and fats. Because all sea lanes were subject to raids from hostile ships, particularly the U-Boat wolf packs, the country faced extreme shortages of essential provender and strict rationing was implemented. All citizen households were issued with ration books containing coupons for various commodities, in weekly proportion as noted below. Other goods were also rationed – petrol, clothing, even the quality of paper was downgraded for the printing of books in wartime.

In the table, Maximum indicates the amounts allowed at the beginning of the war. Minimum amounts were enforced as supplies dwindled and rationing, perforce, became even more austere.

	Maximum	Minimum	April 1945
Bacon and ham	8oz (227gms)	4oz (113gms)	4oz
Sugar	16oz (454gms)	8oz (227gms)	8oz
Loose tea[1]	4oz	2oz (57gms)	2oz
Meat[2]	to the value of:		
	1s 2d	1s	1s 2d
Cheese	8oz	1oz (28gms)	2oz (57gms)[3]
Preserves (per month):			
either marmalade	2lbs (0.91kg)	8oz (227gms)	2lbs
or sugar *or* jam	1lb etc.		
Butter	8oz	2oz	2oz
Margarine	12oz (340gms)	4oz	2oz
Lard	3oz (85gms)	2oz	2oz
Sweets (/month)	16oz	8oz	12oz

Eggs were rationed, (nominally one per week, two for vegetarians), 'allocated to ordinary consumers as available'. In 1944 thirty allocations of one egg each were made. Children and some invalids were allowed three a week; expectant mothers two on each allocation. A packet of egg powder (equivalent to a dozen eggs) was allowed per month.

---

1. Tea bags were not used widely in the UK.

2. 1s 2d bought about 1lb 3 oz (540 g)) of meat. Offal and sausages were only rationed from 1942-1944. Even when sausages were not rationed, the meat needed to make them was so scarce that they were very rarely seen.

3. Vegetarians were allowed an extra 3oz (85gms

The Army Cycling Union training schedule set by Captain Baughan for Olympic cyclists serving in the Army and competing in the Route de France, 4-18 May 1952.

First week

Tuesday 4 March:	Formby to Carlisle via Keswick Accommodation - Depot Border Regiment, Hadrian's Camp.114 miles
Wednesday 5 March:	Carlisle to Catterick via Hexham and Durham. Catterick Camp. 104 miles
Thursday 6 March:	Catterick to Formby via Middleham, Settle and Longridge. 115 miles

Second week

Tuesday 11 March	York via Ripon, Thirsk, Skipton. KOYLI camp Strenshall. 129 miles
Wednesday 12 March	York (circular) via Malton, Scarborough, Whitby. 108 miles
Thursday 13 March	Formby via Harrogate, Skipton. 106 miles

Third week

Tuesday 18 March	Ton Fanau via Corwen, Dolgellau. (Accommodation not yet arranged.) 109 miles
Wednesday 19 March	Trawsfynydd via Harlech, Caernarvon, Bettwys-y- Coed. King's Detachment Trawsfynydd Camp. 97 miles
Thursday 20 March	Formby via Denbigh, Saint Aspah. 98 miles

Fourth week

Tuesday 25 March	Formby-Formby, via Belmont, Chorley. 60 miles
Wednesday 26 March	morning: Western Command 25 mile time-trial afternoon: Bootle cycle track, Liverpool
Thursday 27 March	Formby-Formby, via Chester, Llangollen. 110 miles

Fifth week

Tuesday 1 April	Carlisle, via Kendal, Penrith. 136 miles
Wednesday 2 April	Carlisle-Carlisle, via Cockermouth, Winlatter. 88 miles
Thursday 3 April	Formby via Ullswater, Coniston. 114 miles

Sixth week

Tuesday 8 April	Warwick via Chester, Newport. 135 miles
Wednesday 9 April	Formby via Brownhills, Whitchurch. 135 miles
Thursday 10 April	morning: Bootle track

1950

3rd National Hill-Climb
Championship

1951

1st Thame Valley RR
2nd Dun Laoghaire 100 km RR
2nd National Hill-Climb
Championship

1952

1st Esholt Park 100 km. RR
1st National Hill-Climb
Championship
27th – Olympic Road Race

1954

(Hercules–Ellis Briggs Cycles)
1st Stage 6 Tour of Europe
10th Stage 7
DNF
2nd Tour of Britain
2nd KOM Classification

1955

(Hercules)
1st Tour of the Pennines
4th Flèche Wallonne
4th Spring Classic
4th Tour of Calvados
5th Championship of Great Britain
8th Paris–Nice
23rd Tour of Provinces of South-
East
29th Tour de France
34th Circuit of Morbihan
60th Milan-San Remo
DNF World Championships

1956

(Saint Raphael-Geminiani, Coupry
& Cilo-Saint Raphael)
2nd Saveray
14th Tour de France
3rd Stage 1
7th Stage 8
7th Stage 18
4th Criterium of Europe (Basel)
5th GP Martini (Geneva)
8th Vuelta a España
8th Stage 17
9th Tour of Switzerland
7th Stages 3, 7 & 8
10th Stage 1
9th Criterium des As
12th Paris–Camembert
59th Milan–San Remo
DNF World Championships

1957

(Saint Raphael-Geminiani)
1st G.P. Nice
1st G.P. Forteresse a' Luxembourg
2nd Barcelona
2nd Basel
3rd Milan–San Remo
3rd St. Denis Hotel
3rd Langon
3rd Macon
4th Tour of Luxembourg
2nd Stage 2b & 4
3rd Stage 1
4th Stage 3
4th Tour of l'Ouest
3rd Stage 4
4th Tour of Picardie
4th Stage 2
8th Paris-Nice
2nd Stage 4

3rd Stage 5b
10th Paris–Roubaix
15th Het-Volk
15th Flèche Wallonne
28th Gent–Wevelgem
Abandoned Tour de France on
Stage 5

1958
(Saint Raphael-Geminiani)

1st Stage 7 Tour de France
    6th Stage 13
    6th Stage 14
DNF (Abandoned Stage 20)
1st Double Harness Pursuit with
Jacques Anquetil at Guecho
1st Guecho Omnium with Anquetil
2nd Royan
3rd Rouen
5th Tour de Sud-Est
    1st Stage 5
    2nd Stage 2
5th Bordeaux–Paris
5th Mont Faron
5th Copenhagen
11th Manche-Ocean
12th Het Volk
13th Tour of Luxembourg
    3rd Stage 2
19th Paris-Nice
    1st KOM Classification
    2nd Stage 7
23rd World Championships
35th Paris–Roubaix

1959
(Saint Raphael-Geminiani)

1st Stage 20 Tour de France
    4th Stage 13
    6th Stages 2 & 7
    7th Stage 18
    10th Stage 12
    19th Overall

2nd St. Macarius
3rd Manx Trophy (IOM)
5th Algiers TTT (with Elliott &
Andrews)

1960
(Rapha- Gitane)

1st Stage 2 Tour de l'Aude
    6th Overall
1st Stage 3 G.P. Midi Libre
    2nd Stage 2
    7th Overall
10th World Championships
10th Manx Trophy (IOM)
11th Genoa – Nice
26th Tour de France
    10th Stage 14

1961
(Rapha -Gitane)

1st Criterium du Dauphiné Libéré
    1st Stage 2b TTT
    1st Stage 3
    7th Stage 6
2nd Circuit des Monts d'Auvergne
    1st Stage 2
3rd Stage 4 Durkirk 4-day
3rd Moulins
3rd Annemasse
8th G.P. Midi Libre
9th G.P. Forli (Trofeo Universal)
36th Flèche Wallonne
53rd Tour de France
    8th Stage 10
    9th Stage 3
Abandoned World Championships

1962
(ACBB-Heylett-Saint Raphael)

26th G.P. Midi Libre
30th Tour of the South East
Abandoned World Championships

BIBLIOGRAPHY

BIDOT, Marcel: *L'Epopée du Tour de France*, Olivier Orban

BLONDIN, Antoine: *Tours de France, Chroniques de L'Equipe 1954-82,* La Table Ronde

BOBET, Jean: *Demain on roule*, La Table Ronde

CHANY, Pierre: *La fabuleuse histoire du Tour de France*, Edns. de la Martinière

FALLON, Lucy and BELL, Adrian: *Viva la Vuelta*, Mousehold Press

FIFE, Graeme: *Inside the Peloton*, Mainstream

FIFE, Graeme: *Tour de France: the history, the legend, the riders,* Mainstream

FIFE, Graeme: *Great Road Climbs of the Pyrenees*, Rapha Racing

FIFE, Graeme: *Great Road Climbs of the Alps vol.I*, Rapha Racing

FOTHERINGHAM, William: *Roule Britannia*, Yellow Jersey Press

HEWSON, Tony: *In Pursuit of Stardom*, Mousehold Press

WADLEY, Jock: *My Nineteenth Tour de France*, J.B. Wadley Publications

Journals and magazines:

Coureur

L'Equipe

Les Cahiers de l'Equipe

Miroir Sprint

Dauphiné Libéré

Cycling

Other books published by
Mousehold Press and Sport and Publicity

Master Jacques: the enigma of Jacques Anquetil
Richard Yates

Golden Stages of the Tour de France
edited by Richard Allchin and Adrian Bell

A Peiper's Tale
Allan Peiper with Chris Sidwells

Viva la Vuelta!
Lucy Fallon & Adrian Ball

Indurain; a tempered passion
Javier García Sánchez

In Pursuit of Stardom
Tony Hewson

This Island Race: inside 135 years of British bike-racing
Les Woodland

From the Pen of J. B. Wadley
selected and edited by Adrian Bell

The Sweat of the Gods
Benjo Maso (translated by Michiel Horn)

The Eagle of the Canavese: Franco Balmamion and the Giro d'Italia
Herbie Sykes

Tomorrow, we ride…
Jean Bobet (translated by Adam Berry)

A Racing Cyclist's Worst Nightmare
Tony Hewson

Shay Elliott: the life and death of Ireland's first yellow jersey
Graham Healy with Richard Allchin

Unsurpassed: the story of Tommy Godwin, the world's greatest distance cyclist, Godfrey Barlow

A Bit of an All-rounder: 40 years of Cycling Photography
John Coulson

Dennis Horn - Racing for an English Rose
Peter Underwood

Also available only from Sport & Publicity:

21 Years of Cycling Photography
Phil O'Connor

Ride and be Damned: the glory years of the British League of Racing Cyclists
Chas Messenger